Road Trip to Nowhere

The publisher and the University of California Press Foundation gratefully acknowledge the generous support of the Kenneth Turan and Patricia Williams Endowment Fund in American Film.

Road Trip to Nowhere

HOLLYWOOD ENCOUNTERS
THE COUNTERCULTURE

Jon Lewis

⊞ UNIVERSITY OF CALIFORNIA PRESS

University of California Press
Oakland, California

© 2022 by Jon Lewis

Library of Congress Cataloging-in-Publication Data

Names: Lewis, Jon, 1955- author.
Title: Road trip to nowhere : Hollywood encounters the counterculture / Jon Lewis.
Description: Oakland, California : University of California Press, [2022] | Includes bibliographical references and index.
Identifiers: LCCN 2021042867 (print) | LCCN 2021042868 (ebook) | ISBN 9780520343733 (hardback) | ISBN 9780520343740 (paperback) | ISBN 9780520975132 (ebook)
Subjects: LCSH: Motion picture studios—California—Los Angeles—History—20th century. | Counterculture—California—Los Angeles. | Motion picture actors and actresses—California—Los Angeles.
Classification: LCC PN1993.5.U65 L49 2022 (print) | LCC PN1993.5.U65 (ebook) | DDC 384/.80979494—dc23
LC record available at https://lccn.loc.gov/2021042867
LC ebook record available at https://lccn.loc.gov/2021042868

Manufactured in the United States of America

28 27 26 25 24 23 22
10 9 8 7 6 5 4 3 2 1

For MARTHA, of course

Contents

List of Illustrations *ix*
Acknowledgments *xiii*

Introduction *1*

1 Road Trips to a New Hollywood: *Easy Rider* and *Zabriskie Point* *33*

2 Christopher Jones Does Not Want to Be a Movie Star *98*

3 Four Women in Hollywood: Jean Seberg, Jane Fonda, Dolores Hart, and Barbara Loden *164*

4 Charles Manson's Hollywood *226*

Epilogue *279*

Notes *287*
Index *311*

Illustrations

1. (Left to right) Warren Beatty, Faye Dunaway, and Arthur Penn in Texas in 1967 filming *Bonnie and Clyde*. *4*
2. Elaine (Katharine Ross) and Ben (Dustin Hoffman) worry about the future at the end of *The Graduate*. *8*
3. (Left to right) Sidney Poitier and Rod Steiger in *In the Heat of the Night*. *11*
4. Black Panther Party founder Huey Newton (right) with his bodyguard in 1971. *22*
5. John Wayne presents the Best Picture Oscar to the production team behind *The Deer Hunter*. *27*
6. Quite by accident a fashion photographer (played by David Hemmings) captures on a roll of film what looks like a murder in Michelangelo Antonioni's *Blow-Up*. *36*
7. Michelangelo Antonioni beside a poster for the film that launched his career, *L'Avventura*. *38*
8. In *Easy Rider*, Dennis Hopper (right) and Peter Fonda comfortably embodied their characters. *43*
9. Antonioni's young lovers in love: Daria Halprin and Mark Frechette. *58*
10. The *Zabriskie Point* love-in. *62*
11. Mel Lyman, "the east coast Charles Manson," on the cover of *Rolling Stone*. *83*

12. Dennis Hopper gets his picture taken in Taos, New Mexico, in July 1975. *89*
13. Mark (Mark Frechette) points a gun at a policeman in *Zabriskie Point*. *91*
14. James Dean on the set filming *East of Eden*. *103*
15. Christopher Jones, looking the part as the next James Dean, 1966. *104*
16. The B-movie impresario, Samuel Z. Arkoff. *113*
17. The movie star Christopher Jones in *Wild in the Streets*. *117*
18. Christopher Jones and costar Yvette Mimieux filming *3 in the Attic*. *135*
19. Pia Degermark, Christopher Jones's "love interest" in *The Looking Glass War*. *142*
20. Christopher Jones as Major Doryan in *Ryan's Daughter*. *147*
21. Marlon Brando with Black Panther Captain Kenny Demmon. *167*
22. Jean Seberg in Jean-Luc Godard's *Breathless*. *171*
23. The camera loved Jean Seberg. *175*
24. The offending photograph: Jane Fonda posed astride a North Vietnamese antiaircraft gun in July 1972. *178*
25. Jane Fonda with her husband, the director Roger Vadim. *187*
26. Jane Fonda as Bree Daniels in *Klute*. *192*
27. Left to right: Dolores Hart, Elvis Presley, and Lizabeth Scott on the set of *Loving You*. *198*
28. Dolores Hart (right) as Merritt trying to console her friend Melanie (Yvette Mimieux) after Melanie's rape in *Where the Boys Are*. *201*
29. All that's left of Barbara Loden's performance in *The Swimmer* are some still photographs, including this one with the film's star, Burt Lancaster. *209*
30. Barbara Loden in *Wanda*. *216*
31. The Beach Boys' Dennis Wilson in 1977. *233*

32. The Family posed in the gully where Charles Manson auditioned for Terry Melcher and Gregg Jakobson. *236*
33. Music producer Terry Melcher with actress Candice Bergen at the Whiskey a Go Go in 1967. *241*
34. The Spahn Movie Ranch, where Charles Manson and the Family resided in the summer of 1969. *249*
35. Charles Manson in police custody (again). *258*
36. Damon Herriman as Charles Manson in Quentin Tarantino's *Once Upon a Time in Hollywood*. *272*
37. Margot Robbie as Sharon Tate in *Once Upon a Time in Hollywood*. *278*
38. Sharon Tate (foreground) with costars Patty Duke (left) and Barbara Parkins in a publicity photo for *Valley of the Dolls*. *282*
39. Jim Morrison of the Doors. *285*

Acknowledgments

The final draft of this book was written in lockdown. For most of the past twelve months it's been just me, Tyrone (my cat), and Martha (my best and prettiest friend since July 1985—my, just as Elia Kazan once described Barbara Loden, roulette wheel that never stops turning). Silly as any sentence beginning with, "If I had to be locked down . . ." surely is, if I had to be locked down, I was lucky to have been locked down with the two of you.

I generally keep to a small circle of friends and they get, like it or not, routinely recruited into my book projects. The overlaps between the personal and the professional for me are persistent; such are the benefits of making a life out of watching and talking and writing about movies. Many of these friends are e-mail pen pals; people I see live and in-person all too seldom.

In no particular order: big thanks to Noel King (who sends me things to read, to think about, often anticipating what I need—like the DeLillo piece on *Wanda* for chapter 3), Mark Betz (who offered some, to him, obvious suggestions at an invited lecture at UCL that I would have missed without him), Lee Grieveson (with whom I email most every day; we mostly talk about football and politics, but sometimes also about work—about *the work*—I hope I am nearly as useful to his, work that is, as he is to mine), Murray Pomerance (who weighed in on Antonioni—I so enjoyed the excuse to make contact), and Jonathan Kirshner (with whom I coedited *When the Movies Mattered: The New Hollywood Revisited* for Cornell University Press in 2019, in which I rehearsed many of the ideas played out here).

An even smaller circle of friends assembled more officially and involved actually reading versions of the book: Tom Doherty, Dana Polan, and Eric Smoodin. They can expect to be recruited next time out as well, on or off the books. I am lucky to have such good friends, such brilliant friends. They know me well enough to say what I need to hear even if it isn't always what I want to hear.

I have for over thirty years now enjoyed the support of my friends and colleagues at Oregon State University. I teach what I want to teach, write about what I want to write about. I get paid on time and I feel well respected; not sure what else I'd want or need. For this project, I received from the School of Writing, Literature, and Film some research funding, including a generous grant from the Smith Fund.

Here in Corvallis, another contingent: first, my old friend Tracy Daugherty. Joan Didion's *The White Album* turns up often and meaningfully in this book, and Tracy's to blame for that. Over lunch and drinks, David Turkel and I talked a lot about *Once Upon a Time in Hollywood*. No doubt some of his ideas made their way into this book. And, finally, Kate Dawson, a smart and enterprising grad student, set loose in the archives early on in this project's development; what she found for me offered fuel to the fire, so to speak.

I pitched this book (accompanied by a PowerPoint on my I-Pad) to the University of California Press editor Raina Polivka in a restaurant over a glass of wine and a civilized lunch. I felt like I was onto something that afternoon because I could tell she thought so too. This is the second book we've done together. She gets how I work and how I write—and she tells me what's working and what isn't.

Big thanks as well to the rest of the crew at the University of California Press and at BookComp—Madison Wetzell, Teresa Iafolla, Katryce Lassle, Jon Dertien, and Gary Hamel—and to Nancy Valenti at the Everett Collection for her help with the production stills.

Introduction

Hollywood Encounters
the Counterculture

It is the morning of August 9, 1969. A story begins to circulate about some murders at a house in Benedict Canyon—some people everyone knows. The news spreads quickly, but not always helpfully or accurately. There are conflicting accounts, most of them pinned on the notion that the more sinister aspects of counterculture Hollywood have come home to roost. "I remember all of the day's misinformation very clearly," the essayist Joan Didion wrote in 1979. "And I also remember this, and I wish I did not: *I remember that no one was surprised*."[1]

The so-called Manson murders would become counterculture Hollywood's simultaneous nadir and climax. There was one life in the Hollywood movie colony before August 1969 and another afterward. It would be impossible in the following months and years to shake the crime's impact, to act as if it were not somehow part of a larger story—a larger story told here, in this book.

Hollywood history is anecdotal and improvisational. (I am not apologizing; only explaining.) It is composed in large part of backstories—a malleable term encompassing production histories, star and celebrity biographies, backroom shenanigans (what industry players call "the action," what the trades call deals). These stories take us behind the scenes into a world not so easy to fathom, a world unlike the world most of the rest of us live in. The players in play are "larger than life." We need to keep that in mind.

In the rhetoric of Hollywood history, movie people are said to be "caught up" in events, as if drifting in the wind, as if waking from a dream. Lots of people venture to Hollywood to reinvent themselves—to get or be discovered, to become players. It happens for them or (more often) it doesn't. And if it does (happen, that is), then they run the risk that somewhere, sometime along the way they too will get caught up in something—in another story they most likely didn't see coming. How they react or behave while they're caught up will be news. It will be deemed newsworthy. That is the price they pay for being larger than life, for occupying so much space in the focal point of American pop culture.

The movies—the ostensible product of Hollywood industry—are, in fact, only ever just part of the story. As objects or products they too can get caught up in things, especially when they seem to distill a given moment, when they seem to elaborate a cultural history. From the mid-sixties through the mid-seventies, the counterculture was happening all around Hollywood (and in it too), and plenty of Hollywood's varied players dabbled or dove right in. But for the Hollywood establishment, the manifestations and crosscurrents of the counterculture proved tricky to develop or exploit. So many of its aspects were divisive and controversial, and thus problematic to promote and market.

The studios had a long-term commitment to *their* mass audience and by definition something counter to the dominant culture ran counter to their business plan. Today, the movies from the counterculture era that continue to matter were in their day aberrations, movies that got made *despite* industry policy, movies made elsewhere (overseas, in the B-industry, by independent contractors working on some half-baked deal with a studio)—movies nobody with money and clout at the time gave half a chance at success.

Between 1967 and 1976 (or thereabouts), Hollywood encountered the counterculture. A lucky few made it; they became counterculture celebrities and hung on long enough to make a name for themselves, long enough to exploit the perks of their celebrity. Others got left out, left behind, or more interestingly (for this book, anyway), walked away—as if the Hollywood they had dreamed of and somehow gained admittance into was not all it had been cracked up to be.

Oscar Night 1968: Encountering Hollywood's First Encounters with the Counterculture

The story of the studio industry's first significant encounter with the counterculture begins in 1964 with the screenwriters Robert Benton and David Newman shopping around a script for a film about the Depression-era bank robbers Bonnie Parker and Clyde Barrow.[2] Figuring no one in Hollywood would understand their French New Wave–inspired script; they try to interest the director François Truffaut. The three men meet, and then retire to a screening of the Joseph Lewis noir picture, *Gun Crazy*. The writers figure they've got a deal. But they don't, as Truffaut reconsiders and decides instead to make *Fahrenheit 451*.

Elinor and Norton Wright, the producers of the kiddie TV show *Captain Kangaroo*, option the script. With the Wrights' blessing, Benton and Newman contact Jean-Luc Godard, who loves the script

FIGURE 1. (Left to right) Warren Beatty, Faye Dunaway, and Arthur Penn on location in Texas in 1967 filming *Bonnie and Clyde* (Everett Collection).

and wants to start production immediately. The Wrights tell Godard they don't have the money yet. They can't start production without a distribution deal. Benton adds that they will need to wait for spring anyway, that the weather in Texas in winter is not suitable for production. Godard replies, "Who cares about Texas." He tells Benton he can make the film anywhere, even Tokyo. Benton cringes. Someone calls for a weather report in Texas, which exasperates Godard: "I'm talking about cinema and you're talking about meteorology."

When the Wrights decide not to renew the option, Warren Beatty steps in. He meets with Godard. It does not go well. He then meets with Jack Warner, who, because Beatty is Beatty—that is, a movie star—offers modest financing: $1.7 million. Beatty ponies up the rest. The production decamps to West Texas, far from the prying eyes of the studio.

Several months later Beatty returns to Los Angeles to screen the rough cut. Warner hates it and shouts at Beatty: "What the fuck is this?" Beatty replies, "It is an *homage*"—to the classic 1930s Warner Bros. gangster films. Warner again: "What the fuck is an homage?"

In August 1967, *Bonnie and Clyde* opens in a *limited* release— Warner sees to that. And the film receives poor reviews from the old guard critics. Bosley Crowther at the *New York Times* dismisses the "callous and callow" film as "an embarrassing addition to an excess of violence on the screen."[3] At *Newsweek*, Joseph Morgenstern describes the film as "a squalid shoot-em-up for the moron trade."[4] Then, at his wife (the actress) Piper Laurie's insistence, Morgenstern gives *Bonnie and Clyde* a second chance, this time in a theater with a mostly young audience that absolutely loves the film. Morgenstern pens a retraction.[5] The film's fortunes begin to shift.

For the cover of their December 8, 1967, New Hollywood issue, *Time* magazine commissions a Robert Rauschenberg collage, which the artist assembles from production stills from *Bonnie and Clyde*. A few months later, on Oscar night 1968, the film is up for ten Academy Awards. (It wins two.)

In its initial run, *Bonnie and Clyde* grossed nearly twenty-five times its production budget. It is for Hollywood quite clearly a watershed. But no one at Warner Bros. or at any of the other studios seems to have the slightest idea how or why.

Jack Warner was well into his fifth decade in charge of the family business when Penn and Beatty's film so took him by surprise. He had been running things ever since the studio first experimented with sound, way back when one of the lies executives liked to tell the press, studio talent, and themselves, was that *they* had "the whole equation" in their heads.⁶ That is: a feel for trends, fads, the zeitgeist—a firm grasp of the math (money out and money in). Wishful thinking.

Mike Nichols's *The Graduate* received seven Oscar nominations in 1968. The film was for Hollywood a preliminary narrative exploration of the emerging youth counterculture disguised as a satire of postwar suburbia—an outpost populated in the film by an array of upper-middle-class pseudo-liberals and their offspring: the latter, depicted as a generation adrift, paralyzed by counterculture ennui. The romantic triangle at the heart of the narrative (Ben, Mrs. Robinson, and her daughter Elaine) anticipated the advent of a new regime of film industry censorship (itself an anticipation of social change, a response to the dawning Age of Aquarius). Ben's transition into adulthood runs counter to his upper-middle-class suburban parents' dreamy life and ambitious plans for him—plans epitomized and satirized by the notion that the secret to America's future might be contained in a single, whispered word: "plastics." Asked early on what's troubling him, Ben tells his father: "I'm worried about the future—I want it to be different." By the time we get to the church at the end of the film, we understand why.

Nichols was thirty-six when he made *The Graduate*—for the record, the same age as Anne Bancroft, the actress who played the icon of the affluent and amoral establishment in the film, Mrs. Robinson. (Bancroft was just six years older than Dustin Hoffman, who plays Ben—hardly old enough to be his mother. Just saying.) Nichols was not a baby boomer, and he was not and did not aspire to be a counterculture filmmaker. He was a former sketch comedian, for years partnering with Elaine May. He had recently enjoyed some success as a Broadway stage director with two (what were even then) old-fashioned comedies written by Neil Simon: *Barefoot in the Park* (1963) and *The Odd Couple* (1965).

Nichols's first big Hollywood break came as a result of canny networking; the movie industry was then and still is a relationship business. While working and living in New York, Nichols became friends with the movie stars Elizabeth Taylor and Richard Burton. When Taylor and Burton got tied to a film adaptation of Edward Albee's stage play *Who's Afraid of Virginia Woolf* for Warners, the actors listed Nichols as a director they'd be willing to work with. The studio hired Nichols to keep the star couple happy. And Nichols made the most of the opportunity.

The Graduate was Nichols's second film. And, like *Bonnie and Clyde*, it was a box-office sensation: off a modest budget of $3 million, the film grossed in excess of $80 million domestically and over $100 million globally, astonishing numbers at a time when a $20 million gross qualified a film as a blockbuster. Nichols's film was timely and though essentially a comedy, politically complex. The May-December romance between Ben (Dustin Hoffman) and Mrs. Robinson (Anne Bancroft) that seemed so shocking at the time was for Nichols at once a modern take on the age-old bedroom farce and a commentary on the current generation gap. Mrs. Robinson is one of Ben's parents' friends. She seduces Ben because she despises growing old—because she hates her cushy suburban life with her bourbon-swilling, golf-playing, white-collar husband. She's mostly missed out on the sexual revolution, and she figures Ben is her one last chance to dip in.

The relationship offers for Ben a jolting rite of passage, especially after they split up and Mrs. Robinson becomes a formidable adversary. By then, Mrs. Robinson is something of a caricature—a rather monstrous symbol of an unhappy and lost older generation. Our last images of her at the wedding are meant to exaggerate her failure, her

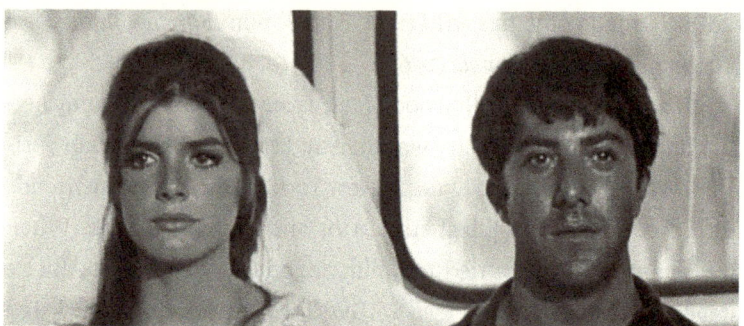

FIGURE 2. Elaine (Katharine Ross) and Ben (Dustin Hoffman) worry about the future at the end of Mike Nichols's *The Graduate* (1967, Embassy Pictures). Plenty of young Americans at the time shared their apprehension and confusion.

futility, and her hypocrisy. She has treated her own marriage with disrespect, yet she has pushed her daughter into the same unsatisfying institution, into marrying a man she doesn't love. Mrs. Robinson wants to be young again, she wants to be part of a counterculture she's only just read about in magazines, a subculture of casual hookups and free sex. She doesn't find what she's looking for. And sadly, Nichols gets us to hate her for trying.

The Graduate ends with a darkly comic set piece: after Ben breaks up the wedding, he and Elaine sit together in the back of a bus, in and of itself (after Rosa Parks) hardly an inadvertent set piece. Seated side by side and captured in a long-take two-shot, they acknowledge through gesture their confusion. This final sequence takes us back to Ben's earlier ruminations in his bedroom at home. He is, he tells his father, worried about the future. He—and here we begin to understand, he is not just speaking for himself—wants things to be different. But he has no idea how to make that happen.

The closest he comes to having a postgraduation plan involves moving to a rented room in a Berkeley boarding house—the better to stalk Elaine into falling back in love with him. (To state the obvious, the scenes of stalking played differently in 1967 than they do today.) The landlord, performed with bug-eyed comic exaggeration by Norman Fell, is anxious about Ben, not because he knows what Ben is up to, but because he's afraid Ben is an "outside agitator" come to stir things up in America's most notorious counterculture college town. Fell makes the most of his brief screen time, and he becomes the fall guy in a series of comic skits. But plenty of older filmgoers shared his anxiety at what was happening in Berkeley and on other college campuses at the time. All to say, in 1967 the Berkeley setting is hardly incidental.

Along with *The Graduate* and *Bonnie and Clyde*, two other films scored big on Oscar night 1968: the topical comedy *Guess Who's Coming to Dinner* (Stanley Kramer) and the trenchant crime-melodrama *In the Heat of the Night* (Norman Jewison), which won Best Picture. All four films were in different ways "counterculture": timely, hip, and political. It was hard for the studio suits to ignore that fact. The fifth and final nominee for Best Picture was the old-fashioned, old-Hollywood *Dr. Doolittle*, directed by Richard Fleischer, a costly and clunky mess that seemed only to emphasize the industry's counterculture rift.

Guess Who's Coming to Dinner (Stanley Kramer, 1967), the year's second-highest-grossing film behind *The Graduate*, and *In the Heat of the Night* both starred the Black movie star Sidney Poitier. Kramer's film cast Poitier alongside Old-Hollywood stalwarts Katharine Hepburn and Spencer Tracy. The film asked a series of topical questions necessarily (per the studio's collective caution) tempered by light comedy. What would a white liberal couple say if their daughter brought home her fiancé and he was Black? And what if he looked like (what if he was someone like) Poitier—handsome, urbane, intelligent? And what if, as the film further poses, he was an MD with a practice in Switzerland? Didn't every married couple in 1967 dream of their daughters marrying doctors?

In the Heat of the Night cast Poitier as a police detective who ventures into the racially segregated South and gets recruited to solve a murder. His task is complicated by a bigoted southern lawman (played by Rod Steiger, who won the Oscar for Best Actor) and by the many racists who occupy the town. The film ends with an unlikely détente possible only in Hollywood's dream version of race relations in late-sixties America.

The box office and Oscar night success of *In the Heat of the Night*, *Guess Who's Coming to Dinner*, *The Graduate*, and *Bonnie and Clyde* spoke to the counterculture predicament in Hollywood at the time. There was, it became quite clear, money to be made and awards to be won making movies that engaged a counterculture audience. But how then to proceed without alienating the so-called silent majority, the establishment folks who in 1968 put Nixon in the White House? It was a question the studio establishment could not answer.

Black Hollywood: Melvin van Peebles's Road to Nowhere

It is (or at least it should be) a source of shame that the movie industry labor force, especially at the top end, was as late as 1968 not yet integrated. And even as white celebrities like Marlon Brando and Paul Newman spoke out on behalf of Black Americans (more on that later), the studios remained cautious about dealing with race on-screen. And they had their reasons. Case in point: the 1965 MGM release, *A Patch of Blue* (Guy Green), which featured an interracial romance between an illiterate, blind, white woman (Elizabeth Hartman) and an educated Black man (Poitier, again). A budding romance was confirmed by an on-screen kiss between the two characters (and stars)—well: they kissed in some versions that some filmgoers saw at some venues. Under pressure from theater owners in the South, MGM distributed an alternate version of the film with the kiss cut out. Two years later: *Guess Who's Coming to Dinner* and

FIGURE 3. (Left to right) Sidney Poitier and Rod Steiger in *In the Heat of the Night* (Norman Jewison, United Artists). The groundbreaking (for white Hollywood at least) civil rights–era film won the Best Picture Oscar in 1968.

In the Heat of the Night were for the moment—arguably, despite the moment—still as far as the studios were willing to go.

In 1969, Black Americans accounted for about 15 percent of the US population. Yet they comprised more than 30 percent of the first-run film audience. Black Americans went to the movies proportionally more than white Americans did. Encouraged by the data and the Best Picture win for *In the Heat of the Night*, studio executives moved cautiously into making movies targeting the Black American audience. They had gotten their feet wet with *Guess Who's Coming to Dinner* and *In the Heat of the Night* and in 1969 they were ready to get in a bit deeper—to their ankles, let's say. To do so, they invested in a small and select group of Black moviemakers.[7]

Among this first group, Melvin van Peebles seems today the most interesting and most important—if only because, to extend the metaphor, with him Hollywood was never just wading in. His story—sudden success followed by a self-inflicted career implosion—was an all-too typical counterculture venture on the road to nowhere. As such, it surely and sadly fits the scheme of this book.

In 1967, after failing to interest a single A- or B-studio in a script based on his novel *La Permission*, van Peebles signed a production deal with the small French company O.P.E.R.A. The retitled adaptation, *The Story of a Three-Day Pass*, told the story of a mild-mannered African American GI stationed in France, who, to celebrate a promotion, takes a rare weekend off the base. On the first day of his three-day pass, he meets a white French shop girl. When she offers to go with him to a resort hotel, he assumes she is a prostitute. She's not, but as they discover together, they both would have been better off had she been one.

Anticipating the release of the film, *Variety* ran a feature on van Peebles under the now well-dated headline: "Saga of a Negro Filmmaker." Rick Setlowe, writing for the trade paper, opened the feature with a fair (thus, cynical) assessment: "The irony is that the novelist-filmmaker [van Peebles] had to exile himself to France to work at all, and the story of his struggle is a commentary on how tough it can be for a talented Negro to break into the film biz." Setlowe highlighted van Peebles's CV: a BA with Honors in literature from Ohio Wesleyan; a stint in the Air Force; a job as a cable-car operator in San Francisco; and, on money earned from selling his car, the producer of three short self-financed films.[8] Van Peebles, Setlowe reported, took his reel to a number of Hollywood executives and agents, but failed to drum up interest. One agent told him, memorably: "If you can tap dance, I might be able to find you some work."[9]

The Story of a Three-Day Pass somehow got van Peebles noticed. And his timing seemed right; he (to indulge the industry use of the term) had "arrived" just as executives were trying build upon *Guess Who's Coming to Dinner* and *In the Heat of the Night*, and he was given a shot at a studio feature: *The Watermelon Man* (1970). The film offered a neat variation on a theme from Franz Kafka's "Metamorphosis," as it tells the story of a bigoted white insurance agent who wakes up one morning to discover that he has been transformed into a Black man. The hook proved timely, and *The Watermelon Man* was a modest hit.

The production went smoothly, with only one significant hitch. Studio executives and van Peebles locked horns over the film's denouement. The executive team at Columbia wanted to soften the film's anti-racist message and commissioned an ending in which the insurance agent wakes to discover that it was all a dream. Van Peebles rejected such an ending as a cop-out. The film was released with van Peebles's ending: the former-white-now-Black-executive enlists in the Black middle class: he buys a house, starts his own company, and most tellingly joins a group of politically aware Black Americans practicing martial arts, preparing for a future in which they might just need such skills.

When the film hit, executives at Columbia quietly put the argument over the ending behind them and offered van Peebles a three-picture deal. But van Peebles had seen enough of the studio process to know it wasn't for him, and moved on. With some of his own and some of his friend Bill Cosby's money he produced, directed, scripted, scored, and starred in the alliteratively titled *Sweet Sweetback's Baadasssss Song* (1971).[10] Had he endeavored to scuttle his career, he could not have produced a more efficient exit strategy.

The film's main character, Sweetback (played by van Peebles) makes his living performing in live sex shows—quite literally performing a white-nightmare version of Black masculinity. When Sweetback witnesses a scene of police brutality, he goes on a rampage. From there, the film takes off—significantly, and if you get on board with van Peebles, and if you consider the identity politics in play—comically into caricature.

The promotional campaign employed by the B-movie distribution outfit Cinemation and then three years later by Roger Corman for the New World rerelease, played off taglines like: "Dedicated to all the Brothers and Sisters who have had enough of the man," "You bled my mamma—you bled my papa—but you won't bleed me," and "Rated X by an all-white jury."[11] The provocative taglines betrayed the film's roots in exploitation—and in this instance, offered some truth in advertising as well.

The mainstream critical response was predictably fraught; *Sweetback* was by design difficult for mainstream (i.e., white) reviewers to evaluate or recommend. In April 1971, the *New York Times* assigned a second-string reviewer, Roger Greenspun to write about the film. It was an unfortunate choice: "In [*Sweetback*] the failure is so very nearly total that the ideas all turn into clichés and positively collaborate in taking things down." The negative review ended with a thud—a gesture of unselfconscious white paternalism; citing the few good moments that "show the director at work in the kind of moviemaking I hope he'll some day complete."[12]

Two weeks later, the *Times* solicited a second review, this time from a Black writer, Clayton Riley, who contended that the only way to write about the film was to "bear witness" to van Peebles's "terrifying vision . . . a vision Black people alone will really understand in all of its profane and abrasive substance."[13] A third review balanced the previous two. Written by Vincent Canby, the review affirmed the film's success "as a contemporary folk parable," but nonetheless qualified that success, noting that for a "film to be art it needs to look better, the acting and the tech work needs to be more professional, the plot must adhere to some semblance of structure. . . . It may be—as some of its supporters claim—the Black experience in America, distilled to its essence [but] my feeling, distilled to its essence, is that that experience deserves a better film."[14]

Van Peebles's Hollywood legacy exceeds the reality of his career. He is often regarded as a Blaxploitation director, but as he was well out of the business by the end of 1971, the genre in fact took off without him. True to its name, Blaxploitation affirmed the anticipated target audience, Black America, and the genre's production style and marketing scheme, B-movie exploitation. Blaxploitation had a short but memorable run with modest hits like *Shaft* (Gordon Parks, 1971), *Super Fly* (Gordon Parks Jr., 1972), *Cleopatra Jones* (Jack Starrett, 1973), *The Mack* (Michael Campus, 1973), *Coffy* (Jack Hill, 1973), *Three the Hard Way* (Gordon Parks Jr., 1974), *Foxy Brown* (Jack Hill, 1974, which made Pam Grier a minor star), and *Dolemite* (D'Urville Martin, 1975, which did the same for the indescribable and indomitable Rudy Ray Moore). But to be fair: the genre was never part of any real plan for any studio's future.

After only five years, Blaxploitation had run its course. A more overtly political, counterculture Black American cinema emerged in its place, further marginalized by and thus marginal to the studio-controlled first-run marketplace. This so-called "L.A. Rebellion"—highlighted by Charles Burnett's experimental, episodic family melodrama *Killer of Sheep* (1978), Haile Gerima's neorealist study of a Black Vietnam vet struggling to readjust to life stateside after a tour in Vietnam, *Bush Mama* (1979); and Jamaa Fanaka's prison-boxing film *Penitentiary* (1979)—was from its outset tied complexly to the American counterculture, emerging as it did out of an uneasy effort at diversity on a local college campus: UCLA.

The story of UCLA's fraught struggle to develop a Black Studies program is worth retelling here as it seems rather a sign of the times. In January 1969, UCLA's Westwood campus became the unlikely site of a shootout involving US, a group of black activists organized by the UCLA PhD candidate Ronald Everett (later, Maulana Karenga) and members of the Black Panther Party. Two Black Panthers—John

Huggins and Alprentice "Bunchy" Carter—were killed in the gunfight, as US and the Panthers vied for control over an unlikely turf: the school's fledgling Black Studies program.[15]

Tense times, then, when even an intradepartmental struggle might evolve into a gunfight. And hardly the sort of subculture or counterculture the fiscally conservative movie studios wanted to be associated with. The civil rights movement may have been much in the news, but the ever-conservative studios only ever dipped into and then quickly got out of topical, race-conscious filmmaking.

Oscar Night 1975: Hollywood Discovers Vietnam

Counterculture Hollywood is fairly framed by two memorable Oscar nights: 1968 and 1975. The 1968 ceremony took place on April 8, bookended by the late-January Tet Offensive in Vietnam (a battle that made clear to many Americans that the Vietnam war could not be so easily won) and the Democratic National Convention in Chicago, a weekend in August that fueled mounting anxiety over irreconcilable divisions between Democrat and Republican (and, eventually, between Hubert Humphrey and Richard Nixon), and between young and old, hip and square, dove and hawk (i.e., anti- v. pro-war) as well.

The 1975 ceremony took place just twenty days before the fall of Saigon. The war was by then nearly over, but only and finally getting a first airing-out in Hollywood. The big moment of that night came when the ex-model Lauren Hutton and the TV comedian Danny Thomas took the stage to announce the award for Best Documentary Feature: "and the winner is . . . [Peter Davis's] *Hearts and Minds*." It was a moment everyone in attendance had been waiting for. And as anticipated the producers of the film were not about to be good winners.

On behalf of the production team, Bert Schneider accepted the award, reading aloud a telegram from the North Vietnamese delegation to the Paris peace talks, thanking the U.S. antiwar movement "for all they have done on behalf of peace." Schneider was speaking on behalf of the industry's politically progressive majority. But his speech struck plenty in attendance as, even though the war was nearly over, a bit too much too soon.

Telegrams—it's 1975, so Western Union was the format du jour for sudden outrage—arrived fast and furious.[16] Frank Sinatra took the stage to read a message on behalf of the Academy of Motion Picture Arts and Sciences (AMPAS): "We are not responsible for any political utterances on this program and we are sorry that this [that is, Schneider's speech] had to take place." The Academy had put the words in Sinatra's mouth. But to be fair: Sinatra and his cohost Bob Hope agreed with them.

Lurking just off-stage and waiting for Sinatra to come their way were Shirley MacLaine (Sinatra's costar in *Some Came Running*, Vincente Minnelli's 1958 film) and her brother Warren Beatty. MacLaine went first: "You said you were speaking for the Academy. Well, I'm a member of the Academy and you didn't ask me!" Then Beatty, with ample snark: "Thank you Frank, you old Republican." It proved to be a watershed moment: the New Hollywood colliding with the old—AMPAS trying to be balanced and fair and failing yet again to be everything to everyone (or to be anything to anyone), because in 1975 balanced and fair was no longer possible.

Sinatra was indeed old, by Hollywood standards at least; he turned sixty in 1975. But he had not always been a Republican. In fact, he had only just become what he was that night: someone well chosen to speak on behalf of an entrenched and embattled Conservative Hollywood, a friend to Richard Nixon and the Reagans, a projection for his older fans of outrage at the rock-and-roll generation and the politics of progressive Hollywood. But it was not always that way.

Sinatra lived a long, public life. His navigation of the political minefield of twentieth-century celebrity was complicated and conflicted. Sinatra was at least at first a working-class Jersey boy made good—a child of immigrants, a survivor of the Great American Depression. His mother, Dolly, was active in Democratic Party circles in New Jersey, and his politics initially matched hers.

When he broke into the music business as a singer on the pop and jazz scenes Sinatra embraced the race politics inherent to an industry that was far more and better integrated than the rest of America at the time. And even when it seemed risky career-wise, he was willing to speak out for racial justice and civil rights. For example, he appeared in the 1945 Oscar winning dramatic short film, *The House I Live In*, written by Communist Party member and future blacklistee Albert Maltz. Reading from Maltz's script, Sinatra tells a bunch of inner-city kids that racial and religious differences in America shouldn't matter, "except to a Nazi or somebody who's stupid." Sinatra sang the film's title song as well, lyrics by Abel Meeropol—the same Abel Meeropol who wrote "Strange Fruit," a poem that protested lynching later put to music and performed by Billie Holiday—the same Abel Meeropol who was a card-carrying member of the American Communist Party member (later blacklisted), who in sympathy to the cause adopted the convicted spies Ethel and Julius Rosenberg's children. In 1945, Sinatra sang Meeropol's lyrics like he meant them—"The house I live in / A plot of Earth, a street / The grocer and the butcher / And the people that I meet / The children in the playground / The faces that I see / All races and religions / That's America to me"—because at the time, he did.

Sinatra supported President Franklin Delano Roosevelt and, only after being disappointed at the progressive Democrat Henry Wallace's failed bid for the nomination in 1948, backed the more conservative Democrat Harry Truman. He joined the Committee for the First Amendment (CFA) that publicly opposed HUAC and appeared conspicuously at fundraisers alongside Hollywood Communists and progressives like Howard Da Silva, John Garfield, Paul

Henreid, Danny Kaye, and Lena Horne. The company you kept mattered a lot in the 1940s, as it would matter a lot again or still that night in the mid-1970s.

According to "The Cumulative Index to Publications of the Committee on Un-American Activities,"[17] during the blacklist era Sinatra's name was named twelve times, albeit by mostly disreputable witnesses, including Walter S. Steele, who had once accused the Campfire Girls of being "Communistic" and Gerald L. K. Smith, a nativist who remarked that Sinatra was "doing some pretty clever stuff for the Reds."[18] Among Sinatra's Communist front activities (as HUAC perceived them) was his stint as vice president of HICCASP (the Hollywood Independent Citizens Committee of the Arts, Sciences, and the Professions). At HICCASP, Sinatra worked with a range of American celebrities, including the Communist screenwriters Dalton Trumbo and John Howard Lawson; the moderate Democrats Groucho Marx and Screen Actors Guild president Ronald Reagan (before *his* change of heart and party affiliation); and the pacifist chemist and two-time Nobel Prize winner Linus Pauling. As HICCASP's VP, Sinatra sat on the organization's board of directors with Orson Welles (a drinking buddy and fellow political progressive), the actress and CFA supporter Katharine Hepburn, and the soon-to-be blacklisted bandleader Artie Shaw. Sinatra was called in to testify before the California State Senator Jack Tenney's "Little HUAC" fact-finding commission investigating un-American Activities in Hollywood, prompting William Randolph Hearst's *L. A. Examiner* to characterize the singer as a Communist sympathizer in league "with advocates of the *down with the rich until I get it* [crowd]; fighting for this or that and almost any goofy thing that comes along."[19]

In the lead-up to the 1960 presidential election, Sinatra lent his considerable celebrity to John F. Kennedy. He was close with Patricia Lawford, Kennedy's sister and wife of the actor and fellow Rat Packer

Peter Lawford. In 1961, Sinatra was enlisted to organize Kennedy's inaugural gala. But when the president's brother, Attorney General Robert Kennedy, took aim at organized crime Sinatra became a family problem. Robert Kennedy's beef with Sinatra concerned more generally the celebrity's many organized crime connections and more specifically the worrisome matter of Judith Exner, whom Sinatra had carelessly introduced to the president *and* to the gangster Sam Giancana. When the Kennedys vacationed in Southern California soon after the inauguration, they holed up with (the Republican and Sinatra's professional rival) Bing Crosby. Sinatra got the message.

In 1968, Sinatra supported the Democrat Hubert Humphrey. But his heart wasn't really in it. Four years later in 1972, with his celebrity waning, and rock and roll stars dominating the charts and the hearts and minds of young music lovers, Sinatra took a career lifeline of sorts, hitching his wagon to Nixon and his silent majority. In doing so, he took a first giant step toward becoming that guy on the Oscar stage in 1975 reading the cranky AMPAS disclaimer. The move to the right amplified the nastier sides of Sinatra's public persona: the hideous misogyny, the insufferable sense of entitlement, the bullying, the boozing, palling around with Nixon and then (more plausibly) the Reagans. Times had changed, and Sinatra had changed with them.

Bert Schneider was mostly unknown to the TV audience that night. But he had a big reputation among the attendees as a major player in the seventies' Hollywood recovery and as one of a new breed of Hollywood progressives. In 1969, Schneider executive-produced the counterculture classic *Easy Rider*, a film that rather set the New Hollywood in motion. With Bob Rafelson and Steve Blauner (with whom he formed the production outfit, BBS) Schneider produced the counterculture Hollywood features *Head* (featuring the stars of the TV show *The Monkees*, which Schneider had coproduced with Rafelson), *Five Easy Pieces*, *Drive He Said*, *The Last*

Picture Show, and *The King of Marvin Gardens*. Sinatra was a bastion of the old Hollywood—Schneider, a power broker in the new.

The production of *Hearts and Minds* had been from the outset fraught; so the fracas on Oscar night seemed only par for the course. Executives at Columbia got nervous quite early in the film's production—so much so, they pulled their money out of the project and terminated the multi-film BBS contract. The decision forced the partners to scramble for financing and to go ahead with production without certain distribution. The well-publicized row marked the end of what Columbia viewed as a counterculture experiment with BBS.

BBS was at the end of its tether anyway; the partners were on their own negotiating the dissolution of the company. Rafelson felt hamstrung by the Columbia contract and the BBS business model—that is, little personal films made for around $1 million. He wanted to step up into bigger films, to become a proper New Hollywood moviemaker, following in the footsteps of fellow BBS auteur Peter Bogdanovich.

Meantime, Schneider had become a very public Hollywood progressive activist, which Rafelson smartly figured jeopardized his ascent. Schneider had gone public with his support for the legal defense of two counterculture icons: the former Pentagon analyst Daniel Ellsberg and the yippie impresario Abbie Hoffman, whom Schneider had helped jump bail. Blauner had become a counterculture warrior as well, albeit more quietly and anonymously, headquartered at his home in the gated community of Bel Air.

In the mid-summer of 1974, just as Columbia cut BBS loose and about eight months before *Hearts and Minds* won the Oscar, Schneider and Blauner put their radical politics to the test, engineering a covert operation to help the Black Panther leader Huey Newton avoid federal prosecution, hatching and then executing a plan to get him out of the United States and into Cuba (to avoid extradition).[20] Newton, who cofounded the Black Panther Party for Self Defense in 1966 with Bobby Seale, was at that moment in plenty of trouble.

FIGURE 4. Black Panther Party founder Huey Newton (right) with his bodyguard in 1971 (Everett Collection).

He had been arrested for an altercation in an Oakland bar during which he and his bodyguard had tussled with two white cops. While out on bail awaiting trial for the assault, he (or so authorities allege) committed a second crime, shooting a seventeen-year-old prostitute named Kathleen Smith. According to the prosecutor in the case, Newton shot her for calling him by his childhood nickname, "Baby." Smith later died from the wounds, leaving Newton on the hook for her murder.

Newton jumped bail and sought sanctuary at Blauner's Bel Air mansion. Newton and Blauner were prominent in very different counterculture circles, of course. But they nonetheless became fast friends, a friendship highlighted by a venture out, as the film historian Peter Biskind tells the story, together and incognito to see the ultraviolent and ultra-right-wing *Dirty Harry* picture, *Magnum Force* (Ted Post, 1973). Oh, to have been a fly on the wall.

Newton was subsequently ferried from Bel Air to a second community associated with white privilege: Big Sur, and the home of Schneider's friend, a movie and TV writer blacklisted in the 1950s named Arthur "Artie" Ross.[21] There, a handful of left-wing Hollywood luminaries convened to plot Newton's escape. They referred to themselves with predictable movie colony grandiosity as "the Beverly Hills Seven," a play on the activist radicals Hoffman, Jerry Rubin, Tom Hayden, Rennie Davis, John Froines, and Lee Weiner (the Chicago Seven, who organized the protests during the Democratic National Convention in 1968). Given Ross's struggle with HUAC, a less obvious but more apropos allusion to the Hollywood Ten seemed in play as well.

The Beverly Hills Seven were amateur criminals, but professional storytellers. So they went about plotting Newton's escape like they were developing a movie script, pitching scenarios and finally going with the best story they could muster. Following the agreed-upon script, Blauner drove Newton to Mexico. Blauner had seen plenty of criminals on the lam in movies, so he knew enough to use cash when he bought gas and snacks. He stopped en route to call his bookie from a phone booth to place bets and to establish an alibi: that he was, like most every other Sunday, betting on the games he was watching on TV. As Blauner recalled to Biskind: "When I got back across the border from Mexico, I pulled over to the side of the road, and stopped. . . . I felt a thousand feet high. 'Cause [it was] the first thing I could think of that I had ever done under conditions of life and death—I could've gotten shot—for only one reason, the love of another human being."[22] As the journalist Lanre

Bakare quipped looking back on the counterculture adventure, the extraction "might have been BBS's most audacious production."[23]

Newton eventually got to Cuba on a boat from Acapulco hired by Schneider, who sealed the deal by agreeing to fully reoutfit the boat captain (a Colombian who went by the colorful nom de guerre "Pirate") should his vessel be seized en route. The boat wasn't seized, but only because, upon entering Cuba's waters, Pirate bailed on the plan. He put Newton and Newton's wife Gwen Fontaine on a dinghy and then hightailed it back home. As Pirate disappeared into the distance, the dinghy capsized. Newton didn't know how to swim, so Fontaine had to help him reach the beach, where the exhausted couple were met and promptly arrested by Cuban authorities.

Once they figured out who he was, Newton was afforded sanctuary. He lived in Cuba for three years, and then returned to the United States in 1977 to protest his innocence in the Smith case. Amid accusations that the Black Panther Party tampered with and threatened witnesses, the State ultimately failed to convict him.[24]

Newton eventually spent time in prison on a firearms charge. While incarcerated, he worked on his PhD, later conferred by the History of Consciousness program at the University of California, Santa Cruz. The title of his thesis: "War against the Panthers: A Study of Repression in America."[25] But Newton did not live to enjoy his freedom for long. In August 1989, in Oakland, California, Tyrone Robinson, a member of the Black Guerilla Family, murdered Newton. After all Newton had been through, it is important to note that the hit was not in any discernable way political. It was not planned or executed by federal authorities, though they had wanted him dead for a while. It was instead a sign of the times in the Black community, which had by then rather moved on from the Panthers. The Black Guerilla Family was a prison gang. And Newton's murder was part of its effort to secure a crack franchise.[26]

Hollywood's Hearts and Minds

Hearts and Minds was BBS's last film—a final counterculture gesture from Hollywood's most successful counterculture production unit. It was also the unit's first and only film independent of Columbia.[27] Absent the studio deal—a situation complicated by a lawsuit filed by the former national security advisor Walt Rostow, who objected to Davis's cut of his interview in the film—Schneider submitted *Hearts and Minds* to Cannes, smartly anticipating the French festival organizers' interest in what was quite clearly an un- and anti-American film.

On May 16, 1974, *Hearts and Minds* opened Cannes. The print arrived at the last minute and only after Schneider, the director Henry Jaglom, and Howard Zuker (the actor also known as Zack Norman) pooled their resources to complete postproduction. After seeing the film at the festival, the American movie reviewer Rex Reed penned a dispatch describing *Hearts and Minds* as "the only film I have ever seen that sweeps away the gauze surrounding Vietnam."[28] Reed was an unlikely but prodigious ally—he was not only a widely read movie reviewer, but also an industry celebrity, a regular on the late-night talk show circuit. Reed's rave review, penned a few weeks later for the politically conservative *New York Daily News*, was pulled by the publication's editors. The attempt at censoring the journalist only helped promote the film. By the time the other New York critics got to write about *Hearts and Minds*, they had the Reed/*Daily News* backstory on their minds. And they embraced the film as a *cause celebre*. The *New York Times*'s Vincent Canby, for example, hailed *Hearts and Minds* "as one of the most all-encompassing records of the American civilization ever put into one film."[29]

Hearts and Minds reached American theaters through Rainbow Releasing (with some additional financing and logistical help from

Warner Bros.). Its first run began with a limited engagement in Los Angeles in the final week of 1974, in time for Academy Award consideration. The timing paid off.

Davis's documentary is a persuasive piece of propaganda, in part because it is so old-fashioned. It is a compilation film—a smartly selected and assembled collection of found footage (from news sources mostly) intercut with interviews conducted by Davis. Included among those interviewed were the men who had overseen the war effort: Rostow, the former secretary of state John Foster Dulles, General William Westmoreland (excerpts from his interview included chilling remarks like: "Vietnam reminds me of a child," and, "The Oriental doesn't put the same high price on life as does a Westerner"—the latter juxtaposed to images of a Vietnamese woman crying inconsolably alongside a grave), General George Patton III (who cheerfully describes his men as "a bloody good bunch of killers"), and the former secretary of defense Clark Clifford (who breaks down during his interview and confesses that his Vietnam War strategies "could not have been more wrong"). The counterculture, anti-war Left was represented as well in the film, as Davis included interviews with Ellsberg and Senator Eugene McCarthy.

The film's breakout star was someone few Americans had ever heard of—the former bomber pilot Randy Floyd, who speaks in the film movingly about the pointless suffering he caused in his nearly one hundred sorties. When the rugged vet Floyd breaks down and cries on camera, filmgoers got an early hint at the enduring cost of the war.[30]

Studio Hollywood came late to Vietnam, finally weighing in a couple of years later with *The Deer Hunter* and *Coming Home*. Both films reached American screens in 1978; well after the war had ended. And both received predictable recognition from AMPAS, on another memorable Oscar night (1979)—together, netting seventeen nominations. *The Deer Hunter* and Cimino took the top awards and Christopher Walken won as well for Best Supporting Actor (over

FIGURE 5. John Wayne (far right, of course) presents the Best Picture Oscar to the production team behind *The Deer Hunter* (Universal), one of the first American features to depict the terrible cost of the war on young American men. Left to right: producer Barry Spikings, producer-director Michael Cimino, producer Michael Deeley (Everett Collection).

Dern, nominated for *Coming Home*). *Coming Home*'s Jane Fonda and costar John Voight won Best Actress and Actor and the former blacklistee Waldo Salt, along with Nancy Dowd, and Robert C. Jones won for their story and script.

Several of the 1979 Oscar-night acceptance speeches addressed Hollywood's late arrival to the war. Dowd, unknown outside Hollywood before Oscar night, made the most of her couple of minutes on stage: "I wrote my screenplay in 1973 when our country was still at war in Vietnam. I was inspired by Vietnam veterans and the women who loved them. They told me about the painful experiences they suffered in the name of patriotism. Tonight, six years later, I have an Oscar. But for the people about whom I wrote, the war still goes on. I am thinking of them tonight." Fonda, by then an icon of the

Hollywood Left, signed (in sign language) the first part of her acceptance speech in solidarity with the disabled community represented in the film. She too put the film in the context of the long struggle to end the war and the struggle ahead, tending to those who survived it: "This film, *Coming Home*, was born in Santa Monica where we live, in the cramped offices of the Indochina Peace Campaign, as a lot of us whose lives have been bound up with the war sat on the floor. And some of them were veterans. I thank—I thank all of them. One of them was my husband, [Chicago Seven defendant] Tom Hayden; one of them was Bruce Gilbert, who has become my partner and is the associate producer of *Coming Home*."

Road Trips to Nowhere: The Book

The history of movie production culture presented in this book focuses on the emblematic and mostly unhappy encounters of young Hollywood talent (actors and directors, mostly) caught up in the youth counterculture as they came into contact with a quite baffled corporate establishment. Of primary interest are those among the young and talented who after getting caught up in the tumultuous times turned their backs on achievable industry success. Many of the cine-artists whose stories I tell did everything right at first; they built their careers much as their predecessors had. In the parlance of the industry: they paid their dues. But just as things seemed well set for their careers to take off, they got *caught up* in something else. And with one notable exception, things did not work out so well for them (in Hollywood, at least) after that.

We begin in chapter 1 with a fairly prosaic Hollywood predicament: a persistent box office slump made all the more maddening for Hollywood executives by the surprising popularity of two films, *Blow-Up* (Michelangelo Antonioni, 1966) and *Easy Rider* (Dennis Hopper, 1969)—the first a foreign-made art film, the second a biker film with obvious and parallel roots in the early-sixties B-movie and Jack Kerouac's fifties-era counterculture novel, *On the Road*.

After seeing *Blow-Up* in 1966, and hoping to get out in front of (and to exploit) a future counterculture genre, executives at MGM negotiated a three-picture deal with Antonioni, investing in the auteur's next project, a proposed American-made counterculture feature based on a scenario by the playwright Sam Shepard—a film eventually titled *Zabriskie Point* (1970). *Blow-Up* exceeded expectations, which only made their disappointment with *Zabriskie Point* worse. *Zabriskie Point* cost about as much as *The Godfather* (released two years later) and grossed less than $1 million. Two different regimes at MGM would struggle to figure out what to do with the film and have in the end only a list of people to blame.

The production backstory of *Zabriskie Point* is fascinating, as it involves a mélange of the powerful and crazy—a toxic mix of G-men, attorneys from the United States Department of Justice, activist national park rangers, Black Panthers, hippie gurus, and pissed-off Teamsters organizing sick-outs on behalf of a location-based crew frustrated and furious at an Italian cineaste they derisively dubbed "that pinko dago pornographer." Antonioni's American adventure began with a sightseeing trip through the desert Southwest, followed by a talent search for a handsome young couple to duplicate his sojourn. And it ended with all parties agreeing that making another American film together would be a terrible idea. Antonioni returned to Italy. MGM put the counterculture on hold. And the film's two stars abandoned their pursuits of stardom; Daria Halprin married Dennis Hopper and hid out with him in Taos, then sought refuge in self-help. She "found herself" finally years later at a mountain retreat proselytizing for dance therapy. Her costar, Mark Frechette, joined a cult, robbed a bank, and died in prison.

Hopper followed up on *Easy Rider* by taking a jailhouse meeting with Charles Manson (about a possible biopic!), then produced the not-at-all ironically named *The Last Movie*—an unwatchable, self-indulgent western that proved impossible to platform and release. Hopper's particular road trip to nowhere evinced a familiar Hollywood second act, with a sex, drugs, and rock-and-roll backstory suited to the times.

Chapter 2 tracks the American actor Christopher Jones's meteoric rise and sudden disappearance from the celebrity scene. His story involves James Dean and Jim Morrison at the start and, as so many of this era's Hollywood stories do, Charles Manson at its climax. Jones did his best work at American International Pictures (AIP), working for the B-movie producers Samuel Z. Arkoff and Roger Corman, joining there a counterculture Hollywood ensemble that included Jack Nicholson, Bruce Dern, Karen Black, and Ellen Burstyn. Among such a talented troupe, Jones seemed at the time the actor most likely to succeed. He did, succeed that is. And then he vanished—off the screen and off the grid.

I segue from Jones's brief Hollywood adventure to concurrent stories of four women, actors on their own very different road trips: Jean Seberg, Jane Fonda, Dolores Hart, and Barbara Loden. Like Jones, both Hart and Loden did everything right to become movie stars, only to decide that movie celebrity just wasn't for them. Both found their calling elsewhere. Hart found peace and love in a convent, shut the door, and never looked back. Loden fashioned herself as an auteur, her eye fixed on making movies that evoked two contemporary realist traditions: direct cinema and the far-out New York underground of Andy Warhol. Such a sensibility was rather doomed to failure in Hollywood. Loden hung around on the margins of the industry for a decade or so burning bridges, so she'd never be allowed back in, refusing time and again the two roles on offer to her: character actor or celebrity wife.

In 1970, the writer Tom Wolfe sneeringly coined the phrase "radical chic" to describe celebrities speaking out on behalf of the downtrodden and victimized.[31] Movie stars pandering to an all-too-gullible celebrity-crazed public seemed to Wolfe the realization of George Orwell's cynical prophecy of "an army of the unemployed led by millionaires preaching the Sermon on the Mount."[32]

Seberg and Fonda endeavored to use their celebrity to endorse and enhance the anti-war struggle, to fight for social and racial justice. They were in fact not dilettantes, even if the Hollywood establishment wanted or needed them to seem so. Jane Fonda has had a long and successful career as an actor and as an activist; hers is a success story spanning half a century. Seberg was not so lucky. For her efforts, J. Edgar Hoover and the FBI ran her out of town and then out of her life.

The book's final chapter focuses on the most famous casualty of counterculture Hollywood: Sharon Tate—murdered by a group of lunatics camped out at a movie ranch in nearby Chatsworth, in the rugged Simi Valley. Awful as the particulars of the case were, Tate's was in fact only the latest in a long and sordid list of encounters between the movie colony and the many and varied and occasionally dangerous in the near outskirts of Hollywood. Tate's murder recalled William Desmond Taylor's in 1922, Elizabeth Short's in 1947, Ramon Novarro's just a few months earlier—not only because the victims were, like her, movie people (or, as in Short's case, a movie industry aspirant), but because the investigations into these murders brought to light the many unsavory characters the victims had encountered, had hung out with, had done business with on their way up—any and all of whom seemed likely suspects. Tate's murder offers a necessary reminder that looming in the nearby outskirts of Hollywood are the sundry rejects and casualties, not so much or not necessarily of the movie and entertainment businesses, but of daily life in America—men and women who ventured west but then failed to find what they were looking for (unless, that is, what they were looking for all along was trouble).

Tate may or may not have ever become a movie star. We will never know. In the summer of 1969, she seemed on her way up, on her way there. Meantime, she was enjoying the ride. With her spouse, the director Roman Polanski, she got *caught up* in in the wonderful, crazy party life of counterculture Hollywood. The parties, some of which were held at 10050 Cielo Drive where Tate would be brutally murdered, featured an array of illegal drugs—drugs supplied by fringe dwellers like Manson and his right-hand man, Tex Watson, or by other unsavory and dangerous characters quite like them. Manson and Watson were not only useful to and tolerated by the counterculture Hollywood party crowd; they were frequently invited guests. They were essential to the daily operation of the Hollywood celebrity subculture because they supplied certain key services, because they manned the supply chain of drugs and sexually willing women.

Tate and her houseguests were collateral damage, slaughtered (at least in part) because the music producer Terry Melcher (who was, not incidentally, the son of the popular singer and movie/TV star Doris Day) had strung Manson along, dangling a recording contract until he got bored or spooked by Manson and his entourage. On August 8, 1969, fully aware that Melcher no longer lived at 10050 Cielo Drive, Manson sent a handful of his followers to that address anyway, to kill a bunch of people he and they didn't know. Manson was sending a message and pretty much everyone in Hollywood got it loud and clear.

It is a sobering conclusion, I know, that the most significant moment in counterculture Hollywood history is a bloody murder scene—a senseless and pointless encounter that, sadly, most everyone in Hollywood in 1969 could relate to. In the days and weeks after, plenty of movie people could say that what happened to Tate could have easily happened to them—and, it could have. In counterculture Hollywood there were any number of road trips, and most of them, like Tate's and Manson's led nowhere, at least nowhere good.

1 Road Trips to a New Hollywood
Easy Rider and *Zabriskie Point*

A perplexing crossroads dilemma for a movie industry on the brink: What can be done to get young Americans back into the habit of going to the movies? The answer as the sixties wound to a close seemed at once apparent and impossible, weirdly tied to two very different movies grounded in two very different traditions: the European New Wave and B-Hollywood. The collective fortunes of studio Hollywood thus fell to two very different men: Michelangelo Antonioni—an Italian cineaste whose career had suddenly changed course thanks to an unlikely global box office hit, the swinging London thriller, *Blow-Up* (1966)—and Dennis Hopper, a veteran B-actor and counterculture scene-maker whose low-budget biker road picture *Easy Rider* (1969) became for Hollywood the most talked-about movie in a decade.

Both *Blow-Up* and *Easy Rider* made a lot of money for their American distributors off small investments—and, indicatively, off virtually no studio involvement in their production. Neither set a course the studios could so easily or reasonably follow. Executives at the studios nonetheless tried. And in trying, they encountered a new breed of Hollywood talent: movie stars who didn't want to be movie stars and movie directors who frankly wanted nothing to do with the studio business model and hierarchy.

Antonioni followed up *Blow-Up* with *Zabriskie Point*, a film MGM paid him to make and then abandoned when it was done. The film's handsome young stars were well out of the business within a year or so of the film's release. And when Antonioni declined to make another Hollywood film, no one tried to change his mind.

After *Easy Rider*, Hopper was quite astonishingly the hottest director in Hollywood. So he decamped to Taos, New Mexico, to tap into vibes from the Native American community that once lived there. He took up artistic residence near the onetime residences of two legendary artists: the writer D. H. Lawrence and the painter Georgia O'Keefe. And then banked his filmmaking future on a ramshackle western made on location in Peru: *The Last Movie*. The title all too aptly spoke to his future in Hollywood.

Blow-Up: Michelangelo Antonioni's Mod Masterpiece

Intoxicated on prerelease buzz about their hip new thriller, *Blow-Up*, executives at MGM planned a holiday-season 1966 North American release. The film premiered in New York just before the New Year, in time to qualify for the Oscars. The reviews were terrific—offering promise (which would be fulfilled) for a wider spring 1967 release.

The spring playoff was buoyed by a nice surprise from the Motion Picture Academy as Antonioni got an Oscar nomination for Best Director. The nomination was unusual for such a fully international production: directed and produced by Italian filmmakers (Antonioni and his producer Carlo Ponti); based on a novel written by Julio Cortazar, an Argentine; shot on location in London for a British production company (Bridge Films); with a cast comprised of a who's who of the swinging London scene—actors David Hemmings and

Vanessa Redgrave, model and actress Jane Birkin, rhythm and blues band the Yardbirds (for-real rock stars who perform live and don't disappoint: guitarist Jeff Beck's amp short-circuits and he quite wonderfully smashes his instrument on-screen), and the German-born supermodel Veruschka. The casting proved canny, the setting well chosen, the vibe spot on.

Even better news followed in May as Antonioni and the film won the Palme d'Or at Cannes. The US theatrical run was by then in full flight and it well exceeded expectations: $20 million domestic off MGM's investment of less than one-tenth that amount. Things were all good with the unlikely arrangement—MGM and Antonioni, that is—until they were bad, really bad. But that was still a few years away.

Blow-Up was unlike anything MGM had in release or development in 1966. Their release slate for that year was headlined by *The Singing Nun* (Henry Koster), a Debbie Reynolds vehicle that's about, well, singing nuns, and the Doris Day spy spoof *The Glass Bottom Boat* (directed by the Looney Tunes/Jerry Lewis vet Frank Tashlin)—two films that exemplified the studio's endemic generation gap. The studio's top grosser for 1966 would be John Frankenheimer's nearly three-hour motor racing melodrama *Grand Prix*—a bloated epic that cost so much to produce it failed to meet the industry's measure for break-even at the box office.

When MGM signed Antonioni to a three-picture contract in 1966, it sent a clear message—a first affirmative move to cash in on a transitioning marketplace, a marketplace driven by the young in fact and at heart. It took into account the astonishing popularity with young filmgoers of the European art picture in general and with Antonioni in particular.

Blow-Up seemed to MGM execs the perfect film—and the negative pickup deal the perfect hedge—to trial run a relationship between Hollywood and the European New Wave.[1] In an industry

FIGURE 6. Quite by accident a fashion photographer (played by David Hemmings) captures on a roll of film what looks like a murder in *Blow-Up* (Michelangelo Antonioni, 1966, Premier Films/MGM).

that favors "ideas you can hold in your hand" (an adage frequently credited to Steven Spielberg, but it had been in play since the twenties), *Blow-Up* also and uniquely fit that bill as well: quite by accident a fashion photographer captures on a roll of film what looks like a murder, and those implicated in that crime endeavor to silence him. *Blow-Up* was a foreign art film the executives actually understand and like.

After the Oscar nominations and the Palme d'Or, and after pocketing the box office revenues, the American executives seemed (finally and for a change) smart. The critics (finally and for a change) were on board too. Andrew Sarris dubbed Antonioni's film, "a mod masterpiece."[2] And Bosley Crowther, the curmudgeonly *New York Times* critic, gave the film a good review, offering a terse characterization of the film that neatly doubled as an elevator pitch: "[*Blow-Up!* is] vintage Antonioni fortified with a Hitchcock twist."[3] Marketing executives at MGM could not have put it better.

Learning to Love the Foreign Art Film

Antonioni first became an important figure on the international scene in 1960 when his film *L'Avventura* was showcased at Cannes. *L'Avventura* was met with open derision by audiences and then won the Jury Prize despite, or (it's Cannes, after all) *because* of the film's frustrated reception. The film then reached American screens in the spring of 1961 along with an even more impactful Italian import, Federico Fellini's *La Dolce Vita*, which grossed nearly $20 million in the United States—an astonishing figure at the time. An American film culture assembled around these two European art films, and much to the studios' collective envy, a niche market emerged for a new wave of foreign films.[4]

The critical response to *L'Avventura* in the United States was rapturous—a harbinger of things to come. Sarris dubbed *L'Avventura* "a sensation."[5] Stanley Kaufman in the *New Republic* described its influence on film language and history as revolutionary: "Antonioni is trying to exploit the unique powers of film as distinct from the theater.... He attempts to get from film the same utility of the medium itself as a novelist whose point is not story but mood and character and for whom the texture of the prose works as much as what he says in the prose."[6] When a panel of international reviewers was asked by the British film journal *Sight and Sound* in 1962 to assemble a list of the Top Ten Best Films of all time, it ranked *L'Avventura* at number two, behind *Citizen Kane*.[7]

Antonioni's subsequent films—*La Notte* (1961), *L'Eclisse* (1962), and *Red Desert* (1964)—offered a steady diet of rich, handsome, and disaffected characters traipsing around a deceptively scenic postwar Europe. The three films are so consistent in their stories, themes, and mise-en-scène that when the director made the move to color in *Red Desert* it was for critics and serious filmgoers a contentious

FIGURE 7. Michelangelo Antonioni beside a poster for the film that launched his career, *L'Avventura* (1960) (Everett Collection).

topic, like Dylan going electric. After four such metaphysical melodramas, *Blow-Up* seemed for the director a sudden change of course, a point of departure. At least that was the view executives at MGM were anxious to take.

Just after *Blow-Up* completed its run, the Motion Picture Association of America (MPAA) president Jack Valenti took to the pages of the trade journal *Variety* to voice concern about the newly inflated value of foreign-made pictures in the American film marketplace. He reproached American film reviewers for failing to support the Hollywood product, for becoming "hung up on foreign film directors whose names end with 'o' or 'i.'"[8] First and foremost on Valenti's mind were Antonioni and Ponti, the brains and the money behind *Blow-Up*. Well repressed, of course, was the essential irony that Valenti's last name also ended in *i*.

Anticipating an obvious question—precisely who stateside in 1966 was prepared to make movies that could capture the interest of the many American moviegoers and reviewers who patronized the European art film—Valenti offered an answer, boldly announcing: "The future of the film business lies on the [college] campus."[9] The prediction proved accurate, as a new generation of film-school-educated auteurs, later dubbed "the movie brats," arrived on the scene. But in an irony likely lost on the MPAA president, these young auteurs—Francis Coppola and Martin Scorsese, to name just the two most prominent—were themselves rather enamored with and influenced by the films of foreign directors whose names ended in *o* or *i*.

Blowing Up the Production Code

To start: dealing with Antonioni was never going to be easy for MGM. He had by 1966 earned a reputation as an uncompromising and pretentious artist, as a singularly independent filmmaker with idiosyncratic methods. After every setup and before every shot, he liked to sit at the camera, thinking, as the cast and crew waited. MGM hadn't had a good year in some time, so we can understand why they were willing to deal with almost anything, almost anyone if they could get back on track. They really wanted *Blow-Up*; they really *needed Blow-Up*. So they entered into to a contract with Antonioni—a contract that explicitly gave the cineaste control over the final cut.

The issue of final cut was from the outset consequential. MGM executives had seen *Blow-Up*. So they knew about the scene at the photographer's studio—a scene that featured full-frontal female nudity. The MGM contract with Antonioni was meant to be the beginning of something. And as things played out, it was the beginning of a lot of things and not just for MGM. A simple rule of thumb: In the movie business, when they say it's not about the money, it's about the money. And when they say it's about public morality, then it's absolutely about the money.

Blow-Up was never going to get a production seal from the MPAA and the executives at MGM knew that going in.[10] And yet they signed the contract anyway.

When MGM released *Blow-Up* without a production seal, they did so appreciating the message they were sending to the other studios—the agreements, policies, and procedures they were defying. A basic and widely shared understanding had prevailed in Hollywood for over three decades: that no one film is bigger than the industry, that sacrificing free expression (for example, cutting an offending scene or line of dialogue) to suit the censors was a fair price to pay to maintain the necessary fiction of social responsibility, to maintain a predictable and amicable marketplace.[11]

MGM tried to be cagey about defying the MPAA. When they distributed *Blow-Up*, the studio's name and logo were conspicuously absent. The film reached theaters under the Premier Films banner, technically a Bridge Films/Carlo Ponti British-Italian coproduction released by an American "independent" distribution company, a company that MGM had in fact created solely to release the film. It was a convenient fiction. And it fooled no one who mattered in the business.

Executives at MGM knew that the Premier Films release was a calculated gamble. It was hard to predict how the management at the other studios might react or how, as a consequence of their decision to subvert MPAA authority, the censors might in the future judge other MGM films. It was also a gamble concerning the nation's exhibitors: would they be willing to present a noncompliant film to their local clientele? Turns out, theater owners were as tired of losing money as the studios were.

When the film hit, Valenti responded the only way he could, by venting his frustration in the trades. In January 1967, about a month into the film's first run, under the catchy *Variety* headline "Valenti Won't 'Blow-Up' Prod. Code for Status Films; No Church Push," Valenti lent his support to the MPAA's decision to deny *Blow-Up* a production seal.[12] (The "no church push" in the headline referred to NCOMP, the National Catholic Office for Motion Pictures, the less formidably named successor to the Catholic Legion of Decency, which had predictably issued *Blow-Up* its Condemned rating.) Two months later, under the headline, "'Blow-Up' B.O. Comforts Metro," *Variety* staff writers explained and explored MGM's success in defying the MPAA.[13] Valenti posted another press release in the same issue, strategically laid out by the magazine on the same page, announcing a plan to test the feasibility of an age-based, exhibitor-enforced classification system, what would become in the fall of 1968 the Voluntary Movie Rating System. MGM's contract to distribute *Blow-Up* had made such a new regime of censorship not only possible, but necessary.

Easy Rider Changes Everything

MGM's plan for a second picture with Antonioni involved committing the studio's financial support and technical expertise to the production of a hip Euro-Hollywood hybrid—a counterculture *American* film. Antonioni prepared for the shoot by taking a road trip across the southwestern United States during which he proposed to divine the *feeling* of young Americans. Meantime, about six months before Antonioni got his American project going, working with far less money and well under the major studios' radar, Dennis Hopper went into production on *his* counterculture road picture, *Easy Rider*. The differences in execution and subsequent popularity and profitability between the two films would in the end be remarkable.

Antonioni was fifty-seven by the time *Zabriskie Point* wrapped. His depiction of an American youth culture on the road seemed more anthropological than experiential. Such a cold and analytical bent had been in evidence in *Blow-Up*, a matter taken up by Pauline Kael in the *New Republic* in her well-titled review of the film, "Tourist in the City of Youth," in which Kael bluntly bemoaned Antonioni's critical distance from the swinging London he filmed. "It's obvious that there's a new kind of non-involvement among youth," Kael wrote, "but we can't get at what that's all about by Antonioni's terms. He is apparently unable to respond to or to convey the new sense of community among youth, or the humor and fervor and astonishing speed in their rejections of older values; he sees only the emptiness of Pop culture. All we can tell is that he doesn't understand what's going on—which is comprehensible, God knows, because who does?"[14]

The talent behind *Easy Rider* had a ready answer to Kael's query, "who does?" Because: Hopper and costar and coproducer Peter Fonda did. Hopper was just thirty-three when he completed work on *Easy Rider*. Fonda was twenty-nine. Together they comfortably embodied their characters. In doing so, they became rebel archetypes of a new and vibrant American youth culture in a very New Hollywood.

"*Easy Rider* is the real thing," the *New Yorker* critic Penelope Gilliat wrote in her review of the film, "Ninety-four minutes of what it would be like to swing, to watch, to be fond, to hold opinions, and to get killed in America at this moment."[15] Per Gilliat's assessment, *Easy Rider* depicted, absent the usual Hollywood hand wringing, the wilder and darker side of American youth culture, and included scenes of brutal interpersonal violence, a fact of life in a divided nation and a real-world anxiety for many young Americans nationwide. The film's biker heroes, Billy (Hopper) and Wyatt (Peter Fonda), find on their road trip an America in tense transition, with stops along the way at a bucolic commune populated by turned-on, dropped-out city kids (at once blissed out and in denial—they may not be ready to bank their lives on the land, but we get why they want no part of

FIGURE 8. In *Easy Rider* (Dennis Hopper, 1969, Columbia), Hopper (right) and Peter Fonda comfortably embodied their characters. In doing so, they became rebel archetypes of a new and vibrant American youth culture.

Nixon's America) and the Deep South (where the hippie-bikers are reviled and eventually murdered).

Easy Rider offered a sixties' counterculture variation on a theme introduced a decade earlier in Jack Kerouac's novel, *On the Road*. Kerouac's book evoked an improvisational energy, akin to fifties' bebop. Its colorful cast of characters thumbed their noses at a moribund establishment that had settled down after the war into cookie-cutter suburbs and unfulfilling bourgeois lives. Hopper's film similarly celebrates an outcast, libertarian spirit at once individualistic (and thus, quintessentially American) and antiestablishment. At the heart of both is a search for freedom—a rather magic word in America for both the Right and the Left. Readers and moviegoers from across the political and social spectrums took to *On the Road* and *Easy Rider* because they believed the counterculture heroes spoke to and for them.

In *Easy Rider*, Billy and Wyatt "do their own thing," but that *thing* makes them unwelcome most everywhere they go. They are in so many of the places they visit victims of snap judgments made about their looks and unconventional lifestyle. That they are judged so harshly and so superficially explains why they (and the actors who play them) captured the attention and affection of so many young filmgoers, so many Americans who felt similarly misjudged and mistreated. Only once during their travels do they feel fully welcome—at the aforementioned commune, where they spend a perfect day in the arms of the hippie counterculture. A better endorsement for hippie culture would be hard to find, hard to imagine. But the production backstory tells a different tale; and it is revealing. During the development stage of the project, Hopper negotiated with the New Buffalo commune in Arroyo Hondo, New Mexico—sited near his future home in Taos. But the young men and women there regarded Hollywood, even the counterculture version of Hollywood that Hopper and Fonda represented, as crass and commercial and declined participation in the film. So Hopper had to fashion a replica, near (of all places) Malibu, California.

Ironic, then, that a town in the Deep South where Billy and Wyatt are most certainly not welcome facilitated the film's most memorable live shoot. The now notorious luncheonette scene was shot direct-cinema style in Morganza, Louisiana, with support from local merchants and "talent." Armed with lightweight hand-held cameras and mobile sound gear, Hopper gave the impromptu cast dialogue ideas and encouraged them to improvise. He got what he was after, capturing the regional and racist tension that abounded in the Deep South. The scene begins as Wyatt and Billy and their new sidekick George (Jack Nicholson) enter at the luncheonette. The waitstaff, per Hopper's off-screen direction, ignores them. (That service would as well be refused to people of color was a parallel too obvious to miss.) Some of the local male diners amuse themselves at the bikers' expense, loudly referring to the trio as "Yankee queers" and "refugees from some gorilla love-in." One young redneck adds: "We should mate them up with black wenches . . . that's as low as you can git." The film's tagline, "A man went looking for America, but couldn't find it anywhere," seems particularly inapt here. In the Deep South, Wyatt, Billy, and George find America all right, in all its hideous, racist glory.

The luncheonette scene presages two moments of horrifying violence. The first follows soon after the heroes leave Morganza. They ride a ways down the road and make camp for the night. Around the campfire, they share a joint and some speculative drug-induced conversation and then bed down under the stars. As they lie asleep, they are attacked (and George is killed) by, we gather, the men at the luncheonette, one of whom had earlier remarked, coldly: "They'll never make it to Parish line."

The second follows an acid-trip in a New Orleans graveyard during which Billy and Wyatt dally with two prostitutes (played by the actress Karen Black and the choreographer/pop singer Toni Basil). On the road again, Louisiana Highway 105 just outside Kotz Springs to be specific, the bikers have one final encounter with two rednecks (played by Johnny David and D. C. Billodeau—two locals called on to play versions of themselves) during which they are gunned down in cold blood. As we witness these murders, we hear the Bob Dylan song, "It's All Right Ma (I'm Only Bleeding")," performed for the film by the Byrds' front man, Roger McGuinn. The song offers an ironic coda: our heroes are certainly bleeding, and they are most surely *not* all right.

The arrival of awards season 1969–1970 brought a few happy surprises for the film's studio distributor Columbia Pictures, which had acquired distribution rights to the film from Raybert Productions (run by Bob Rafelson and Bert Schneider). In May, the jury at Cannes gave Hopper their annual award for Best First Film. And then, several months later, *Easy Rider* got two Oscar nominations: for Best Screenwriting (Hopper, Fonda, and the counterculture writer, Terry Southern) and Supporting Actor (Nicholson).

Executives at Columbia benefitted from the film's success at the box office as well; *Easy Rider* grossed $19 million domestic off a $375,000 production budget. But behind closed doors they had to admit that *Easy Rider* would never have been optioned, developed, or produced in-house and that the studio had no one under contract prepared or equipped to follow up on the film.

The box office success of *Easy Rider*, despite and because of its (B-movie) mode of production, its obvious nod to the youth culture, and its counterculture sensibilities prompted the predictable industry response: panic. The film changed everything. Columbia executives decided to meet the challenge of following up on Hopper's film by outsourcing, entering into a multipicture deal with *Easy Rider*'s production team Raybert, which soon morphed into BBS, as Rafelson and Schneider added a new partner, Steve Blauner.

Meantime, Warner Bros. entered into a development deal with a young film school–educated writer-director lots of folks in town were talking about: Francis Ford Coppola. Warner executives staked Coppola, who had just turned thirty, $600,000 to develop for them the next *Easy Rider*, the next youth-culture hit.[16] The ambitious young filmmaker took the studio's money and ran—to San Francisco. There, under the American Zoetrope banner and with a handful of his talented friends—George Lucas, Carroll Ballard (who would later direct *The Black Stallion*, 1979), the screenwriting team of Willard Huyck and Gloria Katz, Jim McBride (the director of the audacious remake of Godard's *Breathless* in 1983), John Milius (*Conan the Barbarian*, 1982), and Walter Murch (the sound engineer and editor on Coppola's *The Conversation*, 1974 and most of the auteur's films after that)—he set about remaking Hollywood (for the first but not the last time).

American Zoetrope eventually presented Warners with four film projects for future development: (1) a reboot of Antonioni's *Blow-Up* in which a sound engineer discovers evidence of a crime, (2) a war film based loosely on a magazine article about American soldiers surfing in Vietnam, (3) a teenpic about some Northern California kids celebrating their last night of high school, all the while staring down a future deployment to Vietnam; and (4) a dystopian science fiction film about a domed-city in which the population takes high doses of mood-dampening drugs to keep them in line. None of the films sounded to the studio executives much like *Easy Rider*, so they passed on all four—a mistake, as things played out, of astonishing proportions.

Had the Warner Bros. executives exercised their option on the four projects, for roughly $150,000 per project they would have been able to develop *The Conversation* (Coppola), which won the Grand Prize at Cannes in 1974; *Apocalypse Now* (directed by Coppola and adapted from a script penned by Milius), which earned over $100 million domestically and won for Coppola a second Grand Prize at Cannes; *American Graffiti* (written by Huyck and Katz, directed by Lucas, and executive produced by Coppola in 1973), which became a box office sensation; and *THX-1138*, which never did much business but would have put the studio in partnership with Lucas, whose next sci-fi project, *Star Wars* (1977), and its many sequels and reboots have earned billions for Fox and now Disney. Instead of Coppola's proposed line-up, Warners got their $600,000 back—the old Hollywood's failure to comprehend the counterculture in a nutshell.

In 1971, MCA/Universal formed a counterculture production unit in house, moving Ned Tanen from an executive post in the pop-recording division (Uni-Decca) to a supervisory production position at the Universal film studio. The move proved profitable, but not because Tanen tapped into the counterculture vibe and not because he rebooted *Easy Rider*. Tanen, who would eventually become studio president, instead bet studio money on young would-be auteurs. Among the box office hits during his tenure: *American Graffiti* (Lucas, 1973), *Jaws* (Spielberg, 1975), *The Deer Hunter* (Cimino, 1978), and

Melvin and Howard (Jonathan Demme, 1980). After leaving Universal, Tanen shepherded a handful of popular teen pics directed and produced by John Hughes, including *Sixteen Candles* (1984) and *The Breakfast Club* (1985)—tapping a new youth culture for a new generation of filmgoers.[17]

Paramount pursued a variation on Universal's in-house plan. In 1972, studio president Frank Yablans established an elite production unit to exploit the talents of three young filmmakers: Coppola (fresh off the blockbuster success for the studio of *The Godfather*), Peter Bogdanovich (who had just made a name for himself with BBS's Oscar-nominated *Last Picture Show* in 1971), and William Friedkin (an Oscar winner in 1972 for *The French Connection*). The consideration built into the Director's Company contract was clear: the studio secured for the near future the services of three young, ostensibly hip filmmakers. In exchange for hitching their talent to the studio brand, the three filmmakers got secure and guaranteed financing, studio distribution, and a degree of creative autonomy. The timing seemed right, but internal studio politics, beginning with management disputes over Yablans's plan to use Coppola's *Godfather* sequel to launch the company, undermined the project. In the end, the unit laid claim to only three films: Coppola's *The Conversation* (a critical success), Bogdanovich's *Paper Moon* (a box office success in 1973, for which Tatum O'Neill won a Best Supporting Actress Oscar), and *Daisy Miller* (a film Bogdanovich made with his then girlfriend Cybil Shepard miscast in the lead; the film bombed at the box office and was widely panned by movie critics).

None of the three films produced for Paramount and the Directors Company were much about the counterculture. Bogdanovich's two features were period pieces. Coppola's rebooted *Blow-Up* was set in San Francisco but only because that's where he lived and liked to work. The film proved timely and counterculture, but by accident, really. Coppola began developing *The Conversation* in 1969 and went into production in 1973, before much was known about Nixon's affection for audio surveillance and before the so-called Watergate tapes would play such a significant role in his downfall. A quick timeline: The Watergate Committee convened on May 17, 1974 and issued its damning 1,250-page report on June 27. *The Conversation* was shot and cut by then and premiered at Cannes (where it won the Grand Prize) just as the Committee hearings were captivating American audiences on TV. The film opened theatrically in early July. Nixon resigned on August 8.

Elsewhere in Hollywood—this even after *The Graduate* and *Easy Rider* were such big hits—a lot of studio executives viewed the counterculture film as a genre or fad, offering a youth-oriented title or two as part of their diversified release slate. Among the more interesting titles to emerge from this scattershot "strategy": Arthur Penn's hippie anti-war picture for United Artists, *Alice's Restaurant* (1969), based on folksinger Arlo Guthrie's popular song; Haskell Wexler's neorealist Chicago in the summer of 1968 docudrama *Medium Cool* (Paramount, 1969); Richard Rush's darkly comic take on campus unrest *Getting Straight* (Columbia, 1970), a film capped by a hilarious scene of a botched master's thesis defense; *Panic in Needle Park* (Fox, 1970), Jerry Schatzberg's neorealist chamber piece about two young heroin addicts (played by Al Pacino and Kitty Winn), adapted from a script by Joan Didion and John Gregory Dunne; the clunky, overstated (and wildly popular) *Joe*, chronicling a doomed sojourn into New York's hippie subculture by a wealthy ad man and his unlikely sidekick, a bigoted hard hat, directed for Cannon Films, a B-movie outfit known at the time for distributing Scandinavian-made softcore films, by John Avildsen, who would in 1976 direct *Rocky*; Milos Forman's deft satire of upper-middle-class malaise and the dubious attractions of the emerging youth culture, *Taking Off* (made for Tanen at Universal in 1971); and the seedy drug culture melodrama *Cisco Pike* (B. L. Norton, Columbia 1972).

Of all the studio ventures, the aforementioned BBS unit at Columbia proved to be the industry's most successful counterculture project. Raybert, its predecessor had one bomb (*Head*, directed by Bob Rafelson and coproduced by Jack Nicholson in 1968) and one hit (*Easy Rider*) before Columbia went all in. *Head* is composed of a series of energetic and seemingly random skits, like the popular TV show it expands upon, *The Monkees* (also a Raybert invention). In *Head*, the Monkees—Mickey Dolenz, Davy Jones, Michael Nesmith, and Peter Tork—cluelessly wander from one movie set to another, from one tired old-movie genre to another encountering a raft of demi-celebrities: the past-it actor Victor Mature, the gossip columnist Rona Barrett, the former heavyweight-boxing champion Sonny Liston. Mixed-in as well are quite serious and disturbing images from the war in Vietnam, which fit neither the Monkees' TV format nor the tone of the rest of the film.

The *New York Times*'s Renata Adler dismissed *Head* as an "ersatz Beatles' film," as a pointless mash-up of "pot and advertising."[18] Kael weighed in late and predictably didn't mince her words: "The by now standard stuff of girls squealing at pop idols is not even convincing when they're squealing for the Monkees, and when this is intercut with documentary footage of the suffering and horror of war, as if to comment on the shallowness of what the filmmakers are manufacturing and packaging and desperately trying to sell, the doubling up of greed and pretentions to depth are enough to make even a pinhead walk out."[19] Even *Rolling Stone*, a magazine Raybert had hoped would promote the film, piled on, giving the film its "Non-news Story of the Year Award."[20]

The Monkees were by the summer of 1968 at the end of their brief, astonishing run. The band was formed by music and TV executives; the eventual members auditioned as actors, not musicians. The TV show was meant to be a spoof, a comic commentary on the big business of rock and roll. And the band was never supposed to be any good. But—joke is, joke was—they were. All told, the Monkees sold over seventy-five million records, albeit, especially early on, with the help of crack studio musicians and savvy producers. "The Monkees" TV show ran from 1966–1968, and the recorded music, much of it featured on the show, was then cross-marketed through a Columbia-RCA co-venture, Colgems. Raybert had endeavored to lampoon the rock and roll music business. The Monkees instead became major players in that business. With *Head*, Rafelson and Schneider parody the parody at the heart of the TV show and the showbiz phenomenon the Monkees had become. The film seemed designed and executed with one mission in mind: kill the Monkees. And it accomplished its goal.

As to the larger company mission, Rafelson mused in retrospect: "We [at BBS] didn't have any burning ambition or slogan to change Hollywood. We just knew there was a way to do something that was groovier than the way it had been done."[21] That was enough of a business plan for Columbia after *Easy Rider* hit. Rafelson, Schneider, and Blauner kept things groovy for their second feature for the studio: *Five Easy Pieces*. And they did so by handling in-house pretty much everything from development to release: Rafelson directed, Nicholson starred, Black costarred, and Carole Eastman wrote the script based loosely on Rafelson's account of his own youth as an "upper-middle-class rebel."[22] The cinematographer Laszlo Kovacs (whose counterculture cine-credits include *Easy Rider*, *Getting Straight*, *The Last Movie*, *The King of Marvin Gardens*, and *Shampoo*) shot and lit the film, evoking the groovy style and spirit of the otherwise very different *Easy Rider* by embracing Hopper's vision of a new American cinema in which "the whole damn country [is] one big real place to utilize and film."

In *Five Easy Pieces*, Rafelson and Kovacs shot a lot in the direct cinema style in real working-class American locales—bowling alleys, trailer parks, interstate freeways, and (most memorably) greasy-spoon diners—imbuing a counterculture attitude to such off-Hollywood milieus. The Columbia brass were kept happy (and happily away from the production), as costs were kept within contracted limits; the forty-one-day shoot was brought in for around $1 million.

Much as *Bonnie and Clyde* had baffled Jack Warner in 1967, *Five Easy Pieces* confounded the studio; it seemed to them a ragtag downer of a movie that defied a fundamental big-screen rule: there was no one in the film to root for, no one to like. Then, when audiences and critics seemed to dig the film, and seemed to want more films like it, no one at the studio understood why.

Five Easy Pieces begins with Bobby (Nicholson) working on an oilrig. He's called home for family business and reluctantly complies. His girlfriend, Rayette (Black), who wonders aloud why the country-and-western tearjerkers sung by Tammy Wynette so speak to her life, insists on tagging along. Bobby, again reluctantly, complies. Rayette is the hot-blooded opposite of the icy dispassion of Bobby's upper-class family; Bobby loves her in his way, and that's partly why he leaves her at a motel while he handles things at his family's sprawling estate. She gets impatient and lonely and shows up uninvited and in doing so sets the household on its head.

Bobby doesn't fit in anywhere—not with his family and not with his working-class friends. "I move around a lot," he muses, "not because I am looking for anything. I'm getting away from things that get bad if I stay." For young Americans, Bobby's inertia and its counterpoint, his wanderlust seemed a refusal of sorts, stalling entry into the adult establishment. Bobby's similarities to Ben in *The Graduate* are relevant here.

The New York Film Critics esteemed Rafelson's film; they voted *Five Easy Pieces* the year's Best Picture and Black the year's Best Supporting Actress. The critics, though, were a bit ahead of the curve. *Five Easy Pieces* received four Oscar nominations: Best

Picture, Actor (Nicholson), Supporting Actress (Black), and Screenplay (Eastman and Rafelson). But the AMPAS membership skewed (then as now) old, and the filmmakers came away from the night unrewarded.

To whom BBS and the *Five Easy Pieces* team lost rather tells a story. Nicholson lost to George C. Scott, the star of the Coppola-scripted *Patton*—a film predictably adored by Nixon and his ilk. Black lost to the venerable stage actress Helen Hayes in the bloated and awful Hollywood disaster epic *Airport*. *Patton* won Best Picture. And, for irony's sake, Sinatra took home the Jean Hersholt Humanitarian Award—in all, a very good night for the counter-counterculture. There were a couple of moments that seemed to nod to the emerging counterculture, buried deep in the program. Michael Wadliegh's *Woodstock* won Best Documentary. And for *Let It Be*, the Beatles won for Best Music (Original Score).

Drive He Said (1971), BBS's next feature, was developed at the same time as *Five Easy Pieces* and involved much of the same in-house talent: Nicholson directed from a script by Robert Towne. The film was shot mostly on location on the campus of the University of Oregon and elsewhere in the persistently hippie city of Eugene. Nicholson and Towne stuck close to the unglamorous melodrama at the heart of the source material: Jeremy Larner's 1961 novel about inept professors, lecherous professors' wives, free-spirited (free-loving, free-drugging) students, and anxious elite college athletes.[23] The film got some favorable reviews in some significant places. Canby, for example, wrote that the film was "touched with the kind of unexpected sensibility and decency that are rare in movies of this genre."[24] But the film proved a hard sell. Especially after *Five Easy Pieces*, it seemed at once small and personal. And because Nicholson was behind instead of in front of the camera, it got nothing like the box office, critical, or Motion Picture Academy attention.

The next two BBS films came out within a week of each other: Henry Jaglom's *A Safe Place*, which drew walkouts and boos at its New York Film Festival screening, got mostly awful reviews, and then bombed at the box office, and Peter Bogdanovich's *The Last Picture Show*, a film auspiciously (but not so ridiculously) dubbed by Paul Zimmerman at *Newsweek* as "the most impressive work by a young American director since *Citizen Kane*."[25] Bogdanovich's film netted eight Oscar nominations (including Best Picture and Best Director) and won two (for supporting actors Cloris Leachmen and Ben Johnson). Virtually every major critic—Canby, Ebert, Sarris at the *Village Voice*, Stefan Kanfer at *Time*, and Richard Schickel at *Life*—agreed with Zimmerman's assessment. Even the irascible Pauline Kael was charmed by the film's "flatland anomie," its "basic decency of feeling."[26] In the end, *Last Picture Show* would be BBS's one true masterpiece.

Bogdanovich's film is set in Anarene, Texas—an honest-to-goodness ghost town in Archer County. The anxious young men and women who live there are, like so many BBS characters, stuck in limbo—at the end of one thing having not yet arrived at the start of something else. The choice for the kids is simple: get out or get on with it.

The Last Picture Show is steeped in a peculiar counterculture-era futureless-ness, an anxiety that characterizes *Five Easy Pieces* and *Drive He Said* as well. At the end of *Five Easy Pieces*, Bobby abandons Rayette at a truck stop and hitches a ride with a trucker going north. He leaves behind everything he owns—including a winter coat, which, as the driver reminds him, he will surely need. Bobby moves on—though not necessarily forward. The road ahead leads nowhere.

Hector Bloom, the basketball star antihero in *Drive He Said*, spends most of the film distracted from the apparent task ahead (making the NBA) by his mentally ill roommate, Gabriel, who enlists

Hector into the anti-war movement and assorted other antisocial shenanigans, and Olive, the manipulative wife of a professor with whom he falls in love. In the end, like Bobby, Hector is alone and adrift, a futile spectator, as Olive betrays him and Gabriel is carted off to an insane asylum.

Duane (Jeff Bridges) in the final act of *The Last Picture Show* heads off to a pointless war in Korea, which, as in Robert Altman's MASH, released the previous year, is meant to stand in for Vietnam (a conspicuous absence in American cinema at the time). Duane decides to volunteer not because he's a patriot, but because his girlfriend, Jaycee (Cybil Shepard), has dumped him. The cheerful, dim-witted Billy (Sam Bottoms) is run over on the town's main street, to be mourned only by his brother (Timothy Bottoms), who in despair tries to resume a romantic relationship with his high school coach's wife (Leachman). Thanks to a *400 Blows*-like freeze frame that ends the film—the freeze frame seems a veritable trope in counterculture films—the outcome of the encounter is uncertain, here again quite like Bobby's improvised exit that ends *Five Easy Pieces*.

A number of other counterculture films similarly resist easy closure; even George Lucas's superficially more mainstream *American Graffiti* (1973) ends with a gloomy postscript: one of the Modesto teenagers, we are told, will be MIA in Vietnam; another will get killed by a drunk driver. Steve (Ron Howard), the film's most promising and sensible kid, has the opportunity to leave town for college but decides instead to stay in Modesto—Lucas's Anarene. The postscript tells us that after graduation Steve will sell insurance and remain stuck in his hometown with his clingy high school sweetheart. Only one of the teenagers in *American Graffiti*—Curt (Richard Dreyfuss)—gets out. In *The Last Picture Show*, only Jaycee makes it out of Anarene—all the way to Dallas, we are told, miles down the road but rather a world away to those she's left behind.

Antonioni's America: *Zabriskie Point*

When MGM purchased the US distribution rights to *Blow-Up*, they had already seen the finished product—a complete film financed overseas. Had *Blow-Up* flopped, the studio's short-odds could have been shrugged off—the relatively cheap negative pickup was always only an investment in another outfit's film. When *Blow-Up* hit, MGM made money. But they had to share the profit with overseas moneymen. With the contracted follow-up in-house project, Antonioni would be from development through distribution playing with the studios' money. The difference was significant; the risk was steeper but the studio's stake in the potential profits, far greater.

When MGM first proposed a three-picture deal, what executives wanted from Antonioni was an American follow up to *Blow-Up*. Then, after the director started talking about making a road picture about two young Americans, they maybe fantasized that Antonioni would make for them an art-house *Easy Rider*. What they got instead was a desert-southwest *L'Avventura*, a road trip to Death Valley and the continent's geographic low-point: *Zabriskie Point*, a road trip, as we embrace this book's central metaphor, to a geographic and metaphysical nowhere.

In an interview with the film reviewer Roger Ebert in anticipation of the release of *Zabriskie Point*, Antonioni spoke a lot about the film's desert setting, which he characterized as a seeming lunar landscape: "The desert is nothing. It's an enormous area of nothing. We do not have spaces like that in Europe.... The existence of these great spaces so close to the city says something to me about America."[27] Unlike Hopper's evocation of the open road as, akin to Kerouac, a setting for a counterculture adventure; the road trip in and to *Zabriskie Point* by design and intent led to a place that was figuratively and quite literally nowhere.

Easy Rider and *Zabriskie Point* share settings, and they share certain visual and sonic strategies. Antonioni freely acknowledged the parallels. When asked what American filmmakers he liked, Antonioni soft-pedaled: "I don't have any favorites," then, "I was, however, very impressed by *Easy Rider*."[28] Antonioni recognized Hopper's ambitions and artistry, especially Hopper's gestures at the French New Wave (the use of documentary technique in fiction set pieces, the Godardian flash-forward of Wyatt's murder at the end); in other words, he liked the aspects of style and form that were European, not *American*.

Like Hopper and his forerunners in the French New Wave, Antonioni's style and form was rooted in Italian neorealism. It is hard to imagine many American studio executives appreciating or understanding this. In his interview with Ebert, Antonioni talked about using mise-en-scène to evoke "a feeling about a style." It was pretty abstract; it was not what an American director at the time would have said to a newspaper film critic. *Blow-Up*, he said by way of example, was not "about a certain lifestyle in London," and it was not a movie about a crime and the mystery surrounding it—that is, it was not the film MGM executives rather liked. It was instead just "the story of a photographer." That a single photograph so complicates the photographer's life was just a "thing that happened to [the character] . . . in the course of being a professional photographer. . . . Anything could have happened to him; he was a person living in that world with that personality."[29]

With *Zabriskie Point*, Antonioni again set out to produce *a feeling about a style*. "I think [*Zabriskie Point*] is about what two people feel," the director mused, "It is an interior film. Of course, a character always has a background."[30] In this case, that background referred to the many overlaps among the actors Daria Halprin and Mark Frechette and their fictive counterparts, Daria and Mark—a dynamic complicated by the fact that neither Halprin nor Frechette were professional or instinctive actors. They were young Americans playing young Americans. Antonioni figured the plot would

FIGURE 9. Antonioni's young lovers in love: Daria Halprin and Mark Frechette on location in Death Valley during the production of *Zabriskie Point* (Michelangelo Antonioni, 1970, MGM) (Everett Collection).

emerge organically from their—that is, Halprin and Frechette's—relationship. Such a notion of character, actor, and plot was essential to his neorealist project.

Antonioni's sensibility and his sources were thus in a fundamental way foreign; he was after all and in so many ways *not* an American filmmaker. That he was perhaps as well un-American would be for MGM a problem they were unprepared and unable to solve.

Un-American Activities: Counterculture Filmmaking and Its Sundry Risks

Sometime during preproduction, Antonioni circulated a brief outline penned by the American playwright Sam Shepard about real estate speculators and wilderness exploitation in the desert southwest. The director would soon veer away from that scenario, so much so it is fair to wonder if he shared it only because he figured MGM could understand it, because he figured the executives maybe knew who Shepard was. In the end, five writers would earn screenplay credit for *Zabriskie Point*: Shepard, Antonioni, the veteran Italian screenwriter Tonino Guerra (who had worked with Antonioni on *L'Avventura*), the journalist and left-wing political organizer Fred Gardner, and Clare Peploe, Antonioni's girlfriend. Crediting so many screenwriters on the same film is never a good sign; in this case it revealed how much and how far the film veered from the initial pitch. Once location production commenced, far from the prying eyes of the studio, Antonioni seldom communicated with the studio, and when he did, he did so through an interpreter. The metaphor is irresistible here; Antonioni and MGM were never speaking the same language.

Zabriskie Point opens with a meeting of young political activists. They are up to something, but the discussion is unfocused and unproductive. During preproduction, Antonioni conducted interviews with student radicals and employed as an advisor and later as an on-screen extra Kathleen Cleaver, whose husband, the Black Panther leader Eldridge Cleaver, was in 1969 one of the FBI's ten most wanted fugitives, and who was herself at the time an activist in the organization.[31] Antonioni was maybe naive about the risk; that he was keeping dangerous company. Maybe he didn't care. Such was the price of realism, of making a counterculture film.

The cinematographer Alfio Contini shot the scene in the handheld style of direct cinema documentaries, but the aim, or at least the effect, is not, as the style connotes, objectivity. Instead, the technique confers uncertainty and ambivalence. Direct cinema directors used lightweight cameras to facilitate a unique "you were there" style. Contini used instead a heavy 35 mm Panavision camera—the wrong camera for the right look.³² The effect is at once style and a comment on style—vintage Antonioni.

As the film scholar Donato Totaro points out in his scene-by-scene analysis of the film, Antonioni used the "foreshortened, fragmented space" in this opening scene to "underscore the divisions within the group rather than [highlight] the sense of unity."³³ Collective action from these student radicals is not forthcoming—certainly not from or with the engagement or involvement of Mark, who is featured prominently in the scene. The camerawork and the elliptical editing capture Mark's impatience—an attitude later made explicit in Mark's exit line. After one student says they'd die for the cause, Mark quips: "I'm willing to die too, just not of boredom."

Once Antonioni cut away from this scene, he left the direct cinema style behind and for good; in doing so, he left these students and their politics behind as well. "If I had wanted to do a picture about student dissent," Antonioni commented after shooting the film, "I would have continued the direction I took at the opening with the student meeting sequence."³⁴ Antonioni decided instead to make a film about two young people who fall in love—not with the political counterculture, but with each other. And to characterize that relationship—to depict what it might be like to be young and in love in 1969—he endeavored to show their and by extension their generation's lack of shame or guilt about their bodies and themselves. This proved problematic for the studio as well.

However much MGM executives worried about Antonioni's "European sensibility" concerning sex and nudity—the "offending scene" in *Blow-Up* was after all a recent memory—nothing prepared them for *Zabriskie Point*'s signature sequence, the Death Valley love-in: an eight-minute widescreen tableau depicting dozens of naked couples making love in the sand, becoming in some physical and spiritual way part of the landscape of the continent's geographic nadir. Antonioni's initial plans for the scene had "20,000 hippies out there, making love, as far as you can see."[35] He initially planned to cap the scene with a sandstorm—an apocalyptic sequence in which blowing sand engulfed and overwhelmed the lovers—meant to foreshadow the ending of the film. The logistical problems were obvious and insurmountable, so he settled for less—fewer participants and a more peaceful vibe start to finish. Nevertheless the scene was unique and unforgettable. And it would account for a long list of problems and confrontations.[36]

During the complicated production of the scene, MGM was called upon to intervene on Antonioni's behalf in a series of confrontations with angry park rangers and their bosses in the US Department of the Interior, unruly and unhappy day-laborers and Teamsters, ambitious "America love it or leave it" lawyers in the US Attorney General's Office, and the anonymous raters at the MPAA's Classification and Rating Administration (CARA), who, because of this latest "offending scene," denied *Zabriskie Point* an R-rating.[37]

Antonioni found the fuss quite baffling—a lot of noise over a scene that was less (in his view, at least) about the characters (or what they were or weren't wearing) than the landscape they occupied, less about the nudity and sex than how the stripped-down human figures helped express the majesty of the unique landscape of Zabriskie Point. Antonioni found a dramatic location and then exploited it visually. That's what filmmakers were supposed to do, wasn't it?

Zabriskie Point is indeed a breathtaking spot. Named for the entrepreneur Christian Breevort Zabriskie, who mined Death Valley for the Pacific Coast Borax Company, the Point is an erosional landscape situated approximately 280 feet below sea level, composed of sediments from the evocatively named Furnace Creek Lake—a lakebed that dried up some five million years ago. The site proved perfect for Antonioni's characteristic extreme long shots, a visual style enhanced in the film by the flattening, compressing effects of

FIGURE 10. The *Zabriskie Point* (Michelangelo Antonioni, 1970, MGM) love-in—in more ways than one, the film's "offending scene."

Contini's telephoto lens. It was the desert that fascinated Antonioni. The performers: not so much.

To populate the scene, Antonioni cast members of Joseph Chaikin's Open Theater along with extras found in Las Vegas and then trained by the troupe. He then bused them in to perform the scene. Antonioni was acquainted with "California love-in parties" and was at the time impressed by their "absolute calm [and] tranquility." He was impressed as well with the politics of the sexual revolution, which he viewed as "a form of protest, a way of being committed. It shows that violence is not the only means of persuasion."[38]

Casting Chaikin's avant-garde troupe was a canny move as, quite unlike the director, they were by philosophy and practice, counterculture. Chaikin was a major figure in a shaking-up of the American theater scene; he used expressive movement to "get [actors] away from talking," to enable them to "express the inexpressible" through movement. He believed in the emotive power of an actor's body to "transcend language."[39] It was rather put to the test in Antonioni's dialogue-free love-in scene.

Information about the content of the planned scene (a love-in!) was leaked to the Death Valley National Park Rangers and they organized to block access to the site. Studio management, which had secured permits but were as well anxious about the proposed content of the scene and how Antonioni might film it, declined to intervene, hoping that the Rangers' collective action would force Antonioni to abandon his plans and move on. But then an unlikely ally stepped forward: an organized group of environmental activists. Under the false impression that Antonioni was still working from Shepard's anti-developer script, the activists lobbied Park Service officials in Washington, who then ordered the Rangers to stand down.

After the Rangers backed off, the studio was put in the unhappy role of enabling the scene's production, including, what for them and the press would be the height of folly, trucking in finer-grain sand so Chaikin's troupe and the Vegas-based extras might more comfortably cavort under the desert sun. To get the color right—that is, to alter nature to get the look he wanted—Antonioni spent thousands of dollars dyeing portions of the desert various shades of pink and green. At the director's behest, the production designer Dean Tavoularis crop-dusted the hills visible on the horizon with red powder.[40] It was a costly and ultimately futile experiment, serving in the end mostly to annoy MGM. For studio management, the scene and the film as a whole began to take on the form of an object lesson—a lesson they were not so anxious to learn.

After the Rangers stood down, many among the conservative craftspeople and day laborers hired by MGM refused to work on the scene. To express solidarity with the behind-the-scenes crew, the Teamsters stepped in and organized a series of slowdowns and sickouts, job actions that caused production delays. There was as a result a lot of standing around waiting, made all the more obnoxious given the three-digit temperatures routinely reached at the Death Valley location. Locked in a struggle with the very workers he had expected to be on his side—America was, for Antonioni, a baffling place—and forced to negotiate with the ever-impossible reps from the Teamsters with no help from the studio, Antonioni was left to sort things out on his own. And he was well out of his league.[41] The Teamster delays cost MGM a lot of money. And when the film flopped, studio executives blamed Antonioni for going over budget and falling behind schedule.

The labor dispute vexed Antonioni, but it was a sign of the times. Nineteen sixty-nine may have been the dawning of the Age of Aquarius for some, but it was as well the first year of Nixon's first term, a regime built upon a conservative coalition dubbed "the silent majority." Many of the hardhats, hourly workers, and Teamsters hired for the location shoot were Nixon supporters—right-wing nativists, Vietnam War hawks, and social conservatives. According to Beverly Walker, a publicist hired by Antonioni's managers to do damage control during the production, the crew dubbed Antonioni, that "pinko dago pornographer." He communicated with them through an interpreter, and anything the Teamsters or crew didn't want to understand got necessarily lost in translation.

Talking with the *New York Times*'s Guy Flatley, Antonioni addressed the problems with the crew. "The misunderstanding about my anti-Americanism arose from the fact that I am not used to explaining all my intentions to the crew. They saw the airplane all painted up and the kids talking politics, so maybe they thought I was a Communist starting a revolution. . . . As for the scene showing the American flag painted red," Antonioni remarked, referring to an image that struck many of the workers on the set as a desecration, "well I frequently do things like that with colors."[42] Such an explanation, even if he had bothered to share it with the crew, even if he had told them so in English, would not have sufficed.

Even the most routine production arrangements proved problematic. For a scene set in a desert outpost café, Antonioni wanted to use a jukebox recording of Patti Page's cover of "The Tennessee Waltz." The song fit the setting; it's nostalgic, ostensibly country-western, the sort of single that patrons might choose in that establishment. Its lyrics speak to the film's themes of loneliness and lost romance, and it foreshadows the film's final tune, "So Young," performed by another American original, Roy Orbison. Licensing the Page song proved in the end impossible, as state administrators in Tennessee threatened legal action, claiming the song was a state anthem and not the sort of thing to be used in such a controversial film.

Complications persisted well after the production wrapped. The Rangers who had acceded to pressure from their bosses in D.C. commenced a letter-writing campaign, complaining about Antonioni to executives at MGM, to the press, to the FBI, and most effectively, to the US Justice Department. In the late spring of 1969, several months before the film would be released, assorted Rangers, members of Antonioni's production staff, and employees of the studio were subpoenaed to appear before a Grand Jury in Sacramento. At first, the facts of the case were hard to come by. James Simonelli, a spokesperson for the US Attorney's Office in the California state capitol, confirmed only that an investigation into the production was underway: "This is a grand jury inquiry looking into the production of the film, [but] under the law proceedings before the Grand Jury are kept secret."[43]

Speculation about the Grand Jury inquiry circulated widely. More factual news followed more quietly first in the trades and then later in a feature for *Film Comment* written by Walker. The truth proved stranger than fiction, as no one had guessed what the feds were really up to.

The investigation built upon allegations that the extras bused in to appear in the Death Valley scene had been transported across state lines for immoral purposes in violation of the 1910 Mann Act—a law meant to combat turn-of-the-twentieth-century white slavery. Antonioni contested the charges: "I understand that a girl said that

I had asked her to do oral intercourse ... [but] what I wanted were the attitudes, the gestures of love. Those people from Joe Chaikin's Open Theater were acting, not doing."[44] This distinction between simulated and real sex may well have been accurate, but in 1969 the distinction was in fact legally insignificant.[45]

By the time Flatley interviewed Antonioni in February 1970, the director was already on the defensive. And when he tried to defend himself, he didn't make the situation any better. "I wasn't trying to *explain* the country," Antonioni remarked to Flatley, "a film is not a social analysis, after all. I was just trying to feel something about America, to gain some intuition. If I were an American, they would say I was taking artistic license, but because I'm a foreigner, they say I am wrong. But in some ways a foreigner's judgment may be ... not better, necessarily, but more objective—illuminating precisely because it is a little different."

Antonioni's tendency to philosophize about politics further muddied the waters. Americans *have* politics, much as they *have* religion. So there's no point in talking. The "pinko dago pornographer" tag rather stuck, and notions of Communist agitation were still unpopular in the United States in 1969, still bottomed upon notions widely held during the Cold War. If Antonioni was (and if he considered himself to be) a Marxist, he was the sort of Marxist you might have found teaching literature in an English Department at the time. Marxism was for him a philosophy, a way of understanding the materialist underpinning of modern society. (Good luck explaining that distinction to his critics.)

The early scenes in *Zabriskie Point* set at "California State University" were shot at USC in a then-rugged part of downtown—a location close to the site of the 1965 Watts riots. The L.A. we get in the film is not beaches and sand, posh and stylish Beverly Hills retail, movie industry glitz and glamor. It is instead a flat and filthy urban sprawl dominated by outsized billboards hawking pointless products. Antonioni filmed Frechette walking around downtown; he filmed the handsome young actor posed in front of the billboards—a materialist analysis, then, rendered visually. Antonioni would come to hate L.A., and in the end, he would have his reasons. "L.A.," the director offered in a terse refrain after the film wrapped, "is like being nowhere and talking to nobody about nothing."[46]

Materialist aesthetics aside—and they were beside the point in the evolving allegations focused on Antonioni's Communist politics—what interested interviewers and commentators most were the director's views on the cultural upheaval in the United States, on the possibility of violent revolution. Here again Antonioni waxed philosophical. He had spent some time on college campuses, he told the press, interviewing student radicals, and he had his doubts about "the young white children of the bourgeoisie"— their commitment, and more importantly, their (lack of) desperation. "Perhaps in 50 years, things will arrive at a crucial point. Even though a lot of young people talk about violence and revolution, not all of them could do it. It's not so easy to be violent."[47]

Antonioni mooted instead the notion of a "silent revolution." "With many students violence is just an intellectual thing," he concluded, sounding again like a college professor, "something quite different from the violence that comes out of the condition of life in the black ghetto, where there are practical, material forces that push people into violence."[48] Such intellectual musings got lost in the noise circulating about the film.

Looking back on the struggle to get *Zabriskie Point* screened and seen, the film's executive producer Harrison Starr tersely concluded: "[*Zabriskie Point*] was a counterculture film, obviously, and they [that is, MGM, the press, and America's entrenched conservative establishment] just couldn't understand it."[49] But just as likely, they understood the movie and its director perfectly well. Years after his American experience ended in frustration and disappointment,

Antonioni reflected with uncharacteristic clarity: "If I had to sum up my impressions of America, I would list these: waste, innocence, vastness, poverty."[50]

James Aubrey to the Rescue (Really?): Counterculture Studio PR

The *Zabriskie Point* production budget was about $7 million. For context: Paramount spent $8 million to make *The Godfather* a couple of years later. MGM had a lot riding on the film, but very little control over its production.

A first moment of truth arrived in the fall of 1969, when Antonioni screened a rough cut at the studio. Studio executives hated what they saw and decided to postpone the film's release. Complicating matters further were problems with the MPAA, which had refused a production seal, ostensibly rating the film "X." Boardroom discussions ensued; focusing less on how to platform the film's release than on how much of the studio's good marketing money should be thrown after such a bad production investment.

When MGM postponed the release of *Zabriskie Point*, Antonioni responded with predictable petulance: "[MGM] asks me why the film is so expensive, but that's what I'm going to ask them. I'm seeing such a waste of money. It seems almost immoral. . . . They are consumers. They are used to wasting."[51]

In October 1969, when the corporate raider Kirk Kerkorian succeeded in an unfriendly take-over of MGM, *Zabriskie Point* was still stalled in post-postproduction/pre-distribution limbo. Kerkorian had plans for the studio that didn't only or exactly involve making movies, so to downsize studio operations he replaced the MGM management team hired by the previous ownership group (Seagram's Edgar Bronfman Jr. and Time Inc.) with his own and put the studio under the day-to-day control of the former CBS executive

James Aubrey, a notoriously ruthless executive. Tasked with turning the company's fortunes around, Aubrey dramatically downsized the studio, diminishing production and liquidating assets, including the studio's valuable real estate, the vast film library, and a lot of iconic merchandise, including, as the press could not report often enough, the ruby slippers worn by Judy Garland in *The Wizard of Oz*, which were auctioned off for $15,000.

Aubrey inherited *Zabriskie Point* and the many problems that came with it, which at first seemed more bad news for Antonioni. New regimes in Hollywood routinely short-change their predecessors' projects; Aubrey did not need to be reminded that it's not enough to succeed in the movie business, it's necessary as well for those you might be compared to, those you have replaced, to fail. So it surprised no one when Aubrey decided to further postpone the film's release, strategically attributing the delay to the intractable problem of the film's X-rating.[52]

In December 1969, Aubrey began working behind the scenes to change the public perception of *Zabriskie Point*. He enlisted some PR help from Joyce Haber, the popular industry columnist for the *Los Angeles Times*. He was most likely calling in a favor, or perhaps he promised a favor that could be called in some time in the future, as Haber's column began with an implausible hook, especially given Aubrey's well-earned reputation: "Who says the industry's new business-minded bosses aren't creative-minded as well. Take James Aubrey." (Cue industry insiders laughing out loud.)[53]

Haber characterized *Zabriskie Point* as MGM's "farthest out, most contemporary, most experimental film," then dutifully tracked its troubled production history (*under the old MGM management team*), including the Mann Act inquiry, as a lead-in to Aubrey's stubborn refusal to regard the film as "a total loss." Aubrey was looking forward to working with Antonioni, whom, Haber claimed, he admired. The executive had flown to Rome to supervise a beefing-up of the rock and roll music program (that is, the music comprising the soundtrack), hoping to increase the film's appeal to young filmgoers.

There were rumors circulating at the time that the previous regime had implored Antonioni to produce an R-rated cut, absent the love-in scene and with a significantly foreshortened opening sequence (the student activist meeting). Aubrey dismissed any such backroom drama: "It's an X-movie. X in content, language and everything.... If you're going to make a film about young people today, you're going to be X-rated."[54]

Aubrey pushed hard at the "film about young people today" message, telling Haber *he* believed *Zabriskie Point* was "the most exciting film about the contemporary scene that's ever been made." The executive compared the film to (the also X-rated) *Midnight Cowboy* (John Schlesinger, 1969) and (the "hard" R-rated) *Easy Rider*.[55] Like *Easy Rider*, Aubrey contended, *Zabriskie Point* was "with it." As to the difference between the two pictures, well, compared to Antonioni's film, *Easy Rider* was "not particularly well-made." Aubrey was committed, or so he claimed in his conversation with Haber, to a fully funded January 1970 release of an intact director's cut.

Aubrey took the auteur's side against the critics as well, many of whom had seen and panned the film well before the public had a chance to see it and decide for themselves. Pauline Kael dismissed the film as a "pathetic mess," and then highlighted its anti-Americanism: "he has rigged an America that is nothing but a justification for violent destruction."[56] Aubrey countered: "I don't give a damn what the critics—Judith Crist or Pauline Kael—say about [the film]. Antonioni's a genius. That's all." To which Haber added, "When it comes to executives in the New Hollywood, Aubrey just may be [a genius] too."[57] (Ugh.)

In the second week of February 1970, *Zabriskie Point* finally got its North American theatrical release. But contrary to Aubrey's professed belief in Antonioni's genius, the release was by any industry standard limited, a clear signal of the studio's trepidation.[58] To be fair, Aubrey knew there wasn't much of a point in financing a showcase release (built on big-city playoffs and positive word of mouth and reviews) because the critics had already panned the film. By then, Vincent Canby, writing for the *New York Times*, had remarked upon *Zabriskie Point*'s "stunning superficiality."[59] The *Los Angeles Times*'s Charles Champlin described the film as "shallow and obvious . . . unusefully oblique."[60] Richard Cohen, writing for *Women's Wear Daily* dismissed *Zabriskie Point* as "a loathsome and incredibly shoddy film," then mused out loud what many other reviewers had kept more to themselves: "[Antonioni] has offered us [Americans, that is] his contempt." [61] Even Ebert, who had interviewed the director during the production, was dismissive: "[*Zabriskie Point*] is such a silly and stupid movie."[62]

In its first run, Antonioni's film grossed just $900,000. The auteur era had only just begun and MGM already had its *Heaven's Gate*.[63] Kerkorian's plan for the studio morphed accordingly, prioritizing the construction of and investment in hotels and gambling venues. In the scheme of things in Hollywood in 1970, MGM's CEO figured tourism was the safer bet.

Two days after *Zabriskie Point* opened in American theaters, a news item from Oxbridge, England, ran on one of the back pages of the *Los Angeles Times*: "Antonioni Pleads Guilty to Pot Charge." The marijuana in question was found and seized at Heathrow Airport. Antonioni confessed to the crime, paid a $240 fine, and was summarily escorted by Customs Agents onto the next available plane from London to Rome. The not insignificant nine-ounce count found in his possession was, he confided to the agents, purchased for a mere $15 in Los Angeles from a penniless guy on the street for whom the director felt compassion. "The man was hungry," the director quipped blankly. Antonioni's attorney added nonsensically that his client never smoked the stuff.[64] By then, no one at MGM cared much if anyone believed him or not.

Daria Halprin and Mark Frechette: Hollywood's Hot Counterculture Couple

Antonioni decided at the outset of production to cast unknowns to play the young lovers in *Zabriskie Point*. He figured established actors would bring technique and skill and that the baggage of Hollywood celebrity would counter his efforts at authenticity. His vision of an American neorealism was a calculated gamble that, it's fair to say, didn't in the end pay off.

Antonioni "discovered" Daria Halprin in 1968 after seeing her in Jack O'Connell's *Revolution*, a 1968 film about hippies in San Francisco. Halprin had, Antonioni recalled, a "bratty, free, earth-child quality." And on camera, from most any and every angle, she looked beautiful. Daria Halprin was a child of some privilege. Her parents, Ann and Lawrence Halprin, were well-healed progressives from Marin County. Ann was the founder-director of the Dancers Workshop. Lawrence was a successful landscape architect. They sent Daria to a posh private school, where she got good enough grades to get into the University of California, Berkeley. Daria was working on a project in a pottery class at the university when she was asked if she would like to star in Antonioni's film.

Sally Dennison, a volunteer production assistant, headed the national talent search for Halprin's costar.[65] She first explored local, L.A. options with the help of Fred Roos, then a TV casting director.[66] Roos suggested a young actor he knew, Harrison Ford. Dennison liked Ford, but Antonioni passed because Ford was a professional actor(although at the time, only sort of).

The search moved on to the east coast. In Boston, Dennison met a wannabe-actor named Ed Beardsley, a follower of the charismatic cult leader Mel Lyman, the founder of the Fort Hill Community in Roxbury. Beardsley was a frequent contributor to Lyman's counterculture free paper, *Avatar* and knew pretty much everyone in the local hippie scene. Beardsley wanted the role for himself. But when it became clear that that wasn't going to happen, he generously offered to introduce Dennison to other young men in the Cambridge and Boston hippie scenes.

Dennison was riding in a rented limo with Harrison Starr (who would receive an executive producer credit on *Zabriskie Point*) observing the local scene when she spied Frechette at a bus stop. He was engaged in a heated argument. She stopped to watch the confrontation unfold. Afterward, she and Frechette met and talked briefly. Dennison then rattled off a telegram to Antonioni, stating simply: "He's twenty and he hates."

Antonioni asked to see Frechette on camera. So Dennison staged an impromptu screen test. As Frechette later described the audition to a reporter for the *New York Times*: "They put me in front of a camera and said, 'Drink a beer.' I drank a beer. Run up and down the street. Try to break into that car." Antonioni was impressed; he found in Frechette "the elegance of an aristocrat." And there was, he mused, "something mystical about him."[67]

MGM fronted Frechette money for airfare and a per diem for a callback in New York. Frechette pocketed the travel advance and hitchhiked. When he arrived in New York, he was happy he had economized, as he discovered he was just one of forty "finalists," all in contention for the role. "Everyone was giving long lines about their acting experience." Frechette recalled, "but I had none except in the second grade when I was an Indian in a Thanksgiving melodrama." Frechette returned to Boston weirdly confident and pondered what might happen if he actually got the part. "I started thinking of the publicity, of lots of bread. Could I handle that or would it get to me?"[68] He was about to find out.

Frechette did not have to dig deep to understand his character, Mark, in the film. "I never really got to the point where I felt I was acting. I could easily imagine what was in the character's mind. A lot of real tension and anger, the pent-up uptight feelings the character has were what I felt for a long time."[69] But much as Frechette was suited to the role, casting him in such an expensive film was a big risk, especially since he had what might be called, politely, a colorful biography. He had an arrest record for disturbing the peace and, more worryingly, two stints committed to a mental hospital. According to Ryan Walsh in his "year in the life of Boston" cultural history, *Astral Weeks*, MGM eventually got hold of Frechette's hospital records, but by then he was already on the job. Doctors at the mental hospital detailed "a troubled childhood, distorted religious views, and a deep distaste for authority." They advised approaching Frechette "with caution."[70] If only they had.

In May 1969, the MGM marketing team began positioning the film in the marketplace. So they recruited the L.A. Times's Rasa Gustaitas to properly introduce Halprin and Frechette—"the carpenter and the dancer," as she described them, Antonioni's counterculture it-couple. "[They] had been going their own way and doing their own thing... when, Flash! the MGM finger pointed and despite their lack of acting experience or movie ambitions, suddenly, at age twenty—Flash! instant stardom."[71]

Halprin and Frechette, like their screen counterparts, fell in love. On the set, Gustaitas observed Halprin and Frechette "sitting in the coatroom during a break in the shooting, [just] two kids with arms loosely around each other, grooving."[72] The director's plan to shoot a film about two American kids in love was taking shape.

Gustaitas described Antonioni as "a quiet genius," the epitome of the New Wave cineaste. In the coming New Hollywood, she suggested, studio executives would have to learn to deal with the likes of him. Antonioni seemed determined to make such an adjustment difficult. Explaining the film's themes "of encounter and communication," he noted the film's long takes and periods of quiet. "When the astronauts went around the moon," he mused, "all the time I wondered how they talked to each other."[73] Safe to assume, Gustaitas and more importantly no one at MGM had the slightest idea what he was talking about.

Mark Frechette and the East Coast Charles Manson

After the production wrapped, Frechette returned to Boston and talked to a reporter from the *Globe*. He had no idea what Antonioni was up to either: "Antonioni didn't represent reality. It's all surface phenomenon, part of the prehistoric past." Halprin, who was living with Frechette at the time, chimed in as well: "The whole movie embarrassed me."[74]

Frechette told Ebert that he planned to quit acting to go back to carpentry; he had lately seen several of Antonioni's previous films and didn't much like any of them either. Regarding *Zabriskie Point*, Frechette endorsed the critical consensus: "Nothing happens, man; it's just a lot of young people going nowhere." Interviewed for the same article, Antonioni deigned to agree: "What happens to [Daria and Mark] is not important. I could have them do one thing, or another thing. People think that the events in a film are what the film is about. Not true."[75]

At the risk of seeming glib, the high (and low) point in Frechette's post-film press tour was his truly stunning guest spot with Halprin on the "Dick Cavett Show." Cavett had by then cultivated a reputation as *the* hip talk show host. The competition on that score was not exactly fierce; it was not hard to be more hip than Merv Griffin, Johnny Carson, or Mike Douglas. But here he proved to be yet another hack emcee, another shill for the entertainment industry establishment.

Halprin and Frechette amble onto the stage and join the filmmaker Mel Brooks and the film reviewer Rex Reed. (Reed seemed a bit of a setup, as he had panned the film, describing it as "hilariously awful," dismissing the actors' performances as "two of the worst in a decade.") Frechette seems from the outset sullen, pissed-off, anti-establishment. (And maybe he's read Reed's column.) Cavett struggles to get him and Halprin to talk about the film, about Hollywood, about anything. Working from scribbled notes, Cavett asks Frechette to recount the story of his discovery. "I was cast at a bus stop," Frechette replies tersely, "That's about it." Cavett has the full story in the notes his writers or interns have written for him. But Frechette declines to recount them.

Reading again from his notes, Cavett asks both actors about their alternative "hippie" lifestyles—specifically: the Fort Hill Community where both Halprin and Frechette lived at the time—weirdly mispronouncing "commune" as kə-*myün* as if he had never heard the word said aloud. Frechette grimaces; then starts talking. "It is a community, but the purpose of the community is not communal living." Then, as if anticipating incomprehension, his voice trailing off, Frechette completes the thought: "The community is for one purpose, and that is to serve Mel Lyman." Lyman is of no real interest to Cavett. (He isn't in the scribbled notes, perhaps.) So the interview drifts into silence. Halprin and Frechette come off as rude, incomprehensibly ungrateful.

Watching the Cavett segment today, I don't think Frechette was *trying* to be rude; he was in that moment just being candid about something *he* cared about, something Cavett clearly did not care about. Frechette made $60,000 working on *Zabriskie Point*. And he donated the entire amount to Lyman and Fort Hill. Mark Frechette was a serious guy. And he was serious about Lyman and Fort Hill. That too was beyond Cavett's comprehension.

The marketing team at MGM initially tried to exploit Frechette's life in Boston: they tried to work the story about Dennison and Antonioni plucking the young actor out from a for-real counterculture lifestyle. The counterculture backstory helped frame Frechette's impending celebrity. Gustaitas, for example, recounted: "a long string of frustrations [involving] motorcycles, drinking, housewrecking parties, fistfights, and running away," then added that after years of "wandering and odd-jobbing," he had, "found tranquility in Fort Hill."[76] Working from the MGM PR script, Gustaitas enthused at Frechette's time at Fort Hill: "Watch out Hollywood. Here comes Daria. And right beside her, Mark, whose dream is even vaster: A magic theater at the Fort Hill commune where people will enter a completely enveloping environment and perhaps, be transformed. 'We'll start with love and go on from there,' Mark says."[77] Contrary to Cavett's expectations and preconceptions, Frechette was never thinking about the next big role, the next big step in his career. For him, the future was always and only about Fort Hill.

Gustaitas's *L.A. Times* feature ran in May 1969, when the Frechette/Fort Hill story seemed like something the studio might use to highlight the authenticity of *Zabriskie Point*. But by the end of the year, the commune backstory had to be tabled, as alternative communities, especially ones headed by charismatic gurus became recontextualized amid the horrifying reports about a group of hippies camped out on the outskirts of Los Angeles, who, on orders from a charismatic ex-con named Charles Manson, had murdered a handful of Hollywood's rich and connected. By then, every youth cult and alternative community was potentially and irrationally murderous and every charismatic guru was the next Charles Manson.

A quick Fort Hill backstory: In 1963, Bob Siggins, a banjo player in the Jim Kweskin Jug Band, decided to quit the music business to pursue a PhD.[78] It was from such an unlikely scenario that a young musician named Mel Lyman got his first big break. Lyman filled in for Siggins and then stuck with Kweskin long enough to become a minor folk music legend.

The Jim Kweskin Jug Band was a popular outfit on the sixties folk scene. They got booked on the *Tonight Show with Johnny Carson*, and influenced copycat combos like Mother McCree's Uptown Jug Champions, which featured Jerry Garcia and Bob Weir before they formed the Grateful Dead. The folk-scene's then rising star Bob Dylan dubbed Kweskin one of his favorite singers.

Lyman eventually switched from banjo to harmonica, at first just filling in for the band's harp-player David Simon. Lyman so impressed he became one of the band's featured players, and soon after that its spiritual and intellectual leader. Claims concerning Lyman's otherworldliness date to these early days. And Kweskin was one of Lyman's earliest acolytes—so much so Kweskin's interest in his own music career diminished in direct proportion to an increasing fascination with Lyman's spirituality. "He never made a telephone call when the line was busy," Kweskin recalled, "he never called anybody and they weren't home . . . you'd say it was a coincidence, maybe [if it happened] once or twice. But it happened every day."[79]

In 1971, Lyman made the cover of *Rolling Stone* magazine—not for his work as a musician, but instead as the subject of an investigative piece by David Felton, a writer who (with David Dalton) had penned a feature for the magazine on Manson roughly a year earlier.[80] Felton colorfully described the organization of Fort Hill as "acid fascism," and dubbed Lyman, in a phrase that carried a lot of weight at the time, "the East Coast Charles Manson."[81]

Felton focused on allegations of LSD abuse at Fort Hill. Manson had used the drug to curry favor among his "Family" and then used it to control them. The parallel proved rhetorically useful for Felton. But Lyman was no copycat. His interest in LSD predated Manson's. He first encountered the drug at Richard Alpert's house in Cambridge, the veritable birthplace of the LSD counterculture. Alpert was Timothy Leary's research partner on the Harvard Psilocybin Project. And like Leary, he was convinced of the drug's therapeutic and spiritual value.

Lyman absorbed Alpert's riff on the LSD-fueled spiritual adventure, on how a focused, curated psychic drug-enhanced search might bring together the like-minded in a sheltered, alternative community. In 1963, with Leary, Alpert founded just such a community: Millbrook, situated at the Hitchcock Estate in Millbrook, New York. Group LSD sessions were organized there for folks seeking spiritual enlightenment. Alpert left Millbrook after four years and took an extended sabbatical in India during which he met the gurus Bhagavan Das and Neem Karoli Baba (the Maharaj-ji). Upon his return, Alpert changed his name to Ram Dass and began writing books about his spiritual journey.

Whatever we make of Dass/Alpert today, he was in the sixties a true believer (in "acid" and Eastern mysticism). But because he maintained a link between spiritual mentorship and financial entrepreneurship, doubts about his integrity—and about the integrity of his spiritual endeavor—persisted through his death in 2019.[82] Lyman was impressed by Alpert and conflated the seemingly contradictory endeavors—spiritual mentorship and financial entrepreneurship—as well. When asked in 2017 what the Fort Hill Community was all about, Jessie Benton, one of the Community's original members, replied simply: "Money and soul."[83]

What would later become the Fort Hill Community took root in 1966. Using money donated by Kweskin, Jessie and her father (the painter) Thomas Hart Benton, Paul Williams (the founder of the popular music magazine *Crawdaddy*), Faith Franckenstein (the daughter of the writer Kay Boyle), the music industry entrepreneur David Gude (who would help make James Taylor and Carly Simon stars), and Owen DeLong (a speechwriter for Robert Kennedy), Lyman purchased a few rundown houses that together formed an L-shaped plat in the Fort Hill district of Roxbury, a Boston neighborhood in decline. Lyman engaged an ambitious renovation of the property, recruiting young men and women with useful construction and engineering skills—skills that were put to use again when the Community added sites in Martha's Vineyard and Los Angeles, where "Fort Hill" has endured now long after Lyman's still-unexplained disappearance/death in 1978.[84]

Boston was a counterculture hotspot in the late sixties, not unlike the Haight in San Francisco or the Village in New York, bringing together a number of really interesting people: Lyman, Leary and Alpert, the musician Van Morrison (who wrote and recorded the magisterial "Astral Weeks" in Boston in 1968), and the future United States Congressman and gay rights activist Barney Frank, who back then worked as a political operative for Boston's mayor, Kevin White.

The hippie street scene in Boston had by 1968 become a political flashpoint and plenty of locals put Lyman at the heart of the problem. Most every day in the common areas around Boston's many colleges and universities, young men and women assembled to speak out in opposition to the war and in opposition to (especially local) school segregation. The scene featured plenty of houseless young runaways, some of whom earned pocket money from Fort Hill hawking copies of the community magazine *Avatar* to passersby.

Frank cultivated a reputation for talking with and listening to the young people who congregated in the Commons, so much so that Dr. Stanley Klein, who studied the local youth scene, dubbed Frank the "hippie whisperer."[85] Frank was no doubt whispering warnings about Lyman and Fort Hill to his boss. And he had his reasons. *Avatar* spoke for Lyman and his expanding community, and it was issue after issue quite something: provocative, blasphemous, obscene, pornographic, pro-drug, and anti-war.

Felton's piece in *Rolling Stone* brought Lyman's local act to the national stage. Less than a year after the *Rolling Stone* cover article, Hunter S. Thompson dropped Lyman's name, predictably alongside Manson's, in *Fear and Loathing in Las Vegas*: "First 'gurus.' Then, when that didn't work, back to Jesus. And now, following Manson's primitive/instinct lead, a whole new wave of clan-type commune Gods like Mel Lyman, ruler of Avatar, and What's His Name who runs "Spirit and Flesh."[86]

Felton surmised a dark project at work at Fort Hill—"a pattern of spiritual infiltration" that permeated "nearly every Lyman Family enterprise." It seemed to him very *1984*. Felton used the term "family" to describe Lyman's entourage, which was hardly inadvertent. The "east coast Manson" thing was, for him, indeed *a thing*.

Particularly effective in Felton's feature is the story he tells about Kweskin's conversion from bandleader to avid follower, as he relinquished to his sideman, Lyman, credit and glory for past, present, and future accomplishments. The liner notes to *Jim Kweskin's America*, a 1971 album with an indicative subtitle, "co-starring Mel Lyman and the Lyman Family," outline the quasi-mystical, astrological underpinning to Lyman's vision: "The soul that is born in Cancer must always find its completion in Aires, when God and man become one. You can read the story of it in *Mirror at the End of the World* by Mel Lyman. It is the story of life from the moment it doubts itself and receives its first intimations of immortality to the time it becomes God ... as it grows from Cancer to Aires. You can hear that story in this album if you will step aside and let your soul listen. I am singing America to you and it is Mel Lyman. He is the new soul of the world."

Kweskin's degree of devotion worried Felton; for him, it resembled what he had previously observed in "Jesus freak sects." "There are thousands of them out here who are, you know, just waiting for Mel Lyman." Kweskin told Felton, "He's like the rock that's dropped in the pond, he's going to have more communities. He's going to have hundreds of communities. Before you know it, the whole world is going to be his community." Kweskin's testimony seemed at the time a warning—and a threat.

Felton's exposé contradicted Kweskin's description of Fort Hill as a community dedicated to peace and love. Culled from interviews with disengaged and disgruntled former-members, Felton reported on a shrine to Manson prominently exhibited at the Roxbury compound, under which Fort Hill members placed flowers. Community members have long disputed the story, though one conceded to Felton that *if* such a shrine had ever existed it wasn't to lend support to the murderous madman but rather to more generally "stick it to the man."

Felton focused on some of the scarier, crazier runaways hanging around the community. Especially alarming were the poetic musings of one young woman, Melinda Cohen, whom Felton described tersely as "a former mental patient." (So was Frechette, turns out.) What Cohen's poetry meant to and for her, what it meant to her fellow followers of Mel Lyman, was left for another day. Its evocation of pointless violence and death masquerading as enlightenment certainly smacked of Manson and *his* alternative Family. (It thus fit Felton's story line.)

> Laugh and kill, laugh and kill
> play and work then laugh and kill
> on a cold and sunny day take a friend out far away
> take him where the fields are turning
> light a match and set them burning
> tie him to a log to die
> smile so he will wonder why
> drive back home and go to bed
> dream about your friend that's dead

FIGURE 11. Mel Lyman, "the east coast Charles Manson," on the cover of *Rolling Stone Magazine*, December 23, 1971 (Creative Commons 4.0. "File: Evangelist Mel Lyman-RS 98 [December 23, 1971].jpg" by David Gahr is licensed with CC BY 4.0. To view a copy of this license, visit https://creativecommons.org/licenses/by/4.0).

When Frechette first arrived in Boston in 1966, he was, like a lot of young people at the time, just drifting. He stumbled upon the kids hawking *Avatar* in Harvard Square and was quickly seduced by the magazine's oddball amalgam of spirituality, astrology, and counterculture politics. When he finally met the community's spiritual leader in person, he recalled: "there was a humming in my ears.... I mean the whole damn room was humming."[87] Frechette had been waiting all his life for a moment like that.

Lyman's appeal to young Americans was broadly antiestablishment. After visiting Jessie at the Fort Hill complex in 1972, Thomas Hart Benton reflected upon what had so entranced his daughter: "[Lyman's] success is that he represents the revolt against the assembly lines. Not that a commune would suit me, but [the members of the community] have found a solution to the greatest problem of youth: loneliness. They live like artists, separate from society but with a sense of communion. We've got to have alternatives to the life we're living." Benton wasn't much impressed by Lyman—he found him to be "full of crap, of course"—but he nonetheless understood why his daughter had gravitated to him, and why so many young people were so inclined to buy what Lyman was selling.[88]

Antonioni was like Benton instinctively suspicious of cult leaders and gurus. In an interview written while he was editing *Zabriskie Point*, he wondered aloud why so many young people—including his costars—had "structured themselves into mystic groups."[89] Antonioni doubted such spiritual seeking led much of anywhere, at least anywhere good. But like Hart Benton, he understood the sort of loneliness that might make someone like Lyman and the Fort Hill Community attractive. When Ebert asked Antonioni to talk about the story he was telling in *Zabriskie Point*, he replied that the film is about one thing: loneliness. The characters look "for personal relationships that will absorb them" but instead "find little to sustain them.... [In the end] they are [all just] looking for a home."[90] Here the characters and the actors who played them in the film overlap. Antonioni was talking about the mostly fictional "Mark," but may as well have been talking about the real Mark Frechette, a lonely young man who finally found a home at Fort Hill.

Frechette's fallback position during the film's brief publicity tour was a studied disinterest, both in the movie he had just made, and in the Hollywood publicity machine that so depended upon his participation. The only way to get him talking was to ask about Fort Hill. But even then, the reactions were not always helpful. Backstage at the *Merv Griffin Show*, Frechette threw a punch at the Pulitzer Prize-winning journalist Tony Dolan, because he had once written dismissively about *Avatar*. He was willing to talk, not so anxious to listen.

Frechette was initially useful to Lyman because he had a talent (as a carpenter) that could be exploited in the construction of the Fort Hill complex. Later, after Frechette made some money in Hollywood, he became helpful financially too. Lyman offered Frechette shelter and for the first time in his life, a sense of community, a place where he was welcome, where he might feel like he belonged. Frechette was once upon a time a movie star. But the best years of his short life were spent at Fort Hill.

Hollywood's Even Hotter Counterculture Couple: Daria Halprin and Dennis Hopper

After completing the *Zabriskie Point* shoot, Frechette landed two acting jobs, both overseas: *Uomini contro* (directed by Francesco Rosi and scripted by Tonino Guerra, who cowrote *Zabriskie Point*, 1970) and *La grande scrofa nera* (Filippo Otteri, 1971).[91] Neither film made much of an impact in the United States.[92] While Frechette was off in Italy, Halprin hung around Fort Hill—just long enough to figure out it wasn't for her. By the time Frechette returned to Boston, Halprin was gone.

In a September 1985 interview for *Rolling Stone*, Halprin recalled her decision to leave Fort Hill: "It put me in a kind of lifestyle and situation that in many, many ways I wasn't ready to deal with. . . . I was in a lot of trouble, very close to burnout. I just got through by the skin of my teeth."

After leaving Fort Hill, Halprin made a half-hearted attempt at moving on with her film career, landing a featured role in a political thriller set in the Middle East, *The Jerusalem File* (John Flynn, 1972), in which she was cast, per the *New York Times* review, as "a curvaceous Israeli student-activist."[93] Halprin's performance begins and ends with how wonderful she looks in cutoffs and bikini tops, all the while toting an automatic rifle. She exists in the world of the film as an object of desire for the two male leads, played by Bruce Davison and Nicol Williamson, neither of whom is in her league.

Just as *The Jerusalem File* was being prepared for release, Halprin met Dennis Hopper. And they fell in love—together becoming an indisputably gorgeous counterculture "it" couple. They married, and a year later, Halprin gave birth to a daughter, Ruthanna.

They divorced in 1976, and Halprin resumed searching, eventually finding some of what she was looking for at the Big Sur–based Esalen Institute: "I came [to Esalen] as a wild child, and it was [there] that I was inspired to try to understand more about myself and others psychologically, where I got turned-on to become a therapist, and where I ultimately came full-circle back to my artistic roots, finding a kind of embodied creativity that can be transformative."[94] After Esalen, Halprin continued her spiritual journey, joining her mother in Northern California, where they together founded the Tamalpa Institute and pioneered dance therapy, a mode of transformative healing integrating choreographed movement and self-actualization. "It took me a long time to find my way again," Halprin remarked in 1985, "[Then] I began to work on myself. Out of that I came to a new interest in movement therapy and education. My professional interest in those fields came out of my commitment to save myself."[95]

Hopper's search (pre- and post-Halprin) proved more complicated. In 1969 *Easy Rider* established him as a double threat: bankable auteur and movie star. He had worked long and hard to "get there"—over sixty acting credits, mostly on TV, mostly featured (so, not starring) roles, including some respectable work in some reasonably big films like *Rebel without a Cause* and *Gunfight at the OK Corral*. He was making a good living in a tough business. And then, with one film, he was on top of the world.

Celebrity does different things to different people. After *Easy Rider*, Hopper got spooked by success and left Los Angeles for Taos, a mountain enclave renowned for its natural beauty and its history of embracing free-thinking artists; a generation or so earlier, the novelist D. H. Lawrence and the painter Georgia O'Keefe stayed there. According to Marin Hopper, Dennis's daughter (her mother is Hopper's first wife, Brooke Hayward), the appeal of Taos can be traced to Hopper's spiritual quest: "It was the land of American Indians and their mountains . . . their beautiful Pueblo and their blue lake, which was meant to be so spiritual you could land in Tibet if you bore a hole through the bottom of it."[96]

Hopper had big plans for his new life in Taos. To make those plans happen, he purchased the Mabel Dodge Luhan House, a.k.a. Los Gallos, a compound with ten bedrooms and an adjacent carriage house. He planned to renovate the place as a counterculture Hollywood retreat and postproduction studio. Hopper then purchased and renovated the El Cortez, an old movie theater in town.

From the outset, Hopper's post-*Easy Rider* celebrity proved unwieldy, and New Mexico quickly became for him and his unruly entourage a nonstop party destination. At one of these parties, Hopper hooked up with Michelle Phillips from the popular quartet, the Mamas and the Papas. They were married on Halloween night,

1970. And though it seemed at the time a dream Hollywood/rock and roll match, the couple split just eight days later.

Halprin moved in two years later and, especially after Ruthanna was born, brought some much-needed stability. According to Marin, her father was happy with Halprin—as happy as he could be at the time. Hopper opened and curated an art gallery during Halprin's brief stay: Dennis Hopper Works of Art. But although Taos was meant to get Hopper away from Hollywood, even the gallery openings became counterculture *events*, attracting a host of celebrities. And with the celebrities: paparazzi, drug dealers—the very Hollywood sycophants Hopper needed to escape.[97]

At the very apex of his career, Hopper's second Hollywood act began, and with it a familiar and sordid story: drugs, booze, and self-indulgence, climaxed by the postmodern western *The Last Movie*, an utterly awful follow-up to *Easy Rider* that had, again by the time Halprin arrived, pretty much killed Hopper's movie career. The film was much anticipated, and in advance of its American release it somehow won the Critics Prize at the Venice Film Festival. But when executives at Universal got a look at the festival cut, they found it un-releasable. They urged Hopper to reedit the film into a more conventional narrative. He refused, insisting it was the film *his* young audience wanted. It wasn't. Universal opened the picture at the Cinema 1 in New York, hoping to build on word-of-mouth into a wider release. The critics swiftly made such a plan impossible. By the end of the first week, the theater was empty. Universal pulled the film and took the loss, figuring no feat of marketing and promotion could save it.

(*The Last Movie* has been restored and it was rereleased in 2018. It is today as then nearly unwatchable. The Portland Art Museum, where I saw the film in its restored rerelease, distributed decorative pins to filmgoers on the way out of the theater, tokens of gratitude perhaps, but more like awards for surviving the experience to its bitter end.)

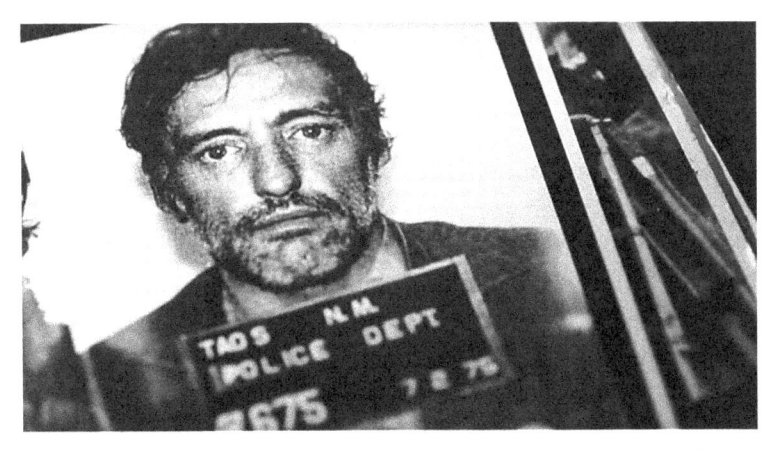

FIGURE 12. Dennis Hopper gets his picture taken in Taos, New Mexico, in July 1975 (Everett Collection).

By the time Hopper began his comeback in the late 1970s, the counterculture that had once embraced and celebrated *Easy Rider* had come and gone. His third Hollywood act would feature a fair share of highlights—no mean achievement after the many years he threw away—including: his vulnerable and self-effacing performance in Wim Wenders's art house feature *The American Friend* (1977), his kinetic cameo in Coppola's 1979 Vietnam epic *Apocalypse Now*, and his blissfully unhinged performance as the nitrous-oxide sniffing maniac Frank Booth in David Lynch's 1984 postmodern thriller *Blue Velvet*.

The Hopper late career narrative is not simply a story of what got lost and then found (in recovery, of course), but a tale as well of endurance, of *surviving* the counterculture. Hopper lived long enough—he died in 2010, age 74—to become a "Hollywood treasure," a term applied to anyone who was once someone—someone who was once upon a time one thing and then another and then another. Hopper was a pretty character actor who became an on-trend artiste, then a lout and a poseur, a has-been, and then a useful character actor again. He was in his later years as well an outspoken Republican.

Mark Frechette: Counterculture Outlaw

In the late afternoon of August 29, 1973, Frechette, along with a fellow Fort Hill resident named Sheldon T. (Terry) Bernhard walked a mile from the Roxbury complex to the New England Merchants National Bank where they hooked up with Chris Thien, who was waiting for them in the bank disguised as a security guard. Frechette approached a bank employee and asked about applying for a $2,500 loan. He was passed on to a second employee, to whom Frechette handed a slip of paper that read: "There are three of us, we're going to rob you, don't get alarmed." The loan officer summoned the bank's real security guard. Frechette showed him his gun and the guard quietly relinquished his firearm. Bernhard and Frechette emptied the till at each teller station. The haul was $10,156.

Frechette, Bernhard, and Thien were undone by a silent alarm. The police arrived while they were still in the bank, still bundling their haul. A patrolman named Daniel Fitzgerald entered first and promptly got into a struggle with Thien, who panicked. A second patrolman, Maurice Flaherty entered a few seconds later and, spying his partner in trouble, fired twice, hitting Thien with both shots. Thien would later die at the hospital. Frechette and Bernhard surrendered.

After his arrest, Frechette characterized the robbery as a revolutionary act, as an act of political protest: "We had been watching the Watergate hearings on television.... We saw the apathy and we felt an intense rage.... Because the banks are federally insured, robbing a bank was a way of robbing Richard Nixon without hurting anybody.... Standing there with a gun, cleaning out a teller's cage—that's about as fuckin' honest as you can get, man." Years

FIGURE 13. Mark (Mark Frechette) points a gun at a policeman in *Zabriskie Point* (Michelangelo Antonioni, 1970, MGM). Life would soon imitate art.

later, Frechette would remain unrepentant, still inclined to view the crime as a countercultural act: "It was a good bank robbery. Maybe it wasn't a successful one, but it was real, ya know."[98]

At his trial, Frechette declined to involve Lyman, and the Fort Hill mystic smartly distanced himself from the former actor. Frechette was found guilty and subsequently incarcerated at the federal prison in Norfolk, Massachusetts, where he continued to obsess about Watergate, at one point producing a play in which inmates read from White House recordings and transcripts. Bernhard, Frechette's accomplice in the robbery, donned a fake nose to play Nixon, and later confided to a local reporter: "I held up a bank and got five to sixteen. Nixon held up a country and he got a pardon."[99]

In March 1975, Frechette got his final notice as a creative artist when the NBC-TV talk show host Tom Snyder spoke briefly about the play and Frechette's role in its production. Barely six months later, Frechette would be discovered dead in a prison exercise room with a barbell crushed upon his throat. A source for the county DA's office termed the circumstances "a little strange," but nonetheless dismissed the possibility of foul play.[100] What, after all, was one dead hippie inmate in the larger scheme of things?

No longer of much interest to anyone anymore was the fact that this particular dead hippie inmate had once upon a time been a movie star—at least, it looked for a year or so like he had a really good chance to become one. But Mark Frechette never became a movie star; instead, he joined a commune, committed a violent crime, and then died in jail. When he was pronounced dead, Frechette was just twenty-seven, not even a has-been—an almost-was.

Two Characters in a Movie by Michelangelo Antonioni

The jailhouse accident/murder offered a fitting coda to Frechette's brief life. And it also eerily suited the loosely fictionalized Mark in *Zabriskie Point*, who is killed in the film by police on a sealed-off tarmac. In the film, the police and assorted onlookers peer dumbly into the cockpit, ogling Mark's dead body. Antonioni resists the usual sequence editing showing the arrival of a medical examiner—the carting off of the body. There is no cut to a somber funeral. Instead we hear the news of Mark's death on Daria's car radio. With Antonioni, always: restraint.

Mark's death in the film, like his obtuse and incomprehensible rebellion, is steeped in anticlimax. His theft of the airplane is neither a crime of passion nor of profit, and his death at the hands of the police is perfunctory and preventable. Mark's politics are vague—his theft, merely a joyride. Whatever larger significance we might attribute to the crime is undercut by Mark's inability to articulate the reasons for its execution. When he returns the plane, he invites confrontation—a seeming suicide that impacts no one, except maybe Daria. Such is Antonioni's America and the existential aimlessness of the counterculture youth who live there.

Daria has a thing—a sexual thing—for Mark in the film; she is fascinated by the notion that he might be (because he looks like) a counterculture outlaw. The same was probably true for the real

Daria Halprin. But as Daria Halprin the actress and Daria the character came to realize, the actor Mark Frechette and Mark, the character he plays in the film, were never so well suited to the role of counterculture outlaw. And after a while, he wasn't so much fun to be around either.

Daria, Antonioni's earth-angel, is given less to do than Mark in the film, but she (not he) is in the end the one who is angry; she is the one who hates. After Mark's death, Daria visits the breathtaking desert compound occupied in the film by some real estate developers and financiers and, ostensibly informed by her adventure with Mark in the film, ponders an act of domestic terrorism. The amazing—and amazingly long—closing sequence in which Antonioni records and replays sequential detonations of the compound and then tracks debris (clothes, appliances, deck furniture, a bag of Wonder Bread) floating into the atmosphere has the look and feel of a fever dream, which is why most filmgoers and critics figure that Daria only *imagines* the detonation.

Contrary to rumors circulating at the time, Antonioni did not blow up the actual house. "We rented the original house, the one in which we shot interiors and some of the exteriors, but naturally the owner was not going to let us blow it up. So we built another one just like it not far away. I believe that the owner sat on his terrace and watched as we blew up that house that looked exactly like his own."

The explosion that caps the film is an aesthetic event, not a human contrivance. But it is nonetheless quite breathtaking. Shot with seventeen strategically placed cameras, the sequence had to be shot live. "It was so difficult to organize the explosion," Antonioni reflected, "with all the wires and cameras—like a war operation." The struggle, then, or at least the memory of the struggle inherent to the film's ending, was for Antonioni logistical and creative, but not political. The audiovisual experience was an end in and of itself: pure cinema.

When Flatley suggested a political reading of the scene in his conversation with the director, Antonioni dismissed the interpretation. Flatley: "Reading between two of the film's final images—a young man being senselessly killed by several policemen and the girl who loved the young man imagining the home of her wealthy employer being blown to smithereens— we might conclude that the point of *Zabriskie Point* is that only through violent revolution can we right the wrongs in our society." Antonioni shrugged, then offered a cryptic, (and for me) funny response: "I wouldn't start a revolution by blowing up a house." For the director, the explosion "is a clear expression of how the girl feels at that precise moment. I am telling *her* story and that is why I don't end [there]. Instead, I show her returning to the car *after* the explosion."[101]

Over the film's final credits, we hear Roy Orbison sing, "So Young." Orbison's soaring falsetto offers the last word on what we have seen and the song he sings comes as close as anything we experience in the film to resolving Antonioni's elliptical narrative and the film's (perhaps, fantasy) denouement. "Time runs out so fast on love too good to last. . . . Zabriskie Point is anywhere." *Zabriskie Point*, as Antonioni noted during the development of the film, is a story about two young Americans who fall in love, and then that love abruptly ends. Zabriskie Point is anywhere, then, and nowhere.[102]

Hollywood's Best-Laid Plans: On Fulfilling a Contract No One Wants Fulfilled

Zabriskie Point was not at all what the MGM executives had mind when they entered into the three-picture contract with Antonioni and not at all what they had in mind when they first contemplated a profitable cinematic encounter with the counterculture. It is not surprising, then, that it would be several years before Antonioni would finally make his third film for the studio; 1975 to be exact, with *The Passenger*, an existential exploration of fate and identity.

The Passenger tells the story of a journalist, played by the American movie star Jack Nicholson, who happens upon a gunrunner's corpse in a North African hotel, and, for reasons never fully expressed or laid out, assumes the dead man's identity. The journalist pockets the dead man's passport and steals his clothes, and then endeavors to face the consequences that come with playing this new character, whatever they may be.

The plot marked Antonioni's return to his preoccupation with the sick soul of the postwar West. And the location work in Algeria allowed for another evocative road trip through a desert. Antonioni's crew filmed in Algeria, Spain, Germany, and England, but not in the United States. Once bitten, twice shy. MGM financed *The Passenger* (per the contract), but modestly at $2.8 million, less than half of the budget for *Zabriskie Point*.

When it was released in 1975, *The Passenger* was widely considered a return to form for Antonioni. The reviews were mostly terrific and at Cannes the film was nominated for the Palme d'Or. Though no one at Cannes, at MGM, or in the art film subculture in the United States was back then apt to point them out, there are some similarities between *The Passenger* and *Zabriskie Point*. Both are modern road pictures set in dramatic landscapes. Both focus on characters whose motivations are muddy, whose identities are in flux. Both create "a feeling about a style" and highlight Antonioni's unique balance of setting, milieu, character, and plot. What was different, for sure, were the expectations. In 1969/1970, *Zabriskie Point* needed to be something—an American *Blow-Up*, an art-house *Easy Rider*—a kind of film Antonioni was never going to make, because he didn't want to. *The Passenger* was a European art film featuring an American movie star—a project more in Antonioni's wheelhouse.

For *Zabriskie Point*, Antonioni worked almost exclusively with non-professionals. His methods baffled his costars, Frechette and Halprin, so much so they appear at once befuddled and beautiful in most every scene. Antonioni's peculiar methods on the set forced an adjustment from the far more experienced and talented Nicholson as well. "I like to provoke the mood I need from [my actors]," Antonioni remarked in a 1973 interview in the *Los Angeles Times*, "I don't think they should know too much about what I want to do, otherwise the actor becomes the director. They overact—in good faith of course, but it's still wrong."

After the production wrapped, Antonioni mused: "Jack, he's such a great guy. He is an extraordinary actor—first of all he has that face, so expressive. And he is so professional. I must say he trusted me. Sometimes he looked a little lost, but I wanted that." Nicholson looked back on the production less fondly, at least at first: "[Working with Antonioni] is like being in the army, something you discipline yourself to get through, not something you enjoy."[103]

Years later, Nicholson was inclined to talk more generously about the film they made together. Appearing in a DVD extra for the Criterion edition of *L'Avventura*, Nicholson reads a selection of Antonioni's theoretical writings on the cinema. At one point, he stops to reflect on his experience with (and these are Nicholson's words) "the maestro." He recalls a take in *The Passenger* that didn't go as planned. Antonioni asked him for a second try: "Jack, nothing wrong, but, for me the actor is a moving thing in space." The Antonioni-ism is briefly suspended as Nicholson takes a pregnant pause—a pause capped by the unmistakable Nicholson laugh, the actor remembering fondly and to himself really, his experience working with (again, in his words) "this particular Italian cat."

The Passenger was more the sort of movie MGM wanted in 1969 than the one they got. And by the time *The Passenger* was readied for release in 1975, American film culture had moved on to a new obsession: the so-called movie brats: Coppola, Scorsese, and after them Spielberg and Lucas. Valenti's vision of an American-led cine-renaissance was underway. Funny thing: the studios would soon enough have problems with these American-born auteurs and *their* bloated auteur road trips—problems that were in 1975 still a few years away.

2 *Christopher Jones Does Not Want to Be a Movie Star*

In 1922, the Universal Studios founder and chief executive Carl Laemmle predicted that movie stars would one-day become "the fundamental thing" in the film business. (He had in 1914, after all, created the first screen star, Florence Lawrence, and had banked profitably on her as the face of his company, IMP.) The remark proved prophetic. Movies became a national pastime, and movie stars proved so useful as marketing attractions that they became the public face of the industry. There were reasons for this—reasons men like Laemmle understood. He and the other first-generation moguls were nouveau riche immigrants, Jewish businessmen. Better to pin Hollywood's public image on the likes of the more wholesome and handsome, on talented and beautiful all-Americans like the lovely girl-next-door Mary Pickford and her husband, the swashbuckling athlete Douglas Fairbanks. Movie stars like Pickford and Fairbanks lived in enviable luxury in a dreamy Hollywood movie colony—like the movies made there, the site par excellence of American aspiration and fantasy.

Our continued fascination with the rise and fall of movie stars speaks to the near-impossible odds against social mobility in America. To become a movie star, to achieve stardom is a rare thing—it takes, to paraphrase the film theorist Andre Bazin, a gift from the fairies and perfect timing. Movie stars are "discovered." Like planets. Origin stories are spun to make movie stars seem all the more magical, a chance encounter at a soda fountain, for example: right place, right time, right look. Stardom is amazing, wonderful, a matter of talent, hard work, and luck. But nothing so good lasts forever. Movie stars are at once invaluable and temporary, indispensable and disposable.

The very year Laemmle spoke so affirmatively about the value of movie stars, the Fatty Arbuckle rape/murder scandal broke and a darker aspect to the celebrity narrative emerged in counterpoint—a reminder to everyone to be careful what they wished for, a reminder that in America the only thing more interesting than success is a counterbalanced decline, a failure that cuts heroes back down to size. The star scandals in the 1920s (Arbuckle, the Wallace Reid heroin overdose, the murder of the producer William Desmond Taylor) were used by studio management to rein in the movie colony. The blacklist thirty years later was used to shut them up—to discourage the many spoiled brat celebrities from speaking out on behalf of the underprivileged, challenging the status quo.

Precious few Americans achieve movie stardom. Some of those who do are able to thrive and enjoy the perks of adulation and wealth. Others seem strangely troubled by their good fortune; they fall into depression, make the wrong kinds of friends and the wrong sorts of decisions. They fail to appreciate the very gifts that have made them who and what they have become. The American dream cuts two ways.

Christopher Jones became a movie star in 1970. He had in the years leading up to that moment done everything right: a stint at the Actors Studio, then TV, a couple of B-movies and a couple of A-films (the second bigger and better than the first). In 1970 he seemed surely to have made it, landing the romantic lead in *Ryan's Daughter*, a sprawling epic directed by the two-time Oscar winner, David Lean. Just seven years into a promising Hollywood career, he had everything. But then, a few months after completing Lean's film, for reasons he never articulated, Jones walked away from the business, away from the money and the celebrity. Forever.

Looking back, Jones's story certainly alludes to a larger disenchantment with celebrity in the counterculture era and with Hollywood as a place, as a construct, as an industry. Jones had pursued and achieved the Hollywood version of the American dream. And then, after achieving success, didn't see anything much to it. A lot of young people in America in 1970 seemed similarly unimpressed (with Hollywood and traditional success).

For two years or so Jones was a counterculture celebrity. In 1968, he appeared in a movie about disillusioned young Americans (too young to vote but old enough to fight in Vietnam) and the following year, a movie set on a college campus (the site of so much of the generational rift in America), in which he stumbled into and struggled with the gender-role confusion prompted by women's lib and the sexual revolution. Off-screen, Jones was never political, not like his idol Marlon Brando. Instead, it was the legendary actor's antisocial tendencies, his anti-Hollywood sentiments that Jones took on. He told an interviewer he wanted to be a movie star so he could make a lot of money and then buy an island (like Brando); he wanted to be so rich and famous he could go his own way, do his own thing—not need Hollywood so much as it needed him. Jones wanted to get to a place where he didn't need to act, where he didn't need the celebrity, where (again, like Brando) he didn't need anyone.

Among the observable differences between Brando and Jones, it is important to note that the former became a star when there was still a star system, still a studio system. Jones arrived nearly two decades later and found everything changed. He became a New Hollywood star—a rock and roll, counterculture star—before there were rules, before such a thing was a thing. His meteoric rise and sudden disappearance offer a provocative case study. He was a young man very much of the moment—with that gift from the fairies ("the camera loved him") and perfect timing (Hollywood was looking, waiting for someone quite like him).

His story—and I will only hint at the particulars here—involved James Dean at the start and, as so many of the era's Hollywood stories do, Charles Manson at its climax. Along the way Jones met and worked with movieland royalty: Bette Davis, Shelley Winters, Ralph Richardson, Anthony Hopkins, and Robert Mitchum. He hung out with rock stars (including his neighbor at the Chateau Marmont, Jim Morrison) and dated some of Hollywood's most talked-about, most sought-after women (including Olivia Hussey, the star of Franco Zeffirelli's sexy 1968 adaptation of *Romeo and Juliet*). Jones did some of his best work with some of the best young talent in Hollywood during his brief stint at American International Pictures (AIP) at a time when the B-movie studio employed a counterculture ensemble that included Karen Black, Ellen Burstyn, Bruce Dern, and Jack Nicholson. Among even such a talented troupe, Jones seemed at the time the actor most likely to succeed. He did, succeed. Briefly. And then he vanished—off the screen and off the grid.

A hint at what follows: Jones's story proved to be a challenge to research and recount. It is more complicated and a lot sadder than I expected, a road trip to nowhere, to be sure. Just not the trip I expected or really wanted to find. A reminder, then: to understand Hollywood we need to get past the bright lights and big pictures—the best and the brightest. We need to focus as well on the things that go wrong, the people who get lost or abandoned, kicked to the side of the road, out of town, out of the business, out of this world. Jones fits this darker historical process, this darker Hollywood history. His story is profoundly revealing about the complexity of counterculture celebrity: its fundamental ambivalences (Hollywood opulence on the one hand, counterculture anti-materialism on the other; the aspirational core of celebrity countered by sixties-era anti-conventionalism) and its fundamental rifts (between an ensconced studio establishment and a very new breed of movie star).

Christopher Jones: The Origin Story

The actor later known as Christopher Jones was born William Franklin Jones in Jackson, Tennessee, on August 18, 1941. Back then, folks called him "Billy." His father, J. G., was a grocery clerk. His mother, Robbie, was a housewife and an amateur artist. Billy had an older brother: Robert. The family lived in a small apartment above a grocery store.

Just as Billy turned four, Robbie's erratic behavior became too much for J. G. to handle so he had her admitted to the state hospital in Bolivar. She would remain there until her death in 1960. When Billy/Christopher got older, he would hardly remember her: "I can remember her picking me up once. But I can't remember what she looked like."[1]

After Robbie's committal, J. G. sent Billy to live with an aunt in Mississippi. But the custodial experiment failed. J. G. then sent both of his sons to Boys Town in Memphis, where Billy stayed until he was sixteen. Jones was in many ways the product of this institutional upbringing and so brought with him (to adulthood, to Hollywood) an array of abandonment issues—issues not so easily resolved by celebrity and success.

Joe Stockton, Billy's mentor at Boys Town, was the first to comment upon Jones's resemblance to James Dean. "I must have been 14 or 15 years old at the time," Jones recalled, thinking back upon being summoned by his mentor, "and I was sure I was going to be punished for something." Instead, Stockton handed Jones a months-old copy

FIGURE 14. James Dean on the set filming *East of Eden* (Elia Kazan, 1955) (Everett Collection).

of *Life* magazine and opened to a photo essay on Dean. "After a long silence he said, 'You know, Billy, you look just like this guy!'" Stockton then took Jones to see *Rebel without a Cause* in Memphis. The experience was revelatory. Jones could finally picture what it was he wanted: "Everything was so clean and uncomplicated in the movies.

FIGURE 15. Christopher Jones, the next James Dean, 1966 (Everett Collection).

All those important people in their big houses. That was my ideal. I wanted to be a movie star."[2]

Jones wanted to be a movie star because movie stars seemed to *belong* in such "a clean and uncomplicated world." His world had been anything but. As a teenager—a teenager who hadn't seen so many films, hadn't read fan magazines or acted in high school plays—what Jones really wanted was out of the institution that housed and educated him, out of a messy and complicated family life, out of the hopelessness of Boys Town and the lower-middle-class American life he had been born into. When Billy Jones dreamed of one day becoming a movie star, the only movie star he knew anything about was James Dean—a young man he, not incidentally, looked a lot like.

What young Billy Jones knew of Dean's off-screen life—that is, the real life of a professional actor and film celebrity—was first culled from the photographs published in *Life* magazine taken by Dean's friend Dennis Stock. They showed the twenty-four-year-old James Dean on his uncle's farm in Indiana posed astride a seven-hundred-pound pig, walking alone on the streets of New York City on a rainy evening cigarette dangling from his lips, just so; backstage on Broadway at the Cort Theater with Geraldine Page, wearing glasses, looking serious, even studious; meeting with his accountant (feet up on the desk, wearing glasses again), and on the set of *East of Eden* (Elia Kazan, 1955) with Julie Harris, happy in Hollywood, or so it seemed. Jones studied the images, apprehending what it took and meant to be James Dean: the working-class kid from Nowheresville, the serious and studious Broadway actor, the successful Hollywood movie star. Accompanying the photographs was a capsule bio that described Dean as the "most exciting actor to hit Hollywood since Marlon Brando," as an actor whose "militantly independent off-stage behavior and . . . scorn for movie convention have studio executives at Warner Bros. apprehensive."[3] We can hardly blame Jones for thinking he could be that sort of movie star too.

The physical resemblance was undeniable. And Dean's "militant independence" was something Jones could appreciate and emulate. Dean's brief Hollywood story made clear that a movie star could be cool. And what lonely teenager, let alone one stuck in an institution for lost and abandoned boys, didn't want to be cool?

In the summer of 1957 Jones turned sixteen and left Boys Town. He lived briefly with his father and his father's new family in Jackson. He helped around the house, babysitting mostly, and then enlisted in the Army. Jones soon tired of the regimentation, the hard work. So he stole a car and went AWOL. He drove from New Orleans to Dean's family home in Fairmount, Indiana, where, at least as Jones told the story, the late actor's aunt and uncle were struck by his resemblance to their nephew and invited him inside.

The army eventually caught up with Jones. He was tried and convicted for leaving his post and served time in the Disciplinary Barracks on Governors Island. Then, after serving his sentence, he took the ferry some eight hundred yards to Manhattan to resume "the next James Dean" narrative.

In New York, Jones committed to a plan of action. He sought out the theater and opera director Frank Corsaro, who in the early 1950s had directed Dean in an off-Broadway production of Percy MacKaye's *Scarecrow*, an early stage performance that had gotten Dean noticed. Corsaro took Jones under his wing. Dean had more talent than Jones. Corsaro recognized that. And he was for sure more disciplined. But Jones had something else, something raw and real.

There were some striking similarities in the two actors' bios. Dean's formative years, like Jones's, were marked by his mother's absence. Dean's mother died when he was nine; Jones's mother was institutionalized when he was four. Winton Dean, like Jones's father, decided he couldn't or shouldn't bring up his son on his own, so he sent the boy to live with his sister and her husband in Fairmount. Dean found stability with his Aunt Ortense and Uncle Marcus and stayed in Indiana through high school graduation and then moved to Los Angeles to attend Santa Monica College and then UCLA. After a single semester, Dean quit UCLA to devote himself to acting full-time. His talent was by then unmistakable.

Both young men had abandonment issues. Both had seen their fair share of loneliness and pain. But there were differences as well. Dean had grown up in a stable suburban home, went to a public high school, and then went to college in Los Angeles, where his talent was encouraged. By the time Dean tried his luck in New York, he could fairly say that he was a professional actor. Jones arrived in Manhattan with a very different résumé: Boys Town, the military, jail. He was, in complicated ways, the real thing: a young man with a past that really did haunt him, a troubled kid with authority issues, discipline issues—a real rebel without a cause.

Dean was far more conventional, and much as he bristled at the daily grind of the movie business, of the celebrity business, he was otherwise locked into fifties notions of success and stardom. There was a wildness in Jones that seemed well suited to the emerging counterculture—a next-generation James Dean, then. But such a role would prove to be hard to play, hard to work out over time.

Jones's relationship with Corsaro quickly paid off as Corsaro cast Jones in a featured role in the first Broadway run of Tennessee Williams's *Night of the Iguana*, a 1961 production headlined by Bette Davis. At first, things did not go smoothly for either of them. Davis engineered the firing of Corsaro shortly before the play opened. Though Jones didn't lose his job as well, Davis mostly ignored him.

When Davis completed her run, Shelley Winters stepped in. And she and Jones hit it off right away. There was, affirmed by both parties, a brief sexual affair. (Winters was sexually notorious. Jones would soon be as well). Winters then introduced Jones to Susan Strasberg, the daughter of Lee and Paula Strasberg, who ran the Actors Studio, where Winters and Dean and Brando had studied. Jones and Susan Strasberg fell in love. The relationship opened doors for Jones—doors that had previously opened for Dean.

In 1963, with Strasberg, the actor Jerry Orbach, and Orbach's wife, Marta, Jones drove cross-country and took up residence at the

Chateau Marmont, a hip West Hollywood hotel frequented by New York actors working in the film business. The Dean reboot seemed still well in play: the director Nick Ray had stayed at the hotel to rehearse *Rebel without a Cause* with Dean, Natalie Wood, and Sal Mineo. Jones certainly knew that.

The Sunset Strip (just south of the hotel, down a block-long private drive) was just then becoming the epicenter of a new Hollywood counterculture. And Jones and Strasberg quickly became it-couple celebrities there. At first, they lived on Strasberg's income; she had found work on TV soon after their arrival. Then Jones landed the lead in *The Legend of Jesse James*, a series produced for ABC by Twentieth Century Fox. In a matter of weeks Jones became a bona fide TV star.

Jones played the outlaw refigured as an American Robin Hood specializing in tormenting executives from the railroad and combatting corrupt law enforcement. The show resumed and updated a narrative introduced at Fox in 1939 for another heartthrob, Tyrone Power. In the Henry King film, titled simply *Jesse James*, the outlaw's criminal activities make allegorical reference to the inequities of the Great Depression. James's efforts at redistributing the wealth, as in *The Adventures of Robin Hood* (Michael Curtiz and William Keighley) released the year before are justified by the systemic oppression he upsets and the exaggerated class divide he tries to reconcile. In the mid-sixties TV version, James as embodied by Jones is a brooding counterculture outlaw, misunderstood and underestimated by a corrupt establishment, living by a code the older generation has sadly abandoned.[4]

The show cast as guest stars a number of young actors who, like Jones, were working their way from the small to big screen. Dennis Hopper, Sally Kellerman, and Gary Lockwood all supported Jones on the show. Also among the featured players in the show's brief run were actors moving in rather the other direction—from big screen to small, earning a steady paycheck in the twilight of their careers. Ann Doran, who played Jesse and Frank James's mother in the series, fell into this latter group. In what seems today a noteworthy coincidence, Doran had played Jim Stark/James Dean's mother in *Rebel without a Cause*. Fair to wonder if she fancied Jones's chances at becoming, as Fox had already begun billing him, "the next James Dean." Fair to wonder if Jones was by then starting to believe in the hype as well.

In 1967, *The Legend of Jesse James* got cancelled, but Jones quickly landed guest star roles on *Judd for the Defense* and *The Man from U.N.C.L.E.* Cast in the pilot episode of "Judd for the Defense," Jones played a charismatic sociopath with a Pied Piper–like effect on a group of local teenagers. Even by Method standards, his performance is flamboyant, his character strategically framed by the episode's creative team in scenes conceived and designed to remind viewers of *Rebel without a Cause* and to play off the actor's resemblance to that film's star.

Titled "Tempest in a Texas Town," the episode begins, like Dean's signature film, in a police station with Jones (as Brandon Hill) an apparently misunderstood teen victim of police authority, accused of abducting and murdering two female teenagers. When Judd (Carl Betz) arrives on the scene and comes, per the series title, to Brandon's defense, he asks Brandon about his relationship with the missing girls. Brandon replies petulantly, "I don't have relationships." Judd follows up, asking what for the times and especially for TV seemed an unthinkable question: "with girls?" Brandon smirks and puts a counterculture spin on the conversation: "with anybody." The echoes of *Rebel*'s teen ennui ("who lives?") are hard to miss.

Jones self-consciously channels Dean's signature mannerisms: the head tilted just so (as if contemplating things the other characters can't imagine), the hunched shoulders and sideways glances (like Dean, Jones never meets anyone's eyes), the endless fidgeting (the serial locomotion, the seeming impatience), the exaggerated body movements (falling to the floor to *show* the depth of his anguish—desperately clinging to the bars in the jailhouse much as Jim Stark/James Dean clung to the bars supporting the banister in the Stark living room after the chickie-run).

Late in 1967, Jones embarked upon a movie career. In those days it was generally one or the other, TV or film, and Jones seemed quite ready for the big-time. The film career ran hot for a while until, after just a couple of years, it didn't run at all.

AIP and the New Hollywood

Jones had a "quiet opening" on the big screen: *Chubasco* (Allen H. Miner) a low-budget melodrama for William Conrad Productions produced in 1967 but not released by Warner Bros./Seven Arts until a year later and then only as the B-feature in a double bill headlined by a Hammer Films/Christopher Lee negative pickup, *Dracula Has Risen from the Grave* (Freddie Francis, 1968). Writing for the *New York Times*, the film reviewer Howard Thompson glibly dismissed *Dracula Has Risen from the Grave*: "Yes, again. And judging by this junky British film in color—asplatter with catsup or paint or whatever, to simulate the Count's favorite color—he can descend again." Thompson was a bit more generous with *Chubasco*, which he deemed "a curious little drama that might have gone places with more care."[5] Given the film's budget, more care was never forthcoming. Still, Jones leaves the impression that he's already too good for the film.

Jones plays a James Dean–style Romeo in *Chubasco* who tries to convince his Juliet's dad he's really OK. It takes a while and only after a little help from a friendly prostitute. Strasberg, Jones's soon-to-be ex-wife, plays the girlfriend. Both do what they can to sell the fiction of a budding romance. *Chubasco* came and went quickly, but still proved a useful stepping-stone. Samuel Z. Arkoff, cofounder of American International Pictures (AIP) spied/stumbled upon the film and gave Jones the big screen break he needed. In a matter of months, Jones became the B-studio's biggest star. And given the ensemble hanging out at AIP, that was no small achievement.

The sixties were difficult for the major studios. Business was a whole lot better at niche-outfits like Arkoff's, where he and his house producer/director Roger Corman churned out low-budget genre pictures that consistently made money. AIP worked faster and cheaper than the studios, and targeted a younger audience. Rather than compete head-to-head for bookings at standalone showcase theaters, AIP smartly booked their films into the over four thousand drive-ins operating in the United States at the time.[6] Most of AIP's early-sixties films were noisy and slapdash—perfect for such venues, as actually watching the movie was for many young drive-in patrons quite beside the point.

When the studios focused on teenagers in the fifties and sixties, they generally did so without much of a sense of humor. Teenagers were, it seemed, a social problem to be solved, evident in three remarkable studio melodramas: *The Wild One* (László Benedek, 1953), *Rebel without a Cause* (Nicholas Ray, 1955), and *The Blackboard Jungle* (Richard Brooks, 1955). Even a madcap comedy like Warner Bros.' 1960 feature *Where the Boys Are* (Henry Levin), which tracked a handful of handsome college kids on spring break in Fort Lauderdale, veered at the end of its second act into cautionary territory, as a date rape and attempted suicide caps the teenagers' misadventure in sunny Florida.

At AIP, filmmakers explored without apology plots and characters the studios were too cautious or out of touch to exploit. Films like *The Wild Angels* (Corman, 1966), *Riot on the Sunset Strip* (Arthur Dreifuss, 1967), *The Trip* (Corman, 1967), *Wild in the Streets* (Barry Shear, 1968), and *3 in the Attic* (Richard Wilson, 1968)—the latter two starring Jones—showed teens behaving badly, absent handwringing or moralizing. And much to the big studios' collective frustration, many of the teen-targeted AIP films (including all of the titles mentioned above) were box office hits.

Even AIP's comically awful *Beach Party* films (seven "official entries" and, all-told, about a dozen thematically interconnected films, many of which starred Frankie Avalon and Annette Funicello) took at least one aspect of the youth culture seriously: rock and roll. The music was treated at AIP as more than a fad or a trend; the studio took seriously rock's counterculture message as well, and used the genre's popularity with and importance to the studio's younger audience to quietly integrate Black soul and R&B into what were otherwise white teen fantasies, much as the music had by then been integrated into the daily lives of white middle-class teenagers nationwide. Among the several soul and R&B acts to perform in AIP's beach party films: Stevie Wonder, the Supremes, and James Brown (who makes the scene at a ski chalet!).

So long as AIP served a small, niche market, the studios figured they could afford to ignore them. But that all changed with Corman's seedy B-biker picture *The Wild Angels*. Shot on location over a hectic fifteen days and completed for a reported $360,000, the film's first run box office exceeded $15 million, a remarkable haul earned despite awful reviews and organized resistance from the members of NATO (the National Organization of Theater Owners, not the North Atlantic Treaty Organization), many of whom, at the organization's national convention, had walked out on Arkoff's preview screening.

Arkoff was a savvy operator and took the walkout in stride. He smartly gauged NATO's reaction as a positive sign for the film's future with American teenagers, so he added a half-hearted disclaimer at the head of the film. Ostensibly designed to appease filmgoers likely to be put off by the film's antisocial violence, the disclaimer was more likely an exploitation industry-styled bait and switch. Under the pretense of appeasement, the disclaimer offered a surefire come-on: "The picture you are about to see will shock and

FIGURE 16. The B-movie impresario, Samuel Z. Arkoff, cofounder of American International Pictures (AIP) (Everett Collection).

perhaps anger you. Although the events and characters are fictitious, the story is a reflection of our times." In other words: "You are about to see some bad teenagers behaving badly." Arkoff was willing to bet: What American teenager could resist that?

The Wild Angels was quickly and cheaply made, with the studio eyeing a quick and modest payoff. But just as the film was being prepared for its US release, a telegram arrived from the organizers of the Venice Film Festival implausibly offering *The Wild Angels* the coveted opening-night slot. Arkoff and Corman could hardly believe their luck. Officials at the US State Department could hardly believe AIP's luck either. The bureaucrats were anxious about the film's antisocial content and urged Arkoff to turn down the invitation. "For a foreign film festival like this," Arkoff replied, "should we only export pictures that reflect the U.S. in a favorable light?"[7] His answer was there in the asking. Arkoff went ahead with the invited screening in Venice, sending a message to his A-picture competitors that the future of American filmmaking would soon *have to* look a lot more like *The Wild Angels* than the studios' top grossers of that same year: *The Bible* (John Huston) and *Hawaii* (George Roy Hill).

The Wild Angels was in many ways a prototype AIP "wild teen" feature; and the studio was well set up to make more films quite like it. Its cast and crew were culled from the ranks of AIP's prodigious stable of young and hungry talent—Peter Fonda, Bruce Dern, Diane Ladd, and Michael J. Pollard. Behind the scenes: Peter Bogdanovich (assistant director), Monte Hellman (editor), and Polly Platt (costume design and Nancy Sinatra stunt double). These talented actors and practitioners would later work on such New Hollywood classics as *Bonnie and Clyde, Easy Rider, The Last Picture Show* (Bogdanovich, 1971), *Two-Lane Blacktop* (Hellman, 1971), *Paper Moon* (Bogdanovich, 1973), *Chinatown* (Roman Polanski, 1974), and *Pretty Baby* (Louis Malle, 1978).

Arkoff and Corman had a keen eye for young talent. And they booked that talent before anyone at the major studios knew any of these talented "kids" existed. Ellen Burstyn, Robert De Niro, Dern, Richard Dreyfuss, Peter Fonda, Barbara Hershey, Don Johnson, Sally Kellerman, Margot Kidder, Jack Nicholson, Nick Nolte, Chuck Norris, Richard Pryor, and Susan Sarandon all worked for AIP before they got big roles in big films. At a time when impenetrable guild regulations and an entrenched old-boy network complicated opportunities at the big studios, Bogdanovich, Francis Ford Coppola, David Cronenberg, Jonathan Demme, Brian De Palma, John Milius, Ivan Reitman, and Martin Scorsese all got production work at AIP.

Historians routinely underestimate Arkoff's role in the advent of the New Hollywood. And he'd have had it no other way. In his memoir, *Flying through Hollywood by the Seat of My Pants*, Arkoff maintained that the key to his success was that he never took the films or himself so seriously. Talking with Ebert after the release of *Q* (Larry Cohen), a 1982 horror film about a giant flying lizard nesting on the rooftops of New York City skyscrapers, Arkoff was characteristically self-effacing:

> EBERT: "Sam... I just saw *Q*! What a surprise! That wonderful method performance by Michael Moriarty, right in the middle of all that dreck!"
> ARKOFF: "Why thank you... the dreck was my idea."[8]

However much and often Arkoff succeeded in providing "the dreck," by the end of the sixties, movie reviewers had started to look at AIP as a viable studio alternative. Such was their frustration at the poor quality of studio films. The *Variety* review published on the last day of 1967 anticipating the national release of *Wild in the Streets*, Jones's first film for the studio, seems a case in point: "An often chilling political science fiction drama, with comedy, [*Wild in the Streets*] considers the takeover of American government by the preponderant younger population. Good writing and direction enhance the impact of a diversified cast headed by Shelley Winters. . . . Actual footage from real-life demonstrations was shot for [the] pic, some of it matched quite well with internal drama. What comes off as a partial documentary flavor makes for a good artistic complement to the not-so-fictional hypothesis, the logical result of an over-accent on youth."[9]

The editors at *Variety* were not the only ones taking AIP and *Wild in the Streets* seriously. On June 16, 1968, Renata Adler, writing for the *New York Times* marked a seeming decisive moment for the A and B industries: *Wild in the Streets*, she proclaimed, was "the best American film of the year."[10] Two months after Adler's declaration, *Wild in the Streets* got booked as part of the "Opera Prima" series at the Venice Film Festival, the second such showcase for AIP in three years. And then, just after the New Year 1969, even more implausibly, the film editors Fred Feitshans and Eve Newman received a call from the Academy of Motion Picture Arts and Sciences telling them they'd been nominated for an Oscar. The B-studio had quite suddenly arrived.

Wild in the Streets: Old Enough to Fight/Old Enough to Vote

In a 2019 interview with the podcaster and stand-up comic Marc Maron, Bruce Dern reflected upon his apprenticeship at AIP, which he dubbed "the University of Corman."[11] It was an exciting time be an actor there, despite the long hours and sub-scale pay. Among such talented and beautiful company (as had assembled at AIP), Dern recollected, in 1968 Jones seemed the most surely destined for stardom.

And it is not hard to see why. Jones debuted for AIP just as *The Graduate* had completed its blockbuster first run and Dustin Hoffman became the picture's unlikely breakout star. Hoffman wasn't

FIGURE 17. The movie star Christopher Jones in *Wild in the Streets* (Barry Shear, 1968, AIP).

leading-man handsome, and executives at United Artists were baffled at his sudden stardom. After *Wild in Streets*, Jones seemed more of a sure thing.

[Mike Nichols was fond of telling the story behind the casting of Hoffman. The studio had wanted to cast Robert Redford—a good actor, of course, but so far as Nichols was concerned all wrong for the part. During Redford's audition, Nichols asked the actor if he'd ever "struck out" with a woman. Redford replied, "Whaddya mean?" (meaning, the answer was "no.") Nichols later asked Hoffman the same question, and got a list.]

The role of Max Frost, the charismatic rock star in *Wild in the Streets* who exploits pop culture fame all the way to the White House, seems today written with Jones in mind. And it is hard to imagine anyone else doing as much or as well with the part. Interesting, then, to consider that Jones was not AIP's first choice. The studio began developing the project eyeing instead the charismatic protest-folk singer Phil Ochs—a terrific bit of stunt casting for the lead role. According to Ochs's biographer Michael Schumacher, the singer wanted to do the film, but Ochs's manager Arthur Gorson advised against taking the part. Gorson worried that Ochs's antiestablishment music fans might see the film as reactionary and right-wing and that any association with Hollywood would seem to them a sell-out.[12]

Ochs was a for-real voice of the counterculture—a heavy on the Greenwich Village folk scene and a news-making political activist. In 1964, Ochs's protest-folk single "Draft Dodger Rag" offered a first-person account from "a typical American boy from a typical American town" wanting no part of the war in Vietnam. A year later, Ochs recorded a second (seeming first-person) anti-war hit, "I Ain't Marching Anymore," which ended with the refrain: "Call it peace or call it treason / Call it love or call it reason / But I ain't marchin' anymore." In Chicago in the summer of 1968 during the street protests during the Democratic National Convention, Ochs delivered a performance that would among anti-war activists become legendary. The yippies (the loose band of counterculture rabble-rousers affiliated with the Youth International Party) had booked Ochs to perform live. Mayor Richard Daley couldn't ban the show, but he could (and did) deny the organizers permits to use proper sound gear. Many of the acts begged off. But not Ochs, who sang his songs into a megaphone held to his mouth by a stagehand.

Assuming he could act, Ochs might have succeeded in making *Wild in the Streets* into an even more politically meaningful film. And he would have brought by his very presence a political commentary on pop celebrity, one that Ochs would soon explore in his own music.[13] Ochs knew firsthand how celebrity could be cumbersome, that it wasn't at all compatible with a counterculture lifestyle, a counterculture identity, a commitment to counterculture politics. He knew how pop stardom might get a narcissist like Max in the film—or a handsome, well-promoted Hollywood actor like Jones—into trouble.

Pop celebrity would indeed get to Ochs as well. In 1967, when AIP began developing the film, the singer-songwriter was at the apex of his career. But he was drinking heavily as well, self-medicating to manage his undiagnosed manic depression/bipolar disease. After the election of Richard Nixon in the fall of 1968, Ochs despaired that his message had had so little impact. So he took his act quite literally on the road: to Chile to express his support for the newly elected Communist-populist leader there, Salvador Allende. Ochs traveled throughout South America and soon found himself in for-real trouble with the junta in Argentina.

By the time he got back to the United States, he was in bad shape. He did a few shows on the benefit circuit: a 1971 concert and rally sponsored by John Lennon to protest the imprisonment of poet/activist John Sinclair, a 1973 concert protesting the CIA assassination of Allende (in which Ochs performed alongside Pete Seeger, Arlo Guthrie, and Bob Dylan), and the 1975 "War Is Over" celebration in New York's Central Park, which drew over a hundred thousand people. The Central Park performance would be Ochs's last of any importance. Later that year, Ochs took on the alter-ego John Butler Train, whom he claimed had murdered the singer Phil Ochs. Train/Ochs lived for a while on the streets: broke, drunk, impossibly and unrecognizably crazy. In 1976, at his sister Sonny's home, Ochs, just thirty-five years old, died by suicide.[14]

AIP's interest in working with Ochs at the height of his counterculture significance rather highlights Arkoff's willingness to court controversy. Vietnam (the war and the domestic resistance to that war) was in 1967 quite completely off-limits at the studios. But it gets mentioned several times in *Wild in the Streets*. And although music popular with young people (several Motown acts, the Beatles, the Rolling Stones, and the Animals) had been featured by then regularly on family-oriented TV variety programs like the Ed Sullivan and Red Skelton shows, the studios remained reluctant to engage with rock and roll music and culture, reluctant to employ and exploit youth culture talent. As a result, there was plenty of room in the marketplace for a movie like *Wild in Streets*, and plenty of room in the fan magazines, in the hearts and minds of young filmgoers, for Jones, who looked the part of a rock star.

Silly as *Wild in the Streets* may have seemed to studio executives still foolish enough to dismiss AIP as trash or schlock, the film was indisputably topical and its pop star fantasy—its critique of entertainment industry celebrity and the corruptive effect of capitalist accumulation—ideologically complex. A precursor and possible inspiration for *Wild in the Streets* was the direct cinema documentary *Don't Look Back* (D. A. Pennebaker) released the previous year, a film that gave filmgoers fly-on-the-wall access to Dylan's 1965 tour of England. In the film, Pennebaker depicts Dylan's discomfort with the paraphernalia of pop stardom: the press, the entourage, the lonely travel from venue to venue, the behind-the-scenes business conducted without the pop star's input or consent. Dylan's notorious irascibility seems after seeing the film not only comprehensible, but also sensible. The press hangs on his every word, fellow musicians desperately desire an audience, fans take his lyrics as gospel. The pressure is impossible—the tour relentless.

Another precursor to *Wild in the Streets* was Peter Watkins's dour, quasi-Marxist pop-star pseudo-documentary *Privilege* (1967). The British art film had a limited release in the United States about six months before *Wild in the Streets*, and the comparison between the two films is irresistible—indeed, in 1968 Ebert reviewed the films side by side: "The connection between politics and the worship of pop idols is fascinating," Ebert opined, "When Paul Newman was stumping for Sen. Eugene McCarthy in Wisconsin, it was hard to say whether his audiences cared about politics at all. They were drawn by the Newman mystique. But can the appeal work the other way? Two recent movies have explored this idea. One is a good film, Peter

Watkins's *Privilege*. One is pretty bad, Barry Shear's *Wild in the Streets*. Of the two, I'm afraid *Wild in the Streets* is more effective because it has a greater understanding of its audience."

Privilege is a fascinating, but off-putting film—a daunting corrective to the ceaselessly upbeat Beatles' feature *A Hard Day's Night* (Richard Lester, 1964). Lester's film depicts Beatlemania as ever so much fun—for the fans *and* for the band. Even as Ringo has a brief bout of celebrity ennui, he recovers quickly, reminded by his bandmates that being a Beatle is pretty terrific. *A Hard Day's Night* climaxes with a Beatles performance on TV with Ringo by then back in the fold, part of something bigger and better than he could ever have imagined.

Watkins's film stars two of swinging London's trendiest swingers: the supermodel Jean Shrimpton and, playing the tortured rock star, Steven Shorter, Paul Jones,[15] the lead singer of the Manfred Mann group, a pop outfit that charted more than once in the mid- to late sixties. But unlike Lester, Watkins takes a cynical view of the British pop scene. Paul Jones was, with Manfred Mann, a charismatic performer. So, we are told, was the character he plays, Stephen Shorter, before we meet him in Watkins's film. *Privilege* begins with Shorter already at the end of his tether, wanting out. Watkins focuses on what happens behind the scenes and so shows Shorter (and, with a little imagination, Paul Jones) being manipulated by his many handlers, who together exploit the pop star's mass appeal, what we would today call the pop star's brand to get Shorter's many fans to conform to Conservative British values and follow Jesus. Watkins demystifies the mechanics and politics of pop stardom, to make, as Ebert describes it, "a self-conscious message film for serious audiences." *Wild in the Streets*, Ebert notes by way of comparison, was "aimed squarely at the younger teenage audience that buys records and listens to the Top 40 stations."[16] That teenage audience had by 1968 become AIP's audience. And it would with *Wild in the Streets* become Christopher Jones's audience as well.

The pop star Paul Jones did not have to dig deep to play the pop star Steven Shorter. Christopher Jones drew easily from his own experiences as well to portray Max, channeling his West Hollywood neighbor Jim Morrison—the front man and lead singer of the Doors. On stage in the film as Max, Jones copped Morrison's (lizard-like) posture, his mannerisms (he cups his ear as he sings), his (as Ebert describes it) "primitive force." The Doors uniquely pit Morrison's poetic lyrics against improvisational jazz and rock accompaniment. AIP had Jones and Max's band, the Troopers, perform more mainstream fare. To get the sound right, Arkoff secured the services of the pop impresarios Barry Mann and Claudia Weill. The songwriters had authored by then a dozen or so pop classics, including: "He's Sure the Boy That I Love," "On Broadway," "Walking in the Rain," "You've Lost That Lovin' Feeling," and "We Gotta Get Out of This Place." Among the songs they wrote for Jones, an allegorical protest number titled "The Shape of Things to Come," got pressed as a single and charted at number 22. As part of Arkoff's deft cross-marketing scheme, the single was credited to Max Frost and the Troopers and not to Jones and the studio musicians hired to back him.[17]

Despite a style steeped in B-movie camp, *Wild in the Streets* did well to register a provocative message about the risks inherent to underestimating and undervaluing America's precocious and increasingly politicized youth—not only in denying them a political voice in the real world, but in denying them a platform, a genre for the filmic expression of the stories and characters and topics they really cared about. The light-comic tone of *Wild in the Streets* was vintage AIP. But it was also a feint of sorts, as the film's fantasy future of rock and roll fascism was smart and deadly serious.

Wild in the Streets opens with a voice-of-God narrator—a disembodied voice similar to the one used so lightheartedly in the *Beach*

Party films—that introduces Max: suburban kid, precocious genius (he makes LSD in his bedroom; later, a bomb to blow up the family Chrysler), teenage rebel (taking a knife to the plastic slipcovered furniture) confessing to an existential crisis: "I'm running away. I'd kill myself if I had to stay here." We then cut to Max's posh rock-star compound a few years later. Here the light comedy gives way long enough for the narrator to tell us that in 1968 pop music and big business work hand-in-hand: "From his palatial Beverly Hills home Max operates fourteen interlocking companies." Max is a counterculture celebrity *and* an American entrepreneur.

We cut to the interior of the compound and see Max luxuriating in a bathtub with "one of [his] latest creature comforts . . . ex-child star, vegetarian, mystic, acid head," Sally LeRoy (Diane Varsi—by 1968 herself already a Hollywood casualty). AIP caught actors on the way up (like Jones) and the way down (Varsi). In 1957, after a well-publicized national search, Varsi was cast to play Alison McKenzie in Mark Robson's big-budget melodrama *Peyton Place*, a performance for which she received an Oscar nomination. It was an auspicious debut, but on her second film, a Gary Cooper western, *Ten North Frederick* (Philip Dunne, 1958), Varsi suffered a nervous breakdown. She soldiered on in two more films—one of them a terrific screen adaptation of the stage play *Compulsion* (Richard Fleischer, 1959)—then walked away from her studio contract. During the sabbatical, she acted in plays in San Francisco, did a stint at the Actors Studio in New York, and then commenced a modest comeback at AIP with featured roles in *Wild in the Streets* and *Bloody Mama* (Roger Corman, 1970)—then walked away again, this second time for good. It is fair to wonder if Jones recognized himself at all in Varsi's struggles. He should have.

The rest of the band and entourage get their casting call as well—an entourage not, per the *Beach Party* formula, composed of a comic band of lily-white beach bum misfits. Instead Max's inner circle is composed of a strategically integrated collection of teenaged overachievers—a rainbow coalition, including the Black academic/activist Stanley X (played by the future stand-up comedy and movie star Richard Pryor), the Asian-American Fuji Ellie (May Ishihara), and a disabled-American (Larry Bishop as "The Hook," who plays trumpet with a prosthetic hand).

The entourage shields Max from the real world, at least at first. They manage the various Max Frost product lines; rock and roll is big business after all. Much the same dynamic is at work with Dylan's management team, which endeavors to protect Dylan's interests and serve his needs. But it's not so easy, as Dylan is irascible, unpredictable, a new sort of pop star. He's counterculture because he seems to care little about what anyone—the press, his entourage, even his fans—thinks of him. One afternoon the folk-pop star Donovan, who has been touted as the new or next Dylan, visits his idol in a hotel room. Donovan plays a song, like some small-time hopeful begging for approval. When he finishes, the real Dylan grabs a guitar and sings "It's All Over Now, Baby Blue." When he gets to the line that ends every stanza—"it's all over now, Baby Blue"—Dylan nods his head to remind the upstart Donovan who's boss, what it means to be in the presence of a star. Despite the occasional put-upon act (and it is an act) with the press, the scene makes clear that there are plenty of days Bob Dylan enjoys being Bob Dylan. The counterculture act cuts only so deep.

In Watkins's dour fantasy, Steven Shorter is a pawn in a political scheme executed by his management team—the bankers, politicians, and clergy, who together endeavor to use Shorter's pop celebrity to distract and manipulate British youth. Unlike either Dylan or Shorter, who delegate business to businessmen, Max is in control of his destiny. His politics emerge out of promotion and marketing, out of a keen understanding of what his fans, his future constituents want to hear. Early on, we see Max engaging concertgoers with a compelling message, one very much in play in the United States in 1968: that at eighteen, American men were old enough to fight and die in Vietnam but too young to vote. (The Twenty-Sixth Amendment would eventually correct that, lowering the voting age from twenty-one to eighteen. But it would not arrive for another three years.) Max writes a song for the occasion, and in it he offers a simple math lesson—that in 1967, 52 percent of the American population was under twenty-five. "We outnumber the fuzz [police], we outnumber the shopkeepers." And then, as he sings a song simply titled, "52 Percent," Max adds smartly, "We're 52 percent and we make big business big."

What the older generation wants to do with Max and his not-so-silent 52 percent majority begins, per Watkins's film, with an attempt at exploitation. But the sillier film here is also the more transgressive. Enter Johnny Fergus (Hal Holbrook), an ambitious politician running for a US Senate seat. In exchange for Max's endorsement (that will surely win the election for him), Fergus agrees to support an amendment lowering the voting age. The proposed deal is politics as usual; but Fergus underestimates his new partner. At a rally at which he is supposed to give Fergus the agreed-upon endorsement, Max goes off-script. Fergus, he points out, is thirty-seven years old: "That's old, man—I don't want to live to be thirty—thirty is death, man." The only thing that "gets you off" when you're over thirty, Max tells the audience (and here this B-film goes where no 1968 A-feature would have dared to go), "is getting guys to kill other guys in another country." Later, Max pushes the argument further: "In the war you're killing every man, woman, and child to get them to vote your way."

Fergus winces. But he wants to win bad enough to tolerate Max's volatility. And he figures he can control or dump the pop star when he needs to. But he can't, because the pop star's celebrity is akin to the Beatles' circa *Hard Day's Night*—boundless, hysterical, inexplicable.

To play Max, Jones channeled Morrison. But off-stage Max is more like the Beatles' John Lennon: smart, outspoken, *and* political.

Key to both *Privilege* and *Wild in the Streets* were controversial remarks made by Lennon in August 1966, when the Beatle mused on the ridiculous popularity of his band: "Christianity will go. It will vanish and shrink. I needn't argue about that; I know I'm right and I will be proved right. We're more popular than Jesus now. I don't know which will go first—rock & roll or Christianity. Jesus was all right, but his disciples were thick and ordinary. It's them twisting it that ruins me." The interview was published in the *London Evening Standard* and that was that. Lennon went on with being a Beatle. The earth spun on its axis.

But then, a few months later, Lennon's remarks were reprinted in the US teen magazine *Datebook*. And the publication sparked a sensational response. Religious groups in the United States sponsored the public burning of Beatles records. At an anti-Beatles rally, young American Christians held signs: "Jesus Loves You. Do the Beatles?" "Beatles Today. What Tomorrow?" "Jesus died for you, John Lennon." Several American radio stations banned the Beatles' music. DJs smashed their records on air. South Carolina's KKK Grand Dragon nailed Beatles albums to a cross and then, because he was a KKK Grand Dragon, set them alight. Alabama's Imperial Wizard Robert Shelton declared the Beatles brainwashed by Communists. Even the Vatican newspaper *L'Osservatore* weighed in: "Some subjects must not be dealt with profanely, even in the world of Beatniks." South Africa and Spain issued official condemnations. Suddenly the Beatles had enemies. Suddenly the Beatles had to answer for their cultural cache, their perceived influence.

A little context: Lennon's "We're more popular than Jesus now" remarks were extracted from a much longer conversation with Maureen Cleave, a journalist and a friend. Lennon had just read Hugh J. Schonfield's book *The Passover Plot*, in which Jesus fakes miracles with the help of his disciples. As fellow Beatle Paul McCartney noted years later, Lennon wasn't boasting, he was instead talking with a friend about a book—and he wanted to show her and her readers, "[he wasn't just a] stupid rock & roll star."

Ringo Starr freaked out at the controversy and wanted to cancel the band's planned American tour. After all, Ringo implored his bandmates: everyone in the United States has guns. To placate Ringo, Lennon backpedaled. "I'm not anti-God, anti-Christ or anti-religion," he told a reporter. "I was not knocking it. I was not saying we're better or greater, or comparing us with Jesus Christ as a person or God as a thing or whatever it is. I happened to be talking to a friend and I used the word 'Beatles' as a remote thing—'Beatles' like other people see us." The press release was an explanation, and not exactly an apology—and it didn't help.

The band went ahead with the US tour. Death threats accompanied their arrival. So Lennon held another press conference: "I wasn't saying what they're saying I was saying. I'm sorry I said it—really. I never meant it to be a lousy anti-religious thing. I apologize if that will make you happy. I still don't know quite what I've done. I've tried to tell you what I did do, but if you want me to apologize, if that will make you happy, then—OK, I'm sorry."[18] Not exactly an apology either, but it worked as well as one.

Wild in the Streets ponders what would happen if a pop star more popular than Jesus mobilized his flock—what would have happened if John Lennon had not apologized, but instead had doubled down. When Fergus introduces Max to his sons; the senator acknowledges his boys' excitement by saying, "Meeting the president didn't mean anything [to them]," after which one of the boys says to Max: "You're more famous than Jesus." The allusion is hardly inadvertent.

Max and Fergus eventually find themselves at odds, and the politician tells the rock star he could "drive a man to drink." It's an idiom, of course, but Max decides not to acknowledge it as such and dismisses Fergus as just another oldster from "the alcoholic generation." Cut to Fergus later that night as he returns home, drunk. He tells his wife about his latest encounter with Max: "I'm part of the alcoholic generation. We pour Napalm on our own men. We do it because we're drunk." Here again it is hard to imagine a big studio film going anywhere near such dialogue.

As the election nears, Max begins to appreciate how little he needs Fergus. He addresses his fans: "We got the old tigers scared, baby." He then tells them about a mass demonstration he's planning on the Sunset Strip: "I want the hippies. I want the heads. I want the two-car kids. I want the all-in-one-bedroom-kids-with-their-mama. I want the ones who can't even stand their old ladies. I want all of you." Max enlists his "troops" (his young fans) to join him on the Strip for the demonstration, a scenario that surely recalled the curfew riots on that same famous street two years earlier.

Teenagers had transformed the Strip in the mid-sixties. When local businessmen wearied of the "new element"—the shaggy-haired kids were, they claimed with some justification, bad for business—they called upon the L.A. County Sheriff's office to step in. And step in they did, with predictable consequences, imposing and then violently enforcing a 10 p.m. curfew for all those under age twenty-one. Debates persist about the extent or even the existence of an actual riot.[19] But whatever we make of what happened on the Strip to protest the curfew, it made for good TV. Teenagers walked around holding protest placards: "We're Your Children! Don't Destroy Us" and "Ban the Billyclub." They blocked traffic, broke a few windows. Sonny and Cher addressed the throng outside the popular nightclub, Pandora's Box—a neat photo op, a neat clip for the six o'clock news.

The newspapers and TV-news divisions did their best to sensationalize the protest. Arkoff did as well—twice. Licensing network news footage, Arkoff hurried into production the inevitably titled *Riot on the Sunset Strip* (Arthur Dreifuss, 1967). A year later, Shear used the same footage in *Wild in the Streets*, adding fake news commentary from the *Variety* columnist Army Archerd (playing himself) to suit the satire. As we see hippies assembling on the street, Archerd reports: "There have been casualties. Three elderly matrons have died of heart attacks in the safety of their homes." History recycled as farce: vintage Arkoff.

Max makes the most of his opportunity to speak to the teenagers on the Strip. Unlike Sonny Bono—who in a neat twist of fate, quit the music business years later to pursue politics, culminating in a successful run to become a United States congressman, a politically conservative congressman at that—Max has more than a photo op in mind. "America has heard you because you are America," he tells his young fans. Max then ups the ante. He orchestrates the unlikely election to Congress of Sally LeRoy to replace an old white guy who has just died in office. His team then doses the D.C. water supply with LSD, enabling Sally to take control of an inebriated legislature—a ridiculous plot, perhaps, but later in the summer of 1968, the Chicago mayor, Richard Daley, made aware of the film scenario, hired National Guard troops to protect his city's water supply, believing rumors that the Yippies were planning a copycat crime.

Shear cleverly stages the LSD-Congress scene to resemble the takeover of the state house by Reconstruction-era Blacks in D. W. Griffith's 1915 racist epic *Birth of a Nation*. The allusion gets a bit lost in the farce, as blissed-out old white men follow Sally's lead to lower the minimum-age requirements for members of the Congress and Senate, vice president, and president—legislation that paves the way for Max to mount a run for the presidency. Sally's blissed-out speech on the floor of Congress puts everything in perspective: "America's greatest contribution has been to teach the world that growing old is such a drag." Fergus's son, who has run away from home just as Max did years earlier, later confronts his father with a similar indisputable logic: "If you don't want to be old, why should we?"

Max wins the election, and he takes his mandate seriously—so seriously he outlines some very big changes in his first State of the Union address: "There's a fly in the ointment... it's not the Communists, it's not the Birchers... there is a villain in history, though... and it's not the Jews, it's not the labor leaders, it's not the bankers, it's not the Russians, and it isn't even the Chinese. Who has caused all of our problems? Those who are stiff, baby... not with love, but with age... they're heavy with honey and they can't fly." Shear holds on a low angle shot of Max, then cuts to Fergus in high angle. The power dynamics are clear. Fergus pulls a gun. But he is thwarted in his attempt to assassinate Max. We then cut to Max, dusted off and more determined than ever.

Max entreats his troops: "You give me the tools, you give me the laws... you give me the power." They do, and he establishes thirty as a mandatory retirement age. Citizens then have five years to get their lives in order. When they turn thirty-five, they are interned in so-called mercy camps, where, to quote Max, "in groovy surroundings, we're going to psych them all out on LSD.... They're not going to hurt you [that is, his young acolytes].... They won't draft us; we'll draft them." Here again in the most ridiculous of scenarios, the filmmakers address the unpopular Vietnam War draft with an audacity their studio counterparts would not have dared.

The film ends on a down note. Acknowledging his complicity in Max's power grab, Fergus hangs himself in a mercy camp. Max, meanwhile, begins to find the job of being a president a drag. So he skips out of town. Beside a creek, he has a brief confrontation with a boy, whom he cruelly bullies. The film ends as the boy looks into the camera and says: "We're going to put everybody over ten out of business."

The coda offers in black-comic exaggeration a reminder of the risks inherent in the current cult of youth. However ridiculous we find Max's mercy camp solution for the generational struggle between the young and the old—it is at the very least, extreme—the film offers beforehand ample satire of older Americans willing to do most anything to get in on the action. Max's mother, for example, played with the comic hysteria Winters reserved for her many B-movie ventures, is an easy target: she has "work" done, and she dresses like a hippie to pass as part of Max's entourage. In the end, she gets her comeuppance, as we find her wandering around the mercy camp telling passersby who are too high to care that she's Max's mom. Less ridiculous (or at least less broadly comic) is Fergus, who panders to Max and his Troops.

Growing up and growing old are of course not the same things. And this too seems at issue here. By the time *Wild in the Streets* screened for American audiences in the spring and summer of 1968, the generation gap was a well-worn topic for cultural historians and social scientists writing for fellow academics *and* for the public at large (reading popular magazines and newspapers).[20] Meantime, the studios trivialized the phenomenon, rather summed up in the popular 1963 film adaptation of the 1960 Broadway musical *Bye Bye Birdie* (George Sidney). The play and film tell the story of a Midwest teenager's despair at the conscription of the rock and roll music star Conrad Birdie (an obvious reference to Elvis Presley, who had famously answered Uncle Sam's call) and her parents' freak-out at her coming of age. The film features a raucous production number titled "Kids," sung by clueless adults asking over and again: "What's the matter with kids today?" The singers ask: "Why can't they [today's kids] be like we were / Perfect in every way?" The current crop of kids, they lament, are "noisy, crazy, dirty, lazy loafers"; but, for the parents who sing the song, a look in the mirror seems on order as well. Per Hollywood's take on the subject at the time, the song runs full circle and concludes with an amiable shrug: "Nothing's the matter with kids" after all.

If only the generation gap were so simple. As the sociologist Paul Goodman wrote in his landmark study, *Growing Up Absurd*, a nonfiction best seller first published in 1960 (back when public intellectuals like Goodman had a wide readership): "It is not that troublesome youth are under-socialized. Perhaps they are socialized perfectly well. Perhaps the social message has been communicated to the young... and it is unacceptable."[21] As the sixties wound down, the young seemed to many adults, "wild in the streets." But as Goodman so curtly contended, they had their reasons.

3 in the Attic

Studio caution about the counterculture was in many ways a matter of policy and procedure. There were reasons why they could not match AIP's topicality. Studio films take longer to develop, produce, market, and distribute; the two industries have different modes of production and different economies of scale. These distinctions between the A- and B-movie industries carry with them assumptions about relative quality, assumptions that in the late sixties were hard to defend. The sad fact of the matter for the studios was that by the time Arkoff's topical sexual revolution satire *3 in the Attic* entered its first run at Christmastime 1968, AIP had become (for the major studios) "the competition" in almost every way that mattered in the American film market.

The generation gap Arkoff had successfully mined in *Wild in the Streets* was by 1968 nothing radical or new. Nor was the war, the grassroots movement to lower the voting age to eighteen, or rock and roll—all front and center in the AIP feature.

The sexual revolution had been in the news as well, and had been for a while. The Kinsey Reports were first published in 1948 and 1953. Masters and Johnson followed in 1956. Then came Vance Packard's 1968 *The Sexual Wilderness*, which brought to a mass audience what the more serious scientific studies provided for more specialized and sophisticated readerships.[22]

Packard spoke to and for a lot of Americans in 1968, many of whom felt less revolutionized than lost—lost in a new public conversation about sex and gender. His previous book, the 1957 bestselling critique of Madison Avenue, *The Hidden Persuaders*, revealed how the advertising industry used manipulative and deceptive psychological techniques to create desire for certain consumer goods and for consumption in general. With *The Sexual Wilderness*, Packard hoped to reach a similar readership with an equally alarmist message about the sexual revolution.

For his sexual revolution book, Packard drew from surveys conducted mostly at American universities from which he discerned a "chaotic state to interpersonal relationships" among American youth, a "sexual wilderness" in which "the whole range of areas where males and females find themselves in confrontation" had dramatically reconfigured. Packard's book was interesting and influential, but not because his reading of the data was particularly astute (it was not). The book's popularity and influence built upon a fundamental resistance among Packard's readership to social change; Packard spoke for the silent majority (which seemed always to have plenty of folks anxious to speak on their silent behalf), lamenting a permissive culture characterized by the apparent decline in parental/generational authority, the wavering role of religious doctrine, the increased availability of birth control, and the unwillingness among college administrators to act responsibly as substitute parents.

Key as well: plenty among the so-called "greatest generation" felt cheated of *their* youth—years lost during wartime. They quietly envied their kids' freedom and opportunity. And they wanted in on all the sex. If it was a better world for their kids, why (and this was the question Mrs. Robinson seemed to be asking) was it not a better world for them too? Packard warned establishment adults against diving in; the consequences were in his view already in evidence.

"You cannot overhaul the status of one sex [by sex, he means gender] without altering the status of the other in the process. Consider the matter of relative power. If a woman gains in power, a man quite obviously must give up some, and make the best of it, or fight back."[23] To Arkoff, such a gambit sounded a lot like an elevator pitch. And he had the perfect young actor under contract—Christopher Jones—to take such a topic on.

AIP put plenty of muscle behind the film, hiring the director Richard Wilson, who had worked for nearly two decades with Orson Welles and the Mercury Theater. The studio's move up-market paid off. By the spring of 1969 *3 in the Attic* was a top-twenty box-office earner and AIP's top grossing film of the decade.

The plot of *3 in the Attic* proved timely and irresistible: campus lothario Paxton Quigley (Jones) is caught three-timing three very different (and of course beautiful) young women: a sensitive and intellectual blonde WASP (Yvette Mimieux as Tobey), a proud, politicized Black woman (Judy Pace as Eulice); and a free-spirited Jewish brunette (Maggie Thrett as Janet). The women discover his infidelity and together decide to teach Paxton a lesson; they lock him in an attic and make him their sex slave. Paxton tires of their demands, goes on a hunger strike, and then, after he is released and recovers his strength, vows to become monogamous with Tobey, the woman who hatched the plot to imprison him.

The film opens with Paxton in voice-over: "You've heard of the sexual revolution; well, I am one of its casualties." The story then unfolds in flashback; we know it won't go so well for our hero and have only to discover how and why. Wilson begins with Paxton's seduction of Tobey. To capture her interest, Paxton quotes Kierkegaard on boredom and "the aesthetic validity of marriage." He toys with her necklace. He says: "Not too many chicks get turned on by the printed page these days.... It's too linear for them." She's quickly hooked. In voice-over Paxton shares some advice: "Some girls you

FIGURE 18. Every picture tells a story: Christopher Jones and costar Yvette Mimieux on location filming *3 in the Attic* (Richard Wilson, 1968) (Everett Collection).

quote Kierkegaard, you quote Genet, you open a book with them and it's like pulling down the covers of a bed."

Eulice and Janet arrive on the scene a bit later, mostly to unsettle Paxton's confidence. Eulice is a painter, and she asks Paxton to pose for her. We see him naked and in full figure from behind in a variable focus shot that offers a clear view of him, an out-of-focus view of her, paintbrush in hand. He is the object of her and our visual pleasure—such is the gender confusion, the film suggests, inherent to the sexual revolution. The role reversal is as well a setup for a joke. Eulice unveils her painting. "It's only my face," he says. That was always the plan, she admits; she just wanted to see him naked.

A sexual encounter is then staged at a motel. Paxton, we gather, has used the motel in the past. But he is careful not to reveal Eulice's identity to the motel clerk; it's the South and they're a mixed-race couple. Paxton and Eulice talk frankly about race. It is hard to imagine a studio film of the era handling the relationship so candidly.

Paxton then meets Janet, who, like Eulice, is more sexually liberated and adventurous than he is. He tells her a phony story about a male swimming coach taking advantage of him. We gather he's used the story before. She seems at first to fall for the ruse and affects a cure. But we soon discover she's only done what she'd intended to do all along. Après sex she doses him with "magic brownies" and draws on his naked back with magic markers. When it comes to men, she tells Paxton, she is "controlled by her Id."

Paxton makes a schedule so he can see all three women. But Eulice and Janet are unpredictable, insatiable. He opts finally for the safety of monogamy with Tobey. The sexual revolution, he decides, is impossible; the old rules protect men not only from their own worst inclinations but from sexually emancipated women as well. For its first hour *3 in the Attic* is a bedroom farce. After that, I'm not so sure. Paxton's decision at the hour mark to commit to a monogamous relationship with Tobey unluckily coincides with the revelation of his previous infidelities. So begins the more seriously enacted final third of the film in which the male fantasy of becoming a sex prisoner of three very different, very beautiful, and very interesting women is shown to be not very much fun.

Paxton's imprisonment ends when a busybody in Tobey's house rats her out to the Dean, who is introduced, in an easy comic jab at women in higher education, smoking a pipe. The Dean worries aloud about the university's' liability, making clear reference to the 1961 Appeals Court decision in *Dixon v. Alabama*, the case that hurried the demise of "*in loco parentis*" (previously compelling universities to take on certain parental responsibilities).[24] She asks Tobey to explain what she has done with Paxton, and then reminds the coed, "A woman's progressive college is not a priori a whorehouse." In saying so she suggests it probably is. The Dean asks Tobey why Paxton hasn't broken down the door. "We've sapped his strength," she replies matter-of-factly. The Dean smiles. "He's not dead, by any chance," the Dean asks. "Dying," Tobey replies. The dean wants only to keep the whole sordid mess quiet for the good of the university. Just release Paxton, no questions asked. But Tobey declines. She won't back down until Paxton tells her *why* he cheated on her. "You can't fake love," she tells the Dean.

We cut to Paxton. He's asleep, dreaming. In the dream, we hear a female professor opine: "A woman's true education happens outside the classroom." A sit-in ensues. (AIP's sixties films were consistently ridiculous *and* timely.) Paxton stands up: "I accuse—those three Nazis." He points at the women who have imprisoned him. The other women in the room sing a song about him, to the tune of the "Battle Hymn of the Republic"—but it's just a dream.

We cut to Paxton on a stretcher carried to safety by paramedics. Fearing bad publicity, the Dean pins the blame on Paxton. He is, as promised in the opening voice-over, "a casualty of the sexual revolution." We resume the farce. In the name of love, Eulice breaks Paxton out of the hospital in time to preempt Tobey's return to her parents' home. The setting for the reunion is a bus station. It is hard to miss the intended allusion to *The Graduate*.

The happy ending of *3 in the Attic* cues one last gag. Set over the closing credits and staged in animation, a wife tells her husband she bets he'd like to be Paxton. "Oh to be nineteen again," he muses. She plays the shrew: "You were never nineteen," then adds: "In my day, a girl would never think of doing such a thing." He reminds his wife that there has been a sexual revolution, to which she responds: "But remember, honey, you're on the losing side." He sees her point: "Paxton Quigley has three girls in the attic, and I've got two sofas, three mortgages, and no girls." Funny, perhaps, and sexist for sure, but the otherwise silly film has in the meantime offered thoughtful commentary on several timely topics: interracial romance (in the South!), higher education (in the post-*loco parentis* era), women's lib, and the sexual revolution. And it has done so more candidly, less nervously than any studio film of the era.

Case-in-point: Columbia Studios' *Bob and Carol and Ted Alice* (released in September 1969), in which the director Paul Mazursky followed through on the marketing tagline, "consider the possibilities." In doing so, in considering said possibilities, he very gently poked fun at two handsome upper-middle-class white couples wanting in on the action. But the counterculture is in all its many iterations comically pretentious and logistically impossible. The couples dabble then discover that the sexual revolution would be fine without them—a sentiment that spoke for the studio industry and their older customers as a whole.

The reviews for *3 in the Attic* were less enthusiastic than they had been for *Wild in the Streets*. But as the *New York Times*' Vincent Canby acknowledged, *3 in the Attic* seemed sure to succeed despite him. In an alliteratively titled review, "Bye, Bye, Beach Bunnies: Bye, Bye, Beach Bunnies," Canby wrote: "[*3 in the Attic* is] more raunchy and less funny than any other AIP film I've seen. It is a fantasizing projection of dearly held contemporary myths about romance, sex, humor, ethics, aesthetics, art and movies. In its eclectic way, it's also in bad taste on an almost staggering number of levels. Wit: 'non-swimmers shouldn't jump bare—into the sea of love.' Incidental decor: a jock strap hanging permanently over a screen in Paxton's pad. Style: a mixed up anthology of jump cuts, Resnais-like memory cuts, blown-up still photographs all backed up by neo-Simon and Garfunkel. Preliminary box office statistics indicate that it's going to be a smash hit."[25]

Christopher Jones Becomes a Movie Star

Jones left AIP in 1969 after landing the lead in a Columbia Pictures adaptation of John Le Carre's Cold War spy novel *The Looking Glass War* (Frank Pierson)—a for real A-studio feature that cast Jones alongside two heavyweights: Anthony Hopkins and Ralph Richardson. The differences in approach and performance among the actors proved remarkable—and for Pierson, useful. Jones plays a Polish defector to England named Leiser; he is a man from another country *and* another generation. Jones thus fit the bill: he was an *actor* from another country and another generation.

Jones dived deep into his arsenal of James Dean mannerisms. His performance is start-to-finish Method, which proved provocative in ways Jones likely didn't anticipate. The "next James Dean" thing had served him well at AIP. But in the seeming big-time, he faced resistance and ridicule, as an institutional bias prevailed in A-Hollywood favoring British-based classical training over the American Method alternative. Consider the Oscar nominations for Best Actor in the era. In 1963, three of the five nominees were classically trained British actors (Albert Finney, Richard Harris, and Rex Harrison); in 1964, four of five (Harrison, Richard Burton, Peter O'Toole, and Peter Sellers); in 1965, two of five (Burton and Laurence Olivier); and in 1966, three of five (Burton, Michael Caine, and Paul Scofield). As late as 1972, when Brando won for *The Godfather*, three of the four other nominees were Caine, Olivier, and O'Toole. In the 1950s, the Method was a signifier of left-wing Hollywood; a decade later, it referred instead, or as well, to an anti-Hollywood Hollywood counterculture, headlined by Brando and reverential to Dean, the two actors Jones most wanted to emulate.

A now famous exchange between Olivier and Hoffman on the set of *Marathon Man* (John Schlesinger, 1976) helps characterize Jones's predicament. Searching for a way to express his character's pain and anxiety, Hoffman asked Olivier for a suggestion. The more classically trained Olivier replied wearily, "My dear boy, why don't you try acting." It was an ungenerous and unkind remark, but it as well spoke volumes on generational prejudices that prevailed in establishment Hollywood at the time.

When movie reviewers took it upon themselves to uphold the standards of some imagined old Hollywood, they resisted the Method as in and of itself counterculture. For example, in his review of the *Looking Glass War* for the *New York Times*, Howard Thompson described Jones's performance as a "symbol of new-generation independence." He didn't mean it as a compliment. "[Jones] slouches across enemy territory with bland indifference," Thompson writes, "wearing dark glasses, staring morosely... [his] all-American mumble coated with a Polish accent."[26]

In my view, Jones more than holds his own opposite Hopkins and Richardson. And as Method as his performance most certainly is, you can't take your eyes off him. Pierson, the film's director, recognized this fact and gave Jones a proper entrance, a terrific first scene. Leiser/Jones is introduced in the film shirtless, tossing a rubber ball against a wall in a squash court—an allusion Pierson no doubt intends to another rebellious American movie icon, Steve McQueen, shown on several occasions tossing a baseball against a wall in John Sturges's 1963 film, *The Great Escape*. The Jones/McQueen comparison did not in 1969 seem implausible, which is to say from the first scene onward, Jones looks every bit (like McQueen) an American movie star.

The Looking Glass War opens with Leiser in custody. The British spies want to know why he has jumped overboard. "Very boring on ship," is his brief reply. They ask why he has decided to defect. "Vote in free elections, practice free enterprise, be a millionaire . . . sleep with movie stars." Flat affect; he is already bored with England. A more believable reason for the defection emerges—more believable given the free love sixties Leiser has indulged in—more believable given Jones's on- and off-screen persona. On a previous shore leave, Leiser met a young British woman, and she is pregnant. He has jumped ship to do right by her and the baby. The spies propose a deal: they will grant him permission to stay in London if he performs for them a clandestine mission in East Germany. Leiser catches on: "You are spies," he says, smiling, "That is wonderful."

Leiser agrees to perform the mission. Whatever we make of the slouching and mumbling, we believe in Jones's performance because the film so clearly identifies him as the focal point of visual pleasure. The script further underscores his irresistibility; that is Leiser's and Jones's charismatic appeal. When the spies ask Leiser how come he speaks English (and several other languages) so well, he replies: "Girls teach me . . . English girls. Russian girls. French girls." The spies don't for a minute doubt the explanation. After Leiser arrives in East Germany he falls quickly into a romantic encounter with beautiful local woman, Anna (Pia Degermark). There's plenty of voltage between them and their relationship dominates the second act of the film.

Degermark and Jones became off-screen lovers and, albeit briefly, soul mates. They both as well enjoyed—though that's not the right word here—a brief stardom followed by a far longer struggle with what fame and celebrity did for and to them. Degermark was discovered dancing in a disco with the Prince (later King) of Sweden,

FIGURE 19. Pia Degemark, Christopher Jones's "love interest" in *The Looking Glass War* (Frank Pierson, 1970, Columbia Pictures).

Carl Gustav. After a brief stint as a fashion model, she turned to acting with immediate success; for her debut film, *Elvira Madigan* (Bo Widerberg, 1967), she won the Best Actress Award at Cannes. She fell into Jones's orbit during *The Looking Glass War* shoot and stayed there for a while, costarring with Jones in *A Brief Season* (Renato Castellano, 1969), an Italian spy picture put into production just as *Looking Glass War* wrapped.

Degermark moved to Hollywood. He was the next James Dean—she, the next Ingrid Bergman. What could go wrong? Plenty. Degermark split with Jones soon after her arrival. A decade passed without a single American screen credit. By the time she returned to Sweden, she was in deep trouble physically and mentally, struggling with drugs and anorexia. She briefly got back on her feet in Stockholm, founding an organization to help other women afflicted with eating disorders. But the world wasn't quite done with her yet. Amid accusations of embezzlement and fraud, Degermark fell back into drug addiction and after that, did time in prison.

In 1969, just as *The Looking Glass War* wrapped, the director David Lean began casting his next film, *Ryan's Daughter*. Lean had by then six Oscar nominations for Best Director and two wins (for

Bridge on the River Kwai and *Lawrence of Arabia*). He was known for a certain style of old-school epic—no-expense-spared, star-studded affairs: the "money up there on the screen."

Lean first spied Jones after he had already cast Sarah Miles, John Mills, Trevor Howard, and Robert Mitchum. He described his new find to Miles as "shimmering," and saw Jones as the final piece to a complicated casting puzzle. It was to be the young actor's big break. But Jones failed spectacularly to take advantage. And he would never be the same afterward.

In *The Making of Ryan's Daughter*, a 2005 documentary produced for the thirty-fifth anniversary DVD reissue, Michael Stevenson, Lean's assistant director on the film, blandly summarized Jones's problem: "Sadly the chemistry between Sarah and Christopher didn't work." After seeing the film, it's an observation that is hard to dispute.

The romance between Rosy (Miles) and Major Doryan (Jones) is at the heart of Lean's romantic melodrama. And the key to selling that relationship was a brief and (for Lean) explicit sex scene to be performed by Miles and Jones. A first day's work on the scene proved disappointing. Staged outside in difficult conditions, the actors seemed to Lean uncomfortable with the location and thus uncomfortable with each other. Lean tried to fix the problem by shooting a second day of inserts—mostly close-ups staged in a hothouse, which he planned to edit into the scene. The shots didn't really match, but Lean used them anyway—an amateur mistake really, and Lean should have known better.

Miles later wrote candidly and ungenerously about Jones in her memoir, *Serves Me Right*. As she tells the story: she and Jones never hit it off. She had—and Jones knew that she had—circulated rumors that his lines had been dubbed in *The Looking Glass War*.[27] So he had his reasons. To loosen him up for the love scene, Miles asked Mitchum to secretly spike Jones's drink. He complied. But the plan backfired. Mitchum underestimated the drug's effect and Jones could hardly stay awake.[28]

What Miles and Mitchum didn't know was that Jones had as a child witnessed his mother's mental disintegration. When the drug kicked in, Jones freaked out; he wondered what had suddenly gone wrong with him. He figured he was having a nervous breakdown (like his mom). Neither Mills nor Mitchum ever bothered to tell him the truth.

Jones was out of his depth in other ways as well. And he was all on his own without a friend or mentor in the company. Miles and Lean were friends and for a lot of the shoot Jones viewed them as coconspirators. Mitchum and Lean feuded on and off the set. And Jones had no idea how to navigate the social aspects of the shoot.

A Mitchum/Lean behind-the-scenes story is worth telling here—because it's funny, and because it became part of ongoing struggles to come during the long location shoot, struggles that would impact significantly on Jones. Mitchum was Lean's first choice for the role of the aging cuckold Charles Shaughnessy. The casting made no sense (except to Lean), but no one working for the director in 1969 was likely to tell him so. To get Mitchum on board, Lean cold-called the actor and asked what he had next on his schedule. Mitchum replied, "suicide." Lean went with the gallows humor, offering to pay for the funeral so long as Mitchum agreed to play Charles, so long as he waited (to kill himself) until after the film wrapped. Mitchum took the job, though it is hard to imagine what he made of Lean's plan to cast him so against type. As production commenced, the two men fell out, spectacularly. The cast and crew split into two camps—Lean's and Mitchum's—separately headquartered at the director and star's caravans (trailers). Jones fit in neither camp. He kept to himself. He was in well over his head.

The initial shooting schedule called for twenty-four weeks, about twenty weeks longer than the average AIP production. Bad weather and bad planning pushed it to fifty-two, most of it on location in the remote coastal village of Dingle, Ireland, with an added six-week stint in Cape Town, South Africa. For those with featured roles in the film—and that included Jones—it was for the duration of the shoot impractical to leave Dingle or Cape Town. Life went on in the meantime in the real world, including for Jones news that the Manson family had murdered his friend Sharon Tate, including the postponement of his proposed wedding with Hussey. By the time the production finally wrapped, Hussey had moved on.

A raft of bad publicity attended the unending shoot. And it fatally marked *Ryan's Daughter* as a doomed project, well in advance of its release. Box office returns on the first run were poor. The second run was more respectable. But given the scale and scope of the project, the combined numbers were nowhere near what executives at MGM had hoped for.

The reception by the industry and media establishment was a bit of a mixed bag. Mills and the cinematographer Freddie Young won Oscars. Mills's performance is all but unwatchable today, an offensive portrayal of a disabled person that was the sort of thing the Academy honored in those days. Young was a huge talent and his skill at lighting and shooting in awful conditions duly impressed his peers. As always with Lean: the "money was up there" on the screen. That *Ryan's Daughter* got noticed at all on Oscar night revealed just how hopelessly out-of-date the Academy had become, that its voting members continued to cling to old-fashioned notions about good and great films.

The critics, pretty much all of them, were not so generous. Canby brutally disparaged Lean's pretentions: "[*Ryan's Daughter*] belongs to that school of very classy calendar art supported by airlines, insurance corporations and a few enlightened barber shops. It doesn't transfigure the world. It embalms it." The film had ineptly targeted an imagined midcult mass audience suspicious of the pretenses of the European New Waves and the harder-edged American auteur renaissance; it had catered to folks already (after just two years of the new rating system) "tired of unmotivated violence, of sex without ordering inhibitions." Lean's audience, Canby surmised, was, like the director, hopelessly out of date, "[dreaming] of a world in which there is still a moral order, . . . [pining for] "well made films with a beginning, middle, and end."

Canby did not disparage Jones. "He is, I think, a decent enough actor . . . [though] the character [he plays is] written without much perception." Elsewhere: "The Major [played by Jones] never says very much, but he looks great (like the magazine illustration of a hero)." As to the clumsy love scene, Canby pokes fun at Lean's cold shower/old-fashioned intercutting between the sexual act simulated on-screen (in 1970, still a fairly new wrinkle) and a world of nature that explodes in concert with it: "I suspect that the extraordinary event that one will remember most vividly is Rosy's sexual awakening. As the Major makes love to Rosy in a magical forest, dandelions lose their seeds, the sun peers through the leaves to make an effulgent sign of the cross, and the trees themselves go through a little series of ecstatic shudders. This kind of scenic grandeur does not define depth of emotion (it simply substitutes for it)."[29]

Kael's review for the *New Yorker* was brutal. The film has "no driving emotional energy, no passionate vision to conceal the heavy labor." It is "an expensive movie, [*and*] a cheap romance." Kael had liked Jones's performance in *Wild in the Streets*. But, like Canby, she figures he was never given a chance to be any good in the film. "After an hour or so Lean deposits Christopher Jones on the giant screen like a maimed sun god arriving on earth. He stands there alone for an eternity, with a limp and a scar and a permanently pained expression; soon he begins to shake uncontrollably. Lean has made him such a romantic wreck that the picture never recovers from his landing." Jones is for Kael a victim of the director's "pseudo-aristocratic

[146] CHRISTOPHER JONES DOES NOT WANT TO BE A STAR

FIGURE 20. Christopher Jones as Major Doryan in David Lean's epic *Ryan's Daughter* (1970, MGM).

pulp romanticism," asked to act in a film that is corny and sentimental. And as a consequence, he "is given almost nothing to say; what [in such a scenario] could this figment of soggy romanticism talk about?" Jones is "drained of vitality and remade into a synthesis of exhausted romantic clichés. In addition to the scar and the limp, he has been given a green complexion and dark hair, like the soulful, sickly Sharif of *Zhivago*; the doomed look sits on his wily James Dean face like enamel."

Kael saw Lean's film as a symptom of an American movie business refusing to keep up with the times. "There's no point in asking 'What's it all for?'" Kael writes at the end of her review, "We know what it's for; it's to try to repeat the financial success of *Doctor Zhivago*. The question is 'Can they get by with it?' Will the public buy twinkling orgasms and cosmetic craftsmanship? The emptiness of *Ryan's Daughter* shows in practically every frame, and yet the publicity machine has turned it into an artistic event, and the American public is a sucker for the corrupt tastefulness of well-bred English epics. One begins to feel like a member of a small cabal, powerless to fight this well-oiled reverence."[30]

After the critical lambasting of *Ryan's Daughter*, Lean took a sabbatical. And it would be fourteen years before he would return to the director's chair, and then with just one last film, another old-fashioned romantic melodrama: *A Passage to India*. Story goes, during that sabbatical Lean stumbled upon Kael in New York and the two had words. Lean complained that Kael would only be happy if he shot his next film "in 16 mm and black-and-white." Kael came right back at him: "No, you can have color."[31]

Jones would go on sabbatical too. And he would never find his way back.

Life on the Strip (Is No Longer So Fashionable)

After completing *Ryan's Daughter*, Jones rented a place in Benedict Canyon, near the site of Tate's murder. There, the young actor fell into a funk. His management team, headed by super-agent/personal manager Rudy Altobelli, suggested a retreat at, in Jones's words, "one of those 'I'm OK, you're OK' type of self-help things" in Virginia. It didn't help. As Jones described the experience to Pamela Des Barres in a 1996 interview: "There was no therapy involved—the woman running [the treatment center] was not licensed anything. I realized my manager had kidnapped me. Six guys held me down while this bitch beat me with a board. They kept me there for weeks, literally holding me prisoner, trying to make me into a sex slave. It was like a Manson deal. The bitch in charge kept trying to have sex with me, with six henchmen holding me down.... There was a kid there—they beat him too—so, I said, 'Go out the window tonight and call the police.' He did and the next day the police came."

Asked why he decided not to tell this amazing story at the time, Jones told Des Barres, "Because *Ryan's Daughter* was out and I didn't want any negative publicity."[32] Was he really still thinking about his career? Interesting, if we buy Jones's explanation, that he believed he still had one.

Jones and Des Barres were both scene-makers on the Strip. And they had crossed paths a couple of times before 1996 when Des Barres talked Jones into sitting for an interview. They first met on the Strip in 1969. He was, as Des Barres describes him, "the brooding young actor who'd recently taken Hollywood by storm." She was a semi-famous rock-star groupie. By her own accounting, she hoped he'd become another notch on her belt—another beautiful celebrity to add to her collection. But he was at that moment out of her league. She encountered him again on the Strip just a few years later: "His long hair [was] disheveled, his clothes in tatters, his feet dirty and bare. . . . He was obviously having a private conversation with himself."[33] As a preamble to the interview, Des Barres reminded Jones of the two previous encounters. He reluctantly acceded to the accuracy of her recollection. Frankly, he couldn't remember either night.

Jones told Des Barres that he had a breakdown after Tate's death and that he was shaken again a couple of years later by Morrison's death in Paris. Jones and Morrison knew each other briefly and their ascents and rapid declines coincided. Jones met Morrison in the spring of 1967, just as Jones signed with AIP and Morrison and the Doors signed with Elektra Records. On August 5, 1967, Jones began work on Wild and the Streets, just as "Light My Fire" peaked at number one on the Billboard Hot 100. By the summer of the 1971, Jones had become a houseless drifter on the Strip and Morrison an American in exile, living in a rented flat in Paris, waiting out his appeal on a conviction for indecent exposure and profanity onstage in Florida. Jones was in bad shape, drinking and doing a lot of drugs, barely holding it together. Morrison was in bad shape too, addicted to heroin, living as a recluse, hiding out from the success and fame he had worked so hard to achieve.

On July 3, 1971 Morrison was discovered dead in his bathtub in his Paris apartment. He was twenty-seven.[34] The official cause of death was heart failure, though the cardiac event was likely brought on by an accidental heroin overdose. There, Jones pondered aloud to Des Barres, but for the grace of God go I.

Jones talked as well with Jan E. Morris, who maintained a Jones website, about his affinity with the rock star: "The death of Jim Morrison really upset me.... I felt empathy for him, and I identified with what he was saying. The fact that he died that young really affected me."[35] Jones had channeled Morrison to play Max Frost—the performance that got his movie career started. And at Jones's memorial in 2014, the requisite "a life in pictures" slide show was timed at his request to "The Crystal Ship," a Doors' single from 1967, the B-side to "Light My Fire."

After the bizarre experience in Virginia, Jones became convinced his management team was conspiring against him. The paranoia was not unfounded. Altobelli, Jones's manager, was even by Hollywood standards a piece of work. He represented a number of counterculture movie stars and played favorites, and sometimes played one client against another. There are plenty of stories to tell about Altobelli, but the best (because it shows him at his worst) concerns a house he owned on Cielo Drive, first rented to the music producer Terry Melcher and then to Polanski and Tate. After the Manson murders, Altobelli did what only a Hollywood talent manager would do under the circumstances: he sued Polanski, claiming that the director's comments and photos run in *Life* magazine had diminished the resale value of his house.

Before Altobelli sent Jones to Virginia, he engineered the breakup of Jones's relationship with Hussey. To unpack the melodrama: Jones and Hussey got engaged sometime before he left for Ireland. The wedding was planned and then postponed, Jones claimed, at Altobelli's suggestion so Jones could, absent distraction, complete *Ryan's*

Daughter. But as the shoot dragged on, and for reasons none of the principals agree upon, the relationship fell apart. Depending on whom you believe: before or after the breakup Hussey got involved with Dino Martin (Dean Martin's son) and the couple got married in April 1971. Martin was another of Altobelli's clients. Jones felt betrayed. And it is easy to see why.

Hussey tells a very different version of the breakup story, one that takes us into a much more troubling aspect of Jones's off-screen story. The relationship was over well before she met Martin; indeed, it had reached its nadir during a visit with Jones in Dingle—a final encounter marked by violence. Her story seems all the more believable after reading Susan Strasberg's memoir, *Bittersweet*. "[Jones] was beautiful but a little too wild," Strasberg writes. He was always exciting *and* dangerous, with the latter descriptor overwhelming the former. After they split, Strasberg had to take out a restraining order against Jones because she was scared of him.[36]

Hussey claims that Jones assaulted her during her last visit to the *Ryan's Daughter* shoot. She had flown to Dingle to break things off. Jones was by then in pretty bad shape, so out of kindness she decided to stay and help him finish the shoot. They agreed on separate rooms. Some nights Jones was "near catatonic," Hussey writes; on others he'd want sex and would refuse to take no for an answer. On their last night together, he "[forced] his way into my room and slam[med] me against the wall, muttering horrible things.... I didn't know if he was going to kill me. My face was like a balloon. I had a bloody nose, my lip was split open, and I had a black eye. It was terrifying."[37] Altobelli, who was Hussey's manager and godfather, got involved only so Jones could be kept safely away from her.

Hussey struggled with the trauma caused by her encounter with Jones, recalling at one point in her memoir a challenging shoot from 1990. Cast as Norman Bates's abusive mother Norma in a made-for-Showtime movie, *Psycho IV: The Beginning* (Mick Garris, 1990),

Hussey struggled to get into her troubled character's head. So she revisited her tumultuous affair with Jones. The Actor's Studio technique was something the young Method actor Christopher Jones might well have appreciated, a sense-memory that Hussey worked out with her costar Anthony Perkins, an actor who knew a thing or two as well about channeling inner-conflicts to play a difficult part.

Two decades after the fact, Hussey's sense-memory prompted if not exactly forgiveness, then understanding: "I recalled that even at the height of his madness, when he was lashing out at me at the top of his lungs or seething with rage, there was a panic in his eyes, as if some part of him knew he was out of control and was as terrified by it as I was."[38] Jones had behaved horribly with her. But he was by then in bad shape, on the way out of his career, his life, and his mind.

After Jones split with Altobelli, he signed with a new personal manager, Sherry Dodd, with whom he lived on and off for a few years. He was her only client, and he wasn't working, so the relationship was, to be polite, complicated. As Dodd recalled to the essayist Duke Haney, she and Jones first met in 1974, at Ben Frank's, a Sunset Strip hangout. She had forgotten something in the car and went out to retrieve it. Jones emerged from the shadows and asked to borrow her hairbrush. He looked at the time much as Des Barres had described him, the post *Ryan's Daughter* version of Christopher Jones—that is: long hair, worn-out shoes, rough. Jones told Dodd his name was James. Dodd followed him into an adjacent alley—she knew better but went anyway—where he accosted her. She told him to stop and he did.

As Haney tells the story, "[Dodd] wasn't scared so much as intrigued." Maybe she recognized him. Maybe she didn't care. Before heading back inside, Jones asked for her address and she gave it to him. Soon enough he showed up on her doorstep; "It's me, James." By then she had figured out who he once was. So she invited him in.

Jones's behavior at Dodd's was erratic—his stays, sporadic. Back when he had money, Jones bought a house in the toney Doheny Estates. But he seldom stayed there. In the seventies and eighties he couch-surfed mostly, and spent his evenings and days on the Sunset Strip, according to Morris, "drifting through the strip clubs and reading for hours on sidewalk benches," living in Hollywood but hardly working on a comeback.[39]

When he wasn't at Dodd's house in West Hollywood, Jones sometimes slept in a rented room paid for by his former costar Shelley Winters or in a trailer owned by a friend, Jack Simmons. Every once in a while, Jones would turn up at Dodd's. She never knew what version of him she'd get. One time, after watching *The Looking Glass War* he smashed her TV set. He promised to replace it, but when he returned the following night, he instead attacked her. He burst into the house and grabbed her from behind and by the throat. She struggled and they spilled out onto the lawn. A neighbor intervened. The neighbor was armed, and Jones fled the scene. Dodd then sold the house so Jones couldn't so easily find her again.[40]

Jones then hooked up with a new woman, Carrie Abernathy, with whom he had a son, Christopher Jr., to whom Jones remained devoted. After Abernathy, he settled down with Paule McKenna, with whom he fathered another four children. Jones spent much of the nineties with McKenna in Seal Beach, California, as, quite unlike his own father, a stay-at-home dad. He and McKenna eventually split, and while accounts vary, most agree she provided (as did a few other female acquaintances and former lovers) occasional shelter during his final years on earth.

When Haney began working on his Jones essay, "Catch Me," which appears in his collection, *Death Valley Superstars: Occasionally Fatal Adventures in Filmland*, his goal was to answer the by then inevitable question: whatever happened to Christopher Jones? The former actor was no longer so beautiful; he had at the time the "gaunt and glassy-eyed [look of] a jailhouse junkie." Haney had seen that look before, so he figured he'd better write fast. (Jones denied ever taking drugs—a claim that contradicted stories told over and again by his friends and exes, including Strasberg, who, in her memoir blames Jones's and her own drug abuse for the birth defects suffered by their child together, Jenny.)[41]

Haney viewed Jones as a colorful mess, a victim of the sixties' Hollywood party scene. There were plenty of stories that supported the burnout caricature. One of Haney's sources was Bill Dakota, one of subterranean Hollywood's most notorious gossip writers and the publisher/editor of *The Hollywood Star*. Jones lived for a while in an apartment building Dakota managed. The two became friends, but Jones was never easy to deal with. Dakota eventually had to evict Jones because, in addition to seldom paying rent, the former actor had a bad habit of rescuing snakes and wild birds and setting them free in his apartment. When bird droppings seeped through the pipes into another resident's apartment, Dakota sent Jones packing.[42]

Haney catalogs Jones's many romantic entanglements—his six children with three women. There's a Blanche Dubois vibe to the story line, as he lived for decades off the "kindness of strangers," even as he tended not to be so kind to them.

In conversation with Des Barres, Jones claimed that in 1964 he had an affair and fathered a child with the former B-movie actress Susan Cabot, "best remembered," so Haney (who investigated the story) quips, as the star of *The Wasp Woman*," a 1959 horror-cheapie directed by Roger Corman.[43]

Cabot had by the start of the sixties wearied of the B-movie scene, so she moved to New York to become a stage actress. She maybe met Jones in an acting class, or at an audition. Jones couldn't recall exactly. Both were young and beautiful. And they got around. The stage roles failed to materialize for Cabot, but a string of romantic escapades kept her in the public eye. Among her many lovers was King Hussein of Jordan. Some of the more imaginative rumblings on the Web have Cabot working undercover for the CIA, spying on Hussein. But that's not nearly the strangest story told about her.

In 1964, well after the alleged Hussein affair, Cabot gave birth to a son, Timothy, who was born with dwarfism. She never revealed the name of his father. And to be clear: Cabot never mentioned Jones to anyone, but then again why would she; he was back then just another young and handsome New York wannabe actor—not husband or father material.

Bringing up Timothy was a challenge. And Cabot unraveled emotionally under the strain, especially after splitting with her second husband. She became a recluse, a hoarder. On December 10, 1986, in a house cluttered with newspapers and rotting food, Cabot was beaten to death with a barbell. The police took down Timothy's version of the night's events, but from the start they doubted the story he was telling: that a ninja broke in and murdered his mother. The police pressed and Timothy soon relented. He told them that his mother had attacked him in a psychotic rage, so he grabbed the barbell to defend himself.

He and his mother had a complicated relationship, he told them. When he was younger, she gave him growth hormones so he might appear more "normal." The drugs worked; by the time he stopped growing, he had reached five feet, four inches tall. But well after Timothy stopped needing the pills, his mother continued refilling the prescription, believing the drugs helped her look young. Maybe they did. They also exacerbated her mental illness.

Timothy was tried for murder. But after considering the many extenuating circumstances, the jury convicted him of the lesser charge of involuntary manslaughter.[44] Jones was adamant in his claim to paternity. Why did Jones tell such a story, Haney mused, if he didn't believe it was true?

There is a piece of quite amazing audiovisual evidence of Jones's life post-1970 that can be found still on YouTube—a 1984 "walk on" appearance on a public access TV show, "Skip E. Lowe Looks at Hollywood."[45] Lowe was a Hollywood "character," an unself-conscious and unselective fan of Hollywood's D-list, too sweet to be a gossipmonger, too silly and ridiculous to judge those who, like Jones, had found and then squandered fame and fortune. The scheduled guests for the show that night were the lyricist Adrienne Anderson, who cowrote the disco-era dance hit "I Go to Rio," and an oddball actor-singer who went by the name John Barrymore Jr.

The show began with Lowe and Anderson talking pointlessly about her song. About ten minutes in, Lowe introduced "Barrymore"—first as "John Perkins," then as "John Perkins Barrymore," then "John Barrymore Jr."[46] "Barrymore" ambled onto Lowe's makeshift set wearing a baby blue ruffled tuxedo shirt and a flowered, brocade tux jacket, talking the second he hit the stage, even before Lowe can affix his microphone.

He is doing a cable movie, he tells Lowe; he will soon be singing for the Pope. L.A. Mayor Tom Bradley has asked him to perform the National Anthem at the opening ceremony for the Olympics at the L.A. Coliseum. At the seventeen-minute mark in the half-hour show, Barrymore segues from a discussion of his "half-brother" (I assume: John Drew Barrymore), who is "not getting much work anymore" to "another actor I'd like to see work again, Christopher Jones." Lowe interrupts Barrymore to remark that Jones is sitting in the audience.

Jones walks up onto the set and Lowe introduces him to Anderson. There is no available chair for Jones, so he squats. "What have you been doing with yourself?" Lowe asks. Jones replies: "Escorting Barrymore around." Lowe (to Barrymore): "Is this your protégé?" Barrymore winks outrageously. "I'd like to think so."

LOWE: Last time I saw you, Chris, was with Shelley Winters in New York City. You were in a show called . . .
JONES (FILLING A PREGNANT PAUSE): "*Night of the Iguana.*"
LOWE: "*Night of the Iguana*" with Bette Davis. . . . You don't do theater anymore? (Jones shrugs. Lowe continues) You just do films?
JONES: *Ryan's Daughter* was the last film I did.
LOWE: The last? . . . Why . . . a great actor like you . . . why?
JONES: I don't know. That was just it. I had a bad car accident with a Ferrari.
LOWE: A car accident. Where was this?
JONES: Here. [It wasn't—Jones crashed a Ferrari in Ireland.]
LOWE (NON-SEQUITOR): You were married to Susan Strasberg. . . .

Jones goes cold; his body language changes. Lowe carries on clueless, and describes Jones to Anderson: "Christopher was the young James Dean of the seventies . . . the late sixties and early seventies. . . . He became one of the biggest stars here in Hollywood. . . . So what are you doing with your career?" (The phrasing here is so "Hollywood"—as if a career is like a house or a car.) No reply.

LOWE: I understand you're going to do James Dean's story . . .
JONES: Supposedly.
LOWE: You're back with your agent, Maggie . . . uh . . .
JONES: Abbott. Maggie Abbott.[47]

Jones then reaches for a photograph on Lowe's messy coffee table. It's a lobby card for *Rasputin and the Empress* (Richard Boleslawski), a 1932 feature starring John, Lionel, and Ethel Barrymore. He points at the photograph and Perkins Barrymore perks up. Jones abruptly exits. Total screen time: just over two minutes.

The cameo on "Skip E. Lowe's Hollywood"—out on the town or what was left of it for Jones with the likes of "Barrymore" and the show's poseur *par excellence* host—was the last almost anyone would see of Jones for another decade. As to the ongoing mystery, "whatever happened to Christopher Jones," the interview with Des Barres offers a useful coda here.

> DES BARRES: You came back to L.A. [in 1970] and dropped out?
> JONES: I was trying to let sink in what happened to me. I guess I went a little nuts.
> DES BARRES: You just dropped out . . .
> JONES: I dropped out—before I was ever in.[48]

Once Upon a Time in Hollywood (with Christopher Jones)

About halfway in to Quentin Tarantino's 2019 film *Once Upon a Time in Hollywood*, we hit the streets of Los Angeles. It is the summer of 1969 and we follow a route past a marquee above a downtown theater showing *3 in the Attic*. For Tarantino and his production design crew the marquee is quite literally a sign of the times.

Turns out, Tarantino is a big Jones fan. Haney found out and interviewed the director for his feature. Tarantino recalled to Haney two brief encounters; one when he first tried to cast Jones in *Pulp Fiction* (Jones turned him down—a good thing for both of them really; in the early nineties, he was in no shape to make a movie) and then a chance meeting after the film hit. Both times, Jones seemed genuinely surprised and happy that such a popular filmmaker was interested in him, but had little else to say.

After talking with Tarantino, Haney began toying with a possible through line for his essay about Jones, "based on the mondo movies of the sixties: episodic documentaries like *Mondo Mod* and *Mondo Hollywood* that titillated provincial audiences with gonzo footage of

[158]   CHRISTOPHER JONES DOES NOT WANT TO BE A STAR

trippy parties." All the elements were there: "the Manson case, the Susan Cabot case ... Christopher's homeless period, his apartment with free-range birds and snakes." The approach seemed well suited to its subject, but eventually Haney changed course, surrendering smartly to his better self, deciding finally that the Mondo Hollywood angle would inevitably read like "a sneering slant on someone who was mentally ill."[49] The answer to the question "whatever happened to Christopher Jones" was quite suddenly clear to Haney. And it was no laughing matter.

When I started researching Jones, like Haney I was banking on a certain through line, one that fit a larger story about establishment Hollywood's many clumsy encounters with counterculture celebrities. I figured Jones dropped out because ambition and celebrity ran counter to his counterculture ethos; he made enough money after three years making movies to buy a house and live comfortably. Why work when you don't have to? Why give in to ambition in an industry notorious for devouring its own?

I encountered the stories about Jones's relationship with Tate. The Manson murders had surely rocked the Hollywood celebrity subculture (much more on that in chapter 4), especially those involved (as Jones certainly was) in the illicit drug and Hollywood party scenes. I could easily imagine what the news of Tate's death would have done to Jones, an actor with one foot already out the door. Jones told Des Barres that he and Tate were lovers—that Tate discovered that her husband, Roman Polanski, had had an affair, so she returned the favor by sleeping with him. Tate's murder struck most everyone in the Hollywood party scene in Hollywood as at once inexplicable and predictable. Something was always going to happen to somebody; there were so many drugs and so many shady characters hanging around. If Jones had been in Hollywood (and not in Dingle) that night, he could have been there, in that house. Wrong guy, wrong place, wrong time. It was a lot to live down, a lot to live with.

Hussey and Tate were friends. She and Tate's sister Deborah both dismiss Jones's affair story as impossible, ridiculous. Their accounts are more persuasive than his. By the time Des Barres and Haney caught up with Jones, he had told his version of the Tate story so many times, he probably believed it was true. And it probably wasn't.

So what really happened to Christopher Jones? This is my best guess: in 1970 on location shooting *Ryan's Daughter*, he discovered something about himself that changed his life: that acting in A-features is hard work. And hard work was never why he became an actor. Lean was an awful taskmaster and the supporting cast—Mitchum, Miles, Howard, and Mills—were dismissive and disrespectful. *Ryan's Daughter* hurried a decision that was already in the offing; that is, the decision to drop out. "After a year in Ireland [shooting *Ryan's Daughter*, it] was like getting off Devil's Island," Jones told the Chicago *Tribune*.[50] There is no reason to doubt him on that.

Des Barres asked Jones well after he had abandoned his Hollywood career if he thought he had ever been a good actor. "No," he told her, "I was never consistent.... I was mainly interested in fucking—and becoming famous."[51] Haney appreciated such a frank accounting; he too had tried to make it as an actor and had been briefly touted as the next James Dean. Jones was prettier and more talented than Haney and got closer to getting filmgoers to forget the real thing (the real James Dean, that is). Haney got out and moved on; he found a side gig as a writer. Jones, with no Plan B, disappeared into obscurity.

Haney bluntly characterizes Jones as "a charismatic but unruly actor." That seems about right. *Wild in the Streets* and *Three in the Attic* were always going to be the best anyone was ever going to see from him on-screen. After he graduated to A-pictures Jones never seemed comfortable, never fit in. At the very moment he became a movie star, he realized he was never going to be—that he never wanted to be—"one of them."

[160] CHRISTOPHER JONES DOES NOT WANT TO BE A STAR

Jones was briefly "the next James Dean," Dean's sixties counterculture counterpart. The two men looked a lot alike. Jones would have never become an actor had that not been the case. Both suffered childhood abandonments. But Dean got to grow up on a farm with his aunt and uncle, go to high school, and then college in L.A. Jones got passed around and then dumped into Boys Town, then the Army, then jail. By the time they got to Hollywood, they were very different young men. Dean was intense, ambitious, careerist; those Dennis Stock photos were posed, of course, and they projected an image Dean had chosen for himself—portraits of a young actor as a serious young artist. Jones projected a more easy-going vibe; he was a young man of his times. He was not intense, ambitious, or careerist. He became successful at AIP because he was smartly cast as a version of himself: a young and handsome American having some fun in a new American counterculture. He got swept up and then swept away—and soon enough he was down and out at twenty-nine. When Max speaks off the cuff at the Johnny Fergus rally in *Wild in the Streets*, he intones what hip filmgoers recognized as a New Left refrain: "Thirty is death, man."[52] Given Jones's brief run in Hollywood, the line seems today less political than prophetic.

End of the Road (Trip to Nowhere)

When Jones was twenty-five years old and at the very beginning of his Hollywood career, he told Kevin Thomas from the *L.A. Times* that he was already looking forward to retirement, to a future that would not include working in the movie business: "I just want to be successful enough to buy an island. . . . Acting is only a means towards an end."[53] Movie fans reading the interview in 1968 were not likely to miss the pretentious nod to Brando, whose particular brand or style of anti-celebrity appealed to the "charismatic but unruly" Jones. In 1966—just two years before Jones's *L.A. Times* interview—Brando purchased a ninety-nine-year lease on the Tahitian island of Tetiaroa, an opulent gesture that to someone like Jones symbolized a true counterculture anti-celebrity.

Jones continued to follow the Brando script when he told Thomas: "Acting is just my work. Other things—like painting—are more important." And then, more worryingly and presciently: "I hope it stays that way. If it doesn't [stay that way], I'm in trouble. I'll end up in the psycho ward."[54]

In his interview with Marc Maron, Bruce Dern posed a simple story line: that Jones's career abruptly ended because, "he just went crazy." Sadly, that *is* the most likely scenario—the most plausible explanation for the vanishing act. Jones was a counterculture era movie star. Then, and at the time it seemed quite suddenly, he made a decision: that he wanted something else—at least, he wanted out. So he quit acting for a living, in the process breaking a well-earned multipicture contract with Warners. Lots of different things had got to him: the drugs, the women, the managers, Lean, Manson. He "just went crazy," and while it's a drag, it's not hard to understand why.

Jones was an unruly talent, a beautiful young man who was beautiful even by the steep measure of a town with plenty of beautiful people. But the charisma, the looks, the unruly talent got him only so far. When he lost momentum after *Ryan's Daughter* he decided to disappear, and succeeded in doing so. Between 1970 and his death in 2014, Jones made just one big-screen appearance: a bit part in *Mad Dog Time* (1996). He did it as a favor to a friend, the film's director and former *Wild in the Streets* costar, Larry Bishop (Rat Pack comic Joey Bishop's son).

Mad Dog Time is a bad film and Jones is bad in it; but no worries about the performance tarnishing Jones's legacy, such as it was by then, such as it is today. Not very many people have seen the film. Budgeted at a ridiculous, exorbitant $8 million, *Mad Dog Time*

[162] CHRISTOPHER JONES DOES NOT WANT TO BE A STAR

grossed barely $100,000 in its initial and for all concerned suitably brief first run.

Once upon a time in Hollywood, Christopher Jones was a movie star. For the next three decades he did some other things, well out of sight and off the grid. And then without a whole lot of people noticing, he died—by then long lost on his own particular and private road to nowhere.

3 *Four Women in Hollywood*
Jean Seberg, Jane Fonda, Dolores Hart, and Barbara Loden

Los Angeles and the entertainment businesses that thrive there have always made room for women, albeit in roles suited to shared notions of women's work. Going all the way back to the silent era, women could find work behind the scenes in the costume, makeup, and hair departments and further up the backstage ladder as editors and as readers and writers in studio story departments. Conventional wisdom held that women knew (by instinct, no doubt) about clothes, makeup, and coiffure, and that they were better or at least more avid readers than men, thus likely better evaluators, adapters, writers, and editors (a job that also requires a keen sense of story form and structure).

The best jobs were left to men with ambition and pretention, men in suits, men with money. But for the many American women not in the movie business, the glass or celluloid ceiling wasn't so much of an issue. Because producer and director were not the jobs they dreamed about. Thanks to nearly a century of movie fan magazines targeting young women in particular, their dream involved some chanced Hollywood discovery—of someday becoming a movie star.

"Movie star" is a job title in Hollywood. And with that job comes a dramatic upward social mobility—wealth and celebrity otherwise unattainable for the everyday American woman. Who, then, wouldn't want to be a movie star? The question seemed for a century or so moot.

Jean Seberg, Jane Fonda, Dolores Hart, and Barbara Loden all got discovered. They all got to be movie stars. But it was a sign of the times that each of these women risked their amazing good fortune to say or do things they fervently believed in. And in doing so, with one notable exception—Fonda, of course—in saying or doing what they believed in, they abbreviated their movie careers. Who wouldn't want to be a movie star was for them not such an uncomplicated question to answer.

Seberg, Fonda, Hart, and Loden were women of their times, though in very different ways. All four were searching (as were so many of their peers at the time) for social justice, gender fairness or equity, a spiritually (and not just a materially) better life for themselves and others. To find something more, something better than being *just* a movie star, they were willing, each of them in different ways and to different ends, to risk everything—including walking away from the best job Hollywood and, arguably, America had on offer.

Jean Seberg Is a Black Panther

In 1970, the nonfiction writer Tom Wolfe coined the term *radical chic* to describe (among other things) encounters between pretentious and pampered white celebrities and Black civil rights activists. Wolfe had a jaundiced view of the Hollywood counterculture contingent. The politically outspoken celebrities were in his view dabblers and dilettantes who got on and off the bandwagon as it suited their busy social and professional schedules. He dismissed their progressive political activities as "fraught expressions and manifestations of White Guilt."[1] And in a number of cases he was right. Movie actors after all make ridiculous money in a ridiculous business. They are rich and famous and seldom bother with the mundane tasks of everyday life, let alone the not-so-mundane struggles endured by the poor and disenfranchised for whom they spoke, for whom they wrote checks.

Wolfe was by nature a cynic. For the record: I am not. Moreover, as a historian I find it un-useful to be so dismissive. When white movie stars in the 1960s spoke on behalf of Americans of color, for example, when they gave money to antiestablishment outfits like the Black Panthers, the press, and the wider American public paid attention. There was for these celebrities a quite considerable risk engaged in speaking out—plenty to lose and frankly not so much to gain. But a lot of Hollywood movie stars in the sixties and seventies spoke up anyway. And, though this may sound patronizing (and I don't intend it so), it is hard to doubt they meant well.

The movie star Jean Seberg met Hakim Jamal, an activist who raised money for the Black Panthers, on an airplane in October 1968. Life would from that day forward be different for the both of them. Seberg and Jamal hit it off; a friendship, maybe more than that, developed. The nature of the relationship remains subject to debate. At the time, the FBI assumed they were lovers. And Benedict Andrews in his 2020 biopic, *Seberg*, starring Kristin Stewart in the title role perpetuates that version. Seberg's biographer Garry McGee and Seberg herself contend otherwise, that she and Jamal were platonic friends.[2] What we know for sure is that Seberg was sympathetic to Jamal's cause. Working with Jamal, Seberg bought a bus for a school in Compton (a predominantly Black neighborhood in Los Angeles). And she held a fundraiser for the Panthers in her Los Angeles home, which attracted a progressive Hollywood A-list,

FIGURE 21. Marlon Brando with Black Panther Captain Kenny Demmon at the 1968 funeral for Robert "Lil' Bobby" Hutton, a Panther activist killed by police in Oakland, California. Brando delivered the eulogy (Everett Collection).

including Joanne Woodward, Paul Newman, Lee Marvin, and Jane Fonda.

Jamal had had encounters with Hollywood royalty before—Seberg was not to know that—including Marlon Brando, who on more than one occasion had been generous to the Panthers with his time and money.[3] In Oakland in 1968, Brando delivered the eulogy for Robert "Lil' Bobby" Hutton, a teenage Panther activist killed by police while he was, according to eyewitness accounts, trying to surrender. "I'm not going to stand up and make a speech," Brando began, smartly acknowledging the identity politics in play, "because you've been listening to white people for four hundred years."[4]

The Panthers publicly rejected white collaboration and espoused self-reliance—*armed* self-reliance. Huey Newton, Bobby Seale, Eldridge Cleaver, and the rest of the Panthers' leadership actively solicited money from white Hollywood celebrities. They were no doubt

FOUR WOMEN IN HOLLYWOOD [167]

aware that their solicitation of white Hollywood money contradicted their Black separatist politics. But to invoke an already overcooked phrase, the color of the celebrities' money wasn't black or white; it was green. There are stories about Panthers leaders occasionally assuaging their guilt (learning to live with their hypocrisy as well) by demeaning (in private) their white benefactors. An often-repeated story has Seale pocketing a handful of checks after a fundraiser, then quietly boasting to a fellow Panther: "We took Brando for $10,000, we can take Jean Seberg for $20,000."[5]

Seberg's rumored romantic relationship with Jamal brought her to the attention of FBI Director J. Edgar Hoover. In internal memos, Hoover labeled Seberg "a social nuisance" and subjected her to surveillance and harassment. Agents assembled a narrowly focused biography: Seberg, they noted, had been "leaning Left since she was 14," when, as a Midwest teenager she had joined the NAACP.[6] When Seberg became a Hollywood star—just nineteen after nabbing the title role in Otto Preminger's *Saint Joan* (1957)—she donated some of her first big paycheck to buy basketball uniforms for Native American school kids in Iowa. But what really bothered Hoover about Seberg, and this is clear from FBI correspondence, was not her progressive politics. It was the likelihood of miscegenation—that a popular white actress (Seberg) might be having sex with a Black man (Jamal).

The FBI had for a while been wary of the seductive machismo of the Panthers' young and handsome male leadership. Outfitted in black leather jackets and berets, many of these men recognized and exploited their considerable sex appeal while recruiting in Black neighborhoods *and* while fundraising with white celebrities. Writing for the *Nation* in 2003, the former Berkeley-based activist Steve Wasserman reflected on the sexually charged atmosphere around the Panthers leadership. He recalled meeting Fred Hampton, the Black Panther later murdered by the police in Chicago: "Sometime around midnight, Fred Hampton, clad in a long black leather coat and looking for all the world like a gunslinger bursting into a saloon, swept in with a couple of other Panthers in tow. You could feel the barometric pressure in the room rise.... He had the Panther swagger down pat." Elsewhere: "The erotic aura that the Panthers presented was a not inconsiderable part of their appeal, as any of the many photographs that were taken of them show. And in this department, Huey [Newton] was the Supreme Leader, and he never let you forget it." These were men who (as Wasserman describes Cleaver), "exuded charm and menace in equal measure."[7] That white women, including popular white movie stars might be susceptible to that charm (and menace) was for the FBI a matter of no small concern.

Seberg was a fairly minor player in the larger scheme of things for the Panthers. She wasn't such a big movie star either. But she was nonetheless subjected to a full-on COINTELPRO (FBI COunter INTELligence PROgram) investigation. As internal FBI memos reveal, Hoover set out to "neutralize" Seberg, to take actions that would "cause her embarrassment and serve to cheapen her image with the public." The COINTELPRO investigation was conducted under the strictest secrecy, with agents taking "the usual precautions to avoid identification of the Bureau."[8] In the end, the FBI surveillance and harassment of Seberg had little effect on the Panthers' operation. Its impact on the young actress was, in contrast, significant.[9]

When Seberg got pregnant in 1969, the FBI investigation intensified. At the heart of things was again Hoover's disgust at miscegenation, as he assumed the father was Black. Seberg told friends (and because she was being surveilled, FBI agents as well) that the pregnancy had resulted from an extramarital fling with a Mexican actor; to others, she insisted the baby's father was her estranged husband, the French writer and diplomat Romain Gary.[10] Absent proof of any kind, Hoover rejected both (assumed cover) stories and signed off on a press release to Joyce Haber, a gossip columnist for the *Los Angeles Times* that identified the father as a friend of Jamal's, a Black Panther named Raymond Hewitt. Hoover and Haber most likely knew the story was a lie. But Haber printed the story anyway and Hoover's lie circulated uncontested in the press. Seberg later sued *Newsweek*, which had reprinted the rumor, and won a judgment. But the damage caused by the lie proved impossible to overcome.[11] Hoover's story was meant to "cheapen [Seberg's] image with the public" and it accomplished its goal.

The baby in question—a girl—was born on August 23, 1970. The birth was premature and the baby died a few days later. Seberg tried to manage the unmanageable public relations problem by herself, all the while mourning her daughter's death. She returned to her hometown Marshalltown, Iowa, and held a very public funeral. The tiny casket was left open to display the corpse of her *white* child. Members of the press, along with undercover agents from the FBI and a host of curious locals stopped by to take a look. Seberg took photographs of her dead daughter and sent them to industry columnists. Such was her shame, her grief, her impossible predicament.[12]

In a 1974 interview with the *New York Times*'s Bart Mills, Seberg bravely projected a sense of contentment living on her own in Paris—by then, an apparent survivor of counterculture Hollywood. She used the interview to publicly cut ties with Jamal—who was by then dead anyway, gunned down in his apartment in Boston by, according to the police, members of the De Mau Mau, a loose confederation of Black Vietnam veterans. She cut ties with the Panthers as well, because she believed *she* had become something of a liability for *them*: "I had a very, very bad mental breakdown, and now I realize I wouldn't want a person like me in a group I was a member of, as Groucho Marx would put it."

Mills framed the interview with a familiar Hollywood story line; "Jean Seberg," he writes in the article's lead, "is a living argument

FIGURE 22. Jean Seberg in Jean-Luc Godard's *Breathless* (1960, Janus Films).

against winning a Hollywood talent search." The True or Real Hollywood Story angle was likely necessary by then; Seberg's career had for all intents and purposes been over for a while and it was possible some readers didn't know or remember who she was (past tense intended, here).

The now necessary bio-sketch: Seberg was just seventeen in 1957 when the producer-director Otto Preminger chose her, after a nationwide talent search, to play the lead in *St. Joan*. Carrying such a big film proved to be more than she could handle, and the reviews were unkind. Preminger remained convinced about Seberg's talent and cast her in a second film, *Bonjour Tristesse*, released the following year, this time in a more suitable, more modern role as the free-spirited daughter of a decadent playboy (David Niven). The *Cahiers du Cinema* crowd had by then begun championing Preminger, and François Truffaut and Jean Luc Godard, both on the staff at the magazine, admired Seberg in his films. Truffaut labeled Seberg "the best actress in Europe" (*Bonjour Tristesse* was shot on the French Riviera, and Seberg lingered there after the production wrapped) and when Godard cast her in his astonishing feature debut, *Breathless* (1960), he claimed that "the character played by Jean Seberg [in *Breathless*] was a continuation of her role in *Bonjour Tristesse*. I could have taken the last shot of Preminger's film and started after dissolving to a title: 'Three years later.'"[13]

After *Breathless*, another big Hollywood role came her way: Robert Rossen's melodrama *Lilith* (1964), which earned for Seberg a Golden Globe nomination playing opposite another rising star, Warren Beatty. For reasons tough to figure even in retrospect—bad choices perhaps, bad management, bad reputation (as an independent woman with ideas on the set), bad politics (as they were perceived to be)—Seberg's career stalled. She was just twenty-six years old when *Lilith* rolled out, but good parts in good films seemed no longer on offer. After a featured role in the awful (and wildly miscast) adaptation of the stage musical *Paint Your Wagon* (Joshua Logan, 1969, which featured Lee Marvin and Clint Eastwood singing solos) and in the following year, the bloated Hollywood disaster epic *Airport* (George Seaton), Seberg drifted out of Hollywood and out of the American celebrity scene as well.

Mills met Seberg after the career had run its course. He depicted the now former actress as a once-glamorous woman in exile. But as lives in exile go, and this runs counter to Mills's argument, Seberg seemed in 1974 quite comfortable. She lived in a roomy apartment just off St. Germain on the toney Left Bank of Paris where she presided over a salon of sorts for (mostly left-wing) artists whenever they swung into town. Michelangelo Antonioni stopped by while Mills was writing his piece on her.

Seberg was on her third marriage by then, and this time there was a meaningful left-wing Hollywood backstory. The new husband,

Dennis Berry, was the son of another Hollywood exile, the film director John Berry, who was blacklisted in 1951 after Eddie Dymytrk and Frank Tuttle named his name. After running afoul of HUAC and the MPAA, John Berry decided to dodge the inevitable subpoena; so he left the United States, and then, when his visa was summarily revoked—a familiar scenario—he settled in Paris. Dennis grew up in Paris, while his father hustled film work. In the interview, Seberg describes herself to Mills with characteristic self-deprecation; unlike her new husband's father (who was, ostensibly a proper Hollywood political hero), she calls herself, "a fellow traveler at a distance."

When Mills asks Seberg to look back on her career, she judges herself harshly: "Every time I've gone back to do a film, I've been Miss Submissive. I've let things happen to me." Mills assumes that Seberg is talking about *Paint Your Wagon* or maybe the role as Burt Lancaster's arm candy in *Airport*. But she was referring to all of it, the entire oeuvre from *St. Joan* on. Seberg blames Preminger for setting her off on the wrong track; he's a "charming dinner guest," she tells Mills, memorably, "[but] a sadistic director." But as we read on it's clear she blames herself more. She insists she is happy to be done with Hollywood: "Right now, America seems farther away to me than Singapore."

Another perspective on Seberg's career can be found in Mark Rappaport's 1995 documentary, misleadingly titled *From the Journals of Jean Seberg*—misleading, as there were no journals, and except for film clips and some remarks Seberg made to the press, the film's narration is composed of writing from Rappaport's desk. *From the Journals of Jean Seberg* is less a biopic than a work of cine-criticism. And as such it offers an academic's overview and analysis of Seberg's screen career. Rappaport begins by characterizing Seberg as Preminger's muse and then Godard's; he contends that Robert Rossen used her best (in *Lilith*) and her husband Gary, used her badly in a series of French films that cast her as frigid, as a nymphomaniac, as somehow both.

Godard exploited Seberg's flat affect and her crap French accent to make her appear beautiful but ridiculous: *America* in Godard's view, no doubt. For him, Seberg's Patricia stands in for the many young American women in the early sixties who toured Europe in search of new and different experiences abroad. But Godard saw in Seberg (and in Seberg's Patricia) something else or something more going on behind the absence of affect and the awful Midwestern nasal twang, something the many close-ups in *Breathless* exploited and complicated—close-ups of Seberg that seem to give us permission to stare, rudely, and for a duration of time inappropriate in everyday life.

Putting aside the complicated ethics of Rappaport's pseudo history, *From the Journals of Jean Seberg* does well to reflect upon Godard's quip that cinema is "the history of boys photographing girls." And in that vein, Rappaport makes good use of Laura Mulvey's influential essay, "Visual Pleasure and Narrative Cinema."[14] He contends that Preminger asked Seberg to break a fundamental screen-acting rule and return the camera's gaze. Godard was so taken with the gesture he stole it for *Breathless*. We look at Seberg (as Patricia) closely, but see only the face, the hair, the seeming indifference. When the film ends, we still have no idea what's been going on inside her head—why she hung around with Michel in the first place and then why she betrayed him at the end. It may not be a great performance, but Patricia is certainly memorable, and it is fair to conclude that Seberg gave Godard exactly what he wanted.

This is not the first or last time I will trot out this cliché, but it is certainly true here: the camera loved Jean Seberg. Preminger intuited it. And Godard exploited it. Seberg was never as good an actress as Jane Fonda or Vanessa Redgrave, fellow "fellow travelers at a distance." They were targets as well for Hoover, but better connected and in the end far less fragile emotionally or psychologically. Seberg

FIGURE 23. The camera loved Jean Seberg (Everett Collection).

was quite easily crushed by Hoover—with the aforementioned help from Haber and *Time* magazine.

By the time Mills met Seberg, there was no career left to ruin and more importantly there were no more causes to serve. "Around 1968, I got mixed up in a lot of things that had nothing to do with acting," Seberg reflected, "a profession which was coming to mean no more than getting made up into one kind of Barbie doll or another." Her involvement with the Panthers, looking back, was "exhilarating but disastrous": the inevitable narrative trajectory of radical chic. "I used to believe in fairy tales," she mused, "but part of me has become more realistic." Mills moves from there to the obvious parting question: What might she be doing and thinking about in ten years' time? Seberg shrugs, "I couldn't say."[15] She would not live to find out.

Five years after talking with Mills and three months shy of her forty-first birthday, Seberg was found dead in Paris in her car, parked just a few blocks from her apartment—an apparent suicide. She had long since divorced Gary, but he took her death hard. She had tried to kill herself before, always on or around the anniversary of her (perhaps their) daughter's death. And then, when the American press arrived for one last swipe at her (postmortem), Gary took it upon himself to publicly detail the extent of the FBI surveillance and harassment that had driven her out of Hollywood, out of America, and finally out of her life in Paris.

Gary wanted justice for his late and ex-wife, and to make the FBI pay for what they did to her. He worked tirelessly to convince the Paris police to reopen the investigation. They did and the new investigation led to a revised determination, officially charging "persons unknown" with "non-assistance of a person in danger." Seberg, the police noted, had had such a high blood-alcohol level at the time of her death, another person or persons had to have put her in the car. Said person or persons may not have murdered her, or helped her kill herself, but they certainly didn't do anything to stop or to save her.

Seberg is interred at Montparnasse Cemetery, far from Hollywood. She felt more at home in Paris anyway. At Montparnasse, she is today in good company. Buried there are a host of famous and notorious French intellectuals and artists, including Charles Baudelaire, Marguerite Duras, and Simone de Beauvoir. Alfred Dreyfus is buried there as well. For those who believe in an afterlife, Seberg can finally rest in peace in the company of people who were once upon a time quite like her: artists, feminists, political victims.

Hanoi Jane Fonda

December 20, 2019, front page, *The Hollywood Reporter*: "Jane Fonda is back in cuffs again," protesting the Trump administration's failure to respond to the climate change crisis. Octogenarians—at least those not recently deceased—are seldom page-one news in the *Reporter*.[16] But Fonda's cultural capital remains after all these years astonishingly intact. She's still, to revive a very sixties term, *relevant*.

It's been over half a century since Fonda first made the Hollywood scene, over half-a-century since she first lent her celebrity to a cause. She has outlived and outworked any- and everyone so foolishly inclined to have dismissed her as a dilettante, as yet another spoiled-brat celebrity caught up in radical chic.[17]

On the day after her 2019 arrest, Fonda celebrated her eighty-second birthday in jail, slyly remarking to the *New York Times* that getting arrested at her age "has its hazards, like keeping balanced with bound hands. . . . I'll be without my phone—or adult diapers." With age, they say, comes wisdom—and Fonda had planned ahead. She went to the protest anticipating arrest, so she brought along a thick red coat to double as a mattress cover.

Asked if she thought this latest bit of civil disobedience would have much of an effect on the global climate crisis, Fonda gestured to the many reporters assembling around her: "You are all here. So I think it's working."[18] This time the national press was mostly respectful—one of the perks of being eighty-two. But not everyone at the scene was so inclined. One bystander participating in a counterdemonstration (in favor of global warming?) wore a MAGA (Make America Great Again) hat—as if in character and wardrobe from Central Casting. He heckled from the wings: "Hanoi Jane!" For those of us old enough to remember, the epithet brought us all back to Fonda's Vietnam-era antiwar activism in general and a single photograph in particular: a picture taken in July 1972 showing

FIGURE 24. The offending photograph: Jane Fonda posed astride a North Vietnamese antiaircraft gun in July 1972 (Creative Commons: "Jane Fonda in Vietnam" by manhhai is licensed with CC BY 2.0. To view a copy of this license, visit https://creativecommons.org/licenses/by/2.0/).

the actress seated astride a North Vietnamese antiaircraft gun. As plenty of folks at the time observed, the gun might well have been used the day before to fire upon American jets. The image proved unforgettable—for many, unforgivable.

Fonda contends still, she was not thinking straight that day. She was quite shaken by a lot of what she saw in North Vietnam, by what she was shown—the aftermath of US bombing raids on farms, irrigation dikes, and civilians far removed from military targets—in a carefully orchestrated visit. Horrified at the real-world impact of the American war machine, Fonda agreed to record radio announcements that were later aired on the Voice of Vietnam on which she implored US pilots to put down their arms, to stop the bombings. The PSAs sounded to lots of Americans quite like treason. The photograph, circulated by the AP, proved just as difficult to explain or excuse.

The Nixon administration wasted little time before they weighed in on *the photograph*. Charles Bray, a spokesperson for the State Department: "It is always distressing to find American citizens who benefit from the protection and assistance of this government lending their voice in any way to governments such as the Democratic Republic of Vietnam—distressing indeed." A number of civic leaders and lawmakers condemned Fonda's trip. The Veterans of Foreign Wars passed a resolution demanding prosecution. The Maryland state legislature held hearings to bar Fonda from the state. William Burkhead, a Maryland state delegate, told a reporter from the *Washington Post*, "I wouldn't want to kill her, but I wouldn't mind if you cut her tongue off."[19]

Fonda has had plenty of time to reconsider the visit and the media firestorm that followed. In 2012, she recorded a segment for Oprah Winfrey's "Master Class" series, during which the two women discussed *the photograph*. The segment ran under a title no doubt approved by the actor: "Jane Fonda's Unforgivable Mistake."[20] Six years later she reflected again on her "unforgivable mistake" in a feature for the *Washington Post*: "Here is my best, honest recollection of what took place. Someone (I don't remember who) leads me toward the gun, and I sit down, still laughing, still applauding. It all has nothing to do with where I am sitting. I hardly even think about where I am sitting. The cameras flash. I get up, and as I start to walk back to the car with the translator, the implication of what has just happened hits me. Oh, my God. It's going to look like I was trying to shoot down US planes! I plead with him. You have to be sure those photographs are not published. Please, you can't let them be published. I am assured it will be taken care of. I don't know what else to do. It is possible that the Vietnamese had it all planned. I will never know. If they did, can I really blame them? The buck stops here. If

I was used, I allowed it to happen. It was my mistake, and I have paid and continue to pay a heavy price for it."[21]

In 1972, Fonda was beautiful, glamorous, rich. Her father, Henry Fonda, was a movie star. And so was her brother Peter. She was never going to be drafted. She was not male. Not poor. Not Black. Her efforts on behalf of the unlucky and disadvantaged seemed to her detractors patronizing and easy. And for those more cynically inclined, her activism carried a worrying whiff of PR.

Some pertinent facts: Jane Fonda was *not* a product of the American sixties. She turned eighteen in 1955 and in September of that year enrolled but then barely attended Vassar College, where her activities were mildly rebellious but hardly political. By her own account she whiled away her time sunbathing in the nude, sleeping around, and popping Dexedrine to stay slim.[22] Her political engagement can be traced to her first visits to the Actors Studio in New York a few years later. The Studio was at the time widely assumed to be a Communist front organization. And the rep was well earned; plenty of celebrity communists and progressives studied and hung out there.

Jane's father, Henry, knew a lot of the actors at the Studio. But he was never one of *them*. He was never a Communist; instead, he was just another left-leaning Hollywood New Dealer—a Roosevelt Democrat. In 1947, Henry Fonda joined the Committee for the First Amendment (CFA), which publicly condemned HUAC for smearing Hollywood. Allying with the CFA had professional risks and consequences; Fonda fell out with many of his castmates and colleagues, including the right-wing Motion Picture Alliance figureheads Ward Bond and John Wayne. ("I didn't ever have a confrontation with Duke," Henry Fonda reminisced years later, "When anybody's as crazy as that, you can't argue with them.")[23]

In 1949, Henry Fonda decided not to extend his contract at Fox and left Hollywood for New York, which is where Jane spent her formative years (roughly, age twelve to eighteen). For the next six years, he did not have a single screen credit. In 1955, he returned to Hollywood to reprise on-screen his Broadway stage role in *Mister Roberts*, slipping back in as part of a stage-to-screen studio package.

How much Henry Fonda's political activity impacted his screen career from 1948 to 1955—and as well how much it affected his daughter (she was barely twelve when the family left Hollywood for New York, and her relationship with her father was not exactly close)—is difficult to gauge. It is possible he was black- or gray-listed; but really more likely he was trying to create some distance from the studio-based movie business, testing out an independence from the contract system, which was by that time faltering in Hollywood. Plenty of movie actors in the 1950s (most famously, Marilyn Monroe) left Hollywood for New York, started their own production companies, and demanded points against the profits of the films they starred in.

In 1958, twenty-one years old and quite done with college, Jane Fonda started palling around with Susan Strasberg, with whom she sat in on classes taught by Susan's father, Lee. Included among Fonda's Studio classmates were Dustin Hoffman, Faye Dunaway, and Al Pacino—serious competition with no time to waste on second-generation Hollywood dabblers. But even in such talented company, Fonda thrived. When she became a "Lifetime Member of the Studio" in 1961, she was elated. And she could feel good about the fact that she had earned her way. It was quite something to be part of such an exciting scene, joining the ranks of the professionally successful and (as would become relevant in the years following) politically notorious.

Lee Strasberg recognized Fonda's talent and secured for her a screen test for a lead role in Elia Kazan's forthcoming *Splendor in the Grass* (1961). The role went instead to Natalie Wood, who seemed to the director to want it more than Fonda did. (By her own account, Fonda vowed never to make that mistake again; she would never underplay interest or confidence.) Strasberg then introduced Fonda to the stage and film director Joshua Logan, who had studied with Konstantin Stanislavski (who had first elaborated the Method and was in many ways the godfather of Strasberg's studio).

Logan set up a meeting for Fonda with Jack Warner, after which the two men, impressed by her talent, conspired to remake her into a movie star. When Logan and Warner later met with Fonda, they suggested a plastic surgeon to break and reset her jaw and a dentist to pull her back teeth. Logan figured her nose should be fixed as well; it was, in his view, too "cute" for drama. Stupid and cruel as such an accounting seems today, it was back then rather SOP; it was the Old Hollywood looking at a New Hollywood commodity and having no idea what to make of her—in most every way that phrase can be read.

Logan and Warner's plan to remake Fonda coincided with the arrival in her life of the French filmmaker Roger Vadim. A lucky break, really, for her. Vadim is routinely characterized as a villain, a Svengali figure. A very American media story line prevails: Vadim swooped in and whisked away the much younger Fonda—he was, in case facts matter, nine years older than Fonda (in Hollywood terms, not such a big gap). He stole her away to Paris, bent on using her for publicity to further his faltering career. (The notion was in part true.) The assumption was at the time that Vadim would after he was done exploiting Fonda blithely move on; he had, after all, moved on to Fonda after celebrated liaisons with Bridget Bardot and Catherine Deneuve.

The truth of Fonda and Vadim's personal and professional relationship was at once more complex and a lot less sordid. Contrary to the media story line—and quite a bit less horrific than Logan and Warner's plans for her future—Vadim never wanted to remake Fonda; he certainly didn't want to break her jaw or alter her look. He appreciated her beauty and talent and personality. And he found attractive as well her inner strength and psychological complexity. "[Fonda's] mystery lay in her contrasting moods," Vadim wrote in 1977, "She was both aggressive and vulnerable, intolerant and deeply anxious to understand other people, open and reserved, charming and hard as nails—sometimes all at the same time."[24]

It was with Vadim and his friends, the actors Yves Montand and Simone Signoret, that Fonda first began to think about political activism. One night over drinks and dinner, Fonda found herself engaged by Montand and Signoret as they talked passionately about the former French-colonial possession Vietnam. At the time, Fonda knew virtually nothing about Indochina. Few Americans did. When the 1964 Gulf of Tonkin incident that President Lyndon Johnson used to justify American military escalation in the region came up in the dinner conversation, Fonda recalled: "I wanted to defend [to my new French friends] my country as a great power acting from the highest political and moral motives . . . but suddenly the United States was participating in a war halfway around the world, and to what purpose?"[25] She was coming of age.

A second political awakening occurred stateside the following year, set in motion by a ridiculous flap over of all things, a billboard—albeit an eighty-foot billboard hawking Fonda's 1965 film with Vadim, *Circle of Love*, hung in Times Square by the exhibitor Walter Reade. The billboard depicted Fonda lying on her belly and in the nude. Fonda was as surprised as anyone encountering the billboard. Nonetheless Fonda took a beating from the gossip columnists Earl Wilson and Dorothy Kilgallen, though they certainly knew better—that is, they knew the billboard was Reade's doing, not Fonda's.

Fonda felt quite betrayed—by the system, really. And she resented how Wilson and Kilgallen had depicted and disrespected her. So she turned to her left-wing cohorts at the Actors Studio—Brando, Harry Belafonte, Arthur Penn, and Paul Newman—for solace and advice. She was particularly impressed by Brando; pretty much every young actor at the time was. He seemed to her unabashedly contemptuous of celebrity and of the gossipmongers who fed off the star system, the likes of Wilson and Kilgallen who had treated her so unfairly. And he was unapologetic about his progressive politics: his work on behalf of the Congress of Racial Equality (CORE), his engagement with Dr. Martin Luther King, the NAACP, and the Panthers.

Through Brando, Fonda met the Black comedian/political activist Dick Gregory and the formidable Hollywood actress Rita Hayworth (herself a Latina, born Margarita Carmen Cansino) both of whom were working with Newman and Burt Lancaster on initiatives set in motion by SNCC (the Student Nonviolent Coordinating Committee). Moving easily among these older Hollywood progressives (several of whom knew and liked her father) and engaged by a seeming new Hollywood celebrity that allowed for and maybe even benefitted from political engagement, Fonda volunteered at SNCC.

Though she didn't necessarily need another push, Fonda got one while working on Otto Preminger's *Hurry Sundown* in 1967, shot on location in and around Baton Rouge. The production engaged an integrated cast and crew, unusual for Hollywood at the time, with the Black actors Diahann Carroll and Robert Hooks in starring roles. Preminger's Sigma Productions handled the logistics for the location shoot and booked the cast and crew into a local motel. It was the first time management there had agreed to house nonwhites. On a particularly hot day during the shoot, Hooks took a swim in the motel pool. It was for plenty of the locals a hard image to un-see.

The production later decamped for a location shoot to tiny St. Francisville (population fifteen hundred), and things went from uncomfortable to perilous. Whiling away some down time on the town's one main street, Fonda encountered a little Black boy. The boy gave Fonda a flower. She bent over and kissed him on the cheek. Someone took a picture. The picture made the front page of the local newspaper. On the day the photo was published, just as Preminger set up his first shot, a local sheriff arrived with a message: after Fonda's photo op, he could no longer assure the cast and crew's safety. The cast and crew promptly got into a couple of station wagons and left St. Francisville for Baton Rouge—their hasty exit punctuated by gunshots.

Hurry Sundown was well intentioned but poorly received. The *New York Times*'s Bosely Crowther dismissed the film as tasteless and ham-handed: "While there may be some crude fascination for gullible viewers, the whole thing is mawkish and bathetic. Indeed it is an offense to intelligence."[26] And, in a feature for *Esquire Magazine* focusing on a recent wave of Deep South–set anti-racist Hollywood features into which *Hurry Sundown* snugly fit, the novelist Wilfrid Sheed cannily observed: "There are few sectors so devoid of pull that Hollywood feels free to speak its piece about them, so the South serves a definitive purpose, like Polish jokes. It provides a setting for a certain kind of bad movie [*Hurry Sundown*] and also a certain kind of good movie [*In the Heat of the Night*] that cannot be made elsewhere."[27] Sheed wasn't wrong. The South had indeed become a trope, a most awful version of a culture the counterculture was counter to: think *In the Heat of the Night*, *Easy Rider*, *Deliverance* (1972).

After *Hurry Sundown* flopped, Fonda returned to Los Angeles to star in a light comedy: an adaptation of Neil Simon's *Barefoot in the Park* (Gene Saks, 1967), costarring with another beautiful future Hollywood progressive, Robert Redford. The film proved a boon to Fonda's film career. *Variety* and *Time* singled out her portrayal of the energetic, sexy young wife in the picture as the sort of role she seemed rather born to play, the sort of light comic role that suited her style and look. (Snidely, I might add: this was much as Logan had cruelly predicted: light comedy seemed to suit her nose in particular).

Fonda moved back to France after the release of *Barefoot in the Park*. While there, chaperoned by Signoret, she attended a peace march in Paris, which featured speeches by Jean-Paul Sartre and

Simone de Beauvoir. Fonda's head was officially turned. By then, her life had become positively dyslexic: Hollywood/Paris, Neil Simon/Sartre and de Beauvoir. The American press's struggle to find a through line was apparent in a *New York Times* feature: "Jane Fonda has managed to maintain two different public images simultaneously in France and the United States. Over here, she appears in movies like *Barefoot in the Park* and *Any Wednesday*. She sounds and dresses like the pretty roommate of the girl you dated in college, and everyone thinks of her as Henry Fonda's daughter. In Europe, she stars in movies like *Circle of Love* and *La Curée* and she sounds like the girl you eavesdropped on in a Paris café; she undresses like Bridget Bardot and everyone knows her as the latest wife of Roger Vadim."[28]

In France in the summer of 1967, Fonda and Vadim made *Barbarella*, a light-comic, sci-fi fantasy that exploited and epitomized the sexual revolution. The film marked the apex of Fonda's Vadim-era sex kitten persona, but in a curious quirk of history, it was during the production of this apolitical farce that Fonda first went public with her support for the anti-war movement.

By the time Fonda returned to Los Angeles after the film had opened worldwide, she saw herself as a political celebrity—that is, a celebrity with politics. She took up residence in toney Malibu, strategically next door to the Sutherlands (the actor Donald and his wife Shirley), themselves progressive activists. Seberg was part of the Sutherlands' crowd as well, and it was at Seberg's house in Coldwater Canyon, at a fundraiser for a Panther-run Montessori School, that Fonda met Seberg's occasional companion, the charismatic Hakim Jamal. According to Fonda's biographer Patricia Bosworth, Fonda was, like Seberg, besotted with Jamal and at his behest wrote several checks in support of the Panthers' cause.

Fonda and Vadim became bicoastal, bicontinental jet setters; they had a flat in Paris, a room at the Chelsea Hotel in New York,

FIGURE 25. Jane Fonda with her husband, the director Roger Vadim, on the set of the sci-fi farce *Barbarella* (1967) (Everett Collection).

and a house in Malibu. They moved easily among and between scenes and celebrities of very different stripes at these three locales. There was Signoret and Montand in Paris and the progressive political crowd in L.A., which included the Sutherlands, Seberg, Shirley MacLaine, Newman, and Woodward. They were as well involved in the drug and party scene in Benedict Canyon—a crowd that included Roman Polanski and Sharon Tate. Fonda had her hair done by Jay Sebring, who, along with Tate, would be one of the Manson Family's victims in August 1969.

At the Chelsea in New York, the partying was even more intense than it was in Benedict Canyon. Fonda fell in easily with the celebrity and pseudo-celebrity subcultures headquartered there: the Warhol crowd (Candy Darling, Viva, the underground film actor Eric Anderson, whom Vadim cruelly dubbed "the perverted little elf," which spoke as much to Anderson's polymorphous perversity as Fonda's affection for him), Liza Minnelli and Halston (and the rest of the rich and ridiculous crowd that would years later congregate at Studio 54), and some serious artists like Tennessee Williams, Philip Glass, Patti Smith, and Robert Mapplethorpe. What brought such a diverse crowd together were the drugs, booze, and sex—hedonism disguised and/or expressed as counterculture rebellion.

Bosworth claims that Fonda was "devastated" by Tate's murder, so much so that after hearing the news she withdrew from the Chelsea and Benedict Canyon scenes. "To [Fonda]," Bosworth writes, "the murders symbolized the worst aspects of this turbulent decade: sex—drugs—hippies—evil gurus—Hollywood excess."[29] In the late summer of 1969, Fonda took a brief sabbatical to India, the then-fashionable capital of spiritual enlightenment for post-Beatles counterculture celebrities. When she got back to L.A., she threw herself into her career.

Fonda made things happen career-wise quickly. *They Shoot Horses Don't They* (Sydney Pollack) came out in December 1969 to critical acclaim, and a first Oscar nomination. *Klute*, directed by Alan Pakula, followed just over a year later, and with it Fonda's first Best Actress Oscar. The high-priced call girl Bree Daniels would be for Fonda a career-making, career-defining role. And in case it was not already clear to folks in Hollywood, with *Klute* Fonda proved she was a terrific actor *and* a formidable, political, feminist celebrity.

To prepare for the role, Fonda went full-on Method. She spent weeks trawling Manhattan after-hours bars, picking up on, in her words, "the hierarchy of the prostitute world, from streetwalkers to call girls, madams and pimps." To develop the character, per her Actors Studio training, Fonda tapped as well into her own experience as an actress and as a public persona; she knew that beautiful, talented women are often disregarded as "frivolous and superficial," despite being "serious people."[30]

Klute was upon its release widely hailed as a feminist film—as a movie about female empowerment. It delved seriously into how women think about their personal, sexual, and professional lives. Fonda's off-screen persona enhanced the political subtexts; her investment in the character, her ability to embody the character made Bree's lifestyle and professional choices seem serious and seriously political.

Pakula brought to the project as well a considerable left-wing pedigree, informing how the film should be read. Working with his business partner, the director Robert Mulligan, in the decade leading up to *Klute* Pakula produced the progressive Hollywood feature *To Kill a Mockingbird* (1962), the Hollywood exposé *Inside Daisy Clover* (1965), and the inner-city schoolroom melodrama *Up the Down Staircase* (1967). With *Klute*, Pakula moved into the director's chair and embarked upon his "counterculture trilogy," following *Klute* with the paranoid political assassination picture *The Parallax View* (1974) and the Watergate exposé *All the President's Men* (1976).

Klute takes its title from one of its two main characters, the detective John Klute, played by Fonda's Malibu neighbor, friend, and fellow progressive Donald Sutherland. Klute is hired to investigate the New York City disappearance of a Pennsylvania businessman, an investigation that leads him to Bree. Their complicated relationship sets the narrative in motion. Both—the narrative and their relationship—are fraught with contradictions. Klute's investigation involves watching Bree, including wiretapping and bugging her apartment. His surveillance is meant to protect her, which is from the outset problematic. Bree didn't ask for his help, even though she clearly needs it. "There's someone on the roof," he says to her during an encounter in her apartment. He then orders her to "Sit!" (as one would say to a puppy). And he takes control of the situation. She gets back at him for that and reverses the power dynamics. But we're left to wonder, what does she really want? Problem is: she's not sure.

Klute's surveillance echoes uncomfortably with what Bree experiences every day: the ogling gaze of men as she walks by, the consuming gaze of her clients as they assess the goods; the sadistic gaze of the stalking maniac killer Peter Cable, the corporate executive who, we discover, has killed Tom, the missing person in Klute's case, and a couple of prostitutes from Bree's former "stable" as well. Bree is recognizably Jane Fonda, the glamorous Hollywood actor. She is costumed throughout the film in tight sweaters, slim skirts, and (per women's lib) no bra. She's quite stunning to look at, a "being looked at" she—the character that is—says she enjoys.

But we discover that's not exactly true, at least not all the time, not in every circumstance. The looks she gets are double-edged—flattering and diminishing, exhilarating and dangerous. (Here again the overlaps with Fonda the actress are useful.) The sexual freedom Bree espouses as a perk of her particular line of work in the end fails to diminish the creepier aspects the looks portend. She contends in a therapy session that the control she exerts with clients gives her power. But the control doesn't give her pleasure. And doesn't in the end protect her from maniacs like Cable.

A judgmental male gaze persists in her attempts to become legit, to get out of "the life." At a casting call for a TV commercial, Bree walks on stage with a dozen other tall, thin, beautiful women. A couple of ad execs walk down the row and brutally assess each woman's flaws. Bree is dismissed along with the others and another dozen take their place. When Bree auditions for a play, her compellingly performed monologue is interrupted before it's complete. "Interesting accent," the director says patronizingly. Then he calls in the next actress.

The film offers a commentary on the emerging surveillance culture as well: Big Brother watching our every move. To make his point, Pakula highlights diegetic audio. Klute taps Bree's home phone and bugs her apartment—and he does so without her permission or knowledge. Bree's therapist makes recordings of their sessions as well—recordings that capture her most intimate thoughts and feelings. And Cable plays on more than one occasion a clandestine audio recording of his encounter with Bree in which she, in the performance of her profession, encourages him to let it all hang out. It's a rehearsed riff that we hear her deliver more than once and to more than one client, and it serves only to fuel his anger—at her, at women "like her," and at himself (for getting aroused).

The "whore with a heart of gold" fantasy is certainly in play in *Klute*. But that old patriarchal chestnut is revealed to be contradictory and unsatisfying. Klute has ventured from suburban Pennsylvania to save Bree from the decadent city. And while it becomes clear in the film's second act that she needs saving—from Cable, who intends to kill her and from her sleazy former pimp, who exploits her—Bree's claims to sexual liberation get in the way. Bree is deeply conflicted by Klute's attention and affection. She exploits his protectiveness and seduces him, but only, or so she tells him, to prove that she can get any man she wants and to cut him, with his self-righteous strong and silent façade, down to size. Klute is, as Bree derisively describes him, a "square." But she can't shake the fact that being such a square makes him useful and (though she wishes this wasn't true) attractive.

The film's complex social commentary hinges upon how we read the film's final act. Cable abducts Bree. She is, though maybe it's just bad timing, Klute's decoy to get Cable. Just as Cable is about to assault Bree, Klute arrives and Cable falls, jumps, or is pushed (it is hard to tell) out a window to his death. We then cut to the film's perplexing denouement. Bree is moving out of her apartment. Klute is there with her, quietly laying claim to his reward for saving her. The scene should offer closure but instead introduces a new set of contradictions, all of them rooted in the moment—rooted, that is, in 1971 and in the women's movement taking shape at the time, a

FIGURE 26. Jane Fonda as Bree Daniels in *Klute* (Alan Pakula, 1971, Warner Bros.).

movement embodied in all its complexity and contradiction by Fonda *and* Bree.

Bree is packed and appears ready to leave New York for "Cabbageville," as she has cynically dubbed Klute's Pennsylvania suburb. But her voice-over on the soundtrack complicates and contradicts what we see on-screen. We hear a recording of Bree talking with her therapist, ostensibly being honest, as one, we assume, would be with one's shrink. She relays her thoughts about the moment we see on-screen and her possible future in suburbia: "I'll probably be back in a couple of weeks," she says. A diegetic exchange on the dialogue track adds another seed of doubt. A former john calls just as Bree is about to leave with Klute. She puts the guy off, but not unequivocally, and not right away. We, and the professional detective Klute can't help but notice that her voice noticeably softens as she thinks back on old times. For a moment—and Fonda's performance modulates perfectly here—Bree thinks about being in control again, being a call girl again. It turns her on, but it has a very different effect on him.

Klute was widely viewed as progressive, most notably by a number of feminist film professors and scholars who came of age in the sixties and seventies.[31] The film's gender politics are indeed complicated. Klute is a suburban square, a man's man willing and anxious to domesticate Bree. Pakula depicts him as the film's certain moral center. He wants Bree, but he also wants to change her. Cable is a psychopath, but he's more than that, as he asks us to ponder what the sexual revolution has unleashed upon American men. Cable covets his recording of Bree's invitation to johns wanting something a little "strange," something their wives or girlfriends don't want to do with them. "The only way we can be free is to let it all hang out," Bree tells her clients (including Cable just before he hits her), affirming the same "different strokes for different folks" credo that would underpin *Deep Throat* (Gerard Damiano) a year later. Cable tells Bree when she's his captive that "there are corners in everyone's mind that are best left [untapped]." He blames Bree and free-thinking women like her for triggering his violent fantasies. The corners in Cable's mind are peculiarly dark and scary. But the film nonetheless leaves us to contemplate his rationalizations; we are asked to ponder the consequences (for men and because men are violent, women as well) of counterculture sexual freedom and by extension Women's Lib.

What does Bree learn from her encounter with Cable? Is he why she has agreed to leave New York with Klute? If she leaves New York for Cabbageville, will she accept the role of the faithful suburban wife? Will the other suburban wives accept her? Pakula raises questions he has no interest answering. Earlier in the film, during a montage summarizing Bree and Klute's budding romance, the couple lingers at a farmers market. Bree spies a child and looks longingly at him. Is she ready for motherhood? Is she ready to settle down?

She's not so sure. Pretty much everything women's lib is talking about, protesting over, seems somehow in play and at stake. And in the end, you get the feeling Bree can't win, that patriarchy is not only so ingrained in our culture but also so fucked up it would have to be dismantled before any real progress can be achieved.

After *Klute*, Fonda returned to France, not to work with Vadim, but instead, to star alongside her friend Yves Montand in *Tout va bien*, directed by the left-wing, New Wave icon Jean-Luc Godard. Her involvement in Godard's film *briefly* cemented her progressive reputation with even the most cynical of the new and old left. But "briefly" is the operative word here. By the time *Tout va bien* was screened to open the New York Film Festival in 1972, Godard and his collaborator Jean-Pierre Gorin had cobbled together an altogether unflattering companion piece: *Letter to Jane*, an essay film produced under the auspices of the Dziga Vertov group, their Marxist documentary collective.

Letter to Jane deconstructs a single, grainy, black-and-white photograph of Fonda first published in the August 1972 issue of *L'Express*. The American actress faces the camera and is shown listening attentively to a North Vietnamese woman, whose face is mostly obscured. As the American movie critic Jonathan Rosenbaum writes, Godard and Gorin examine how such a picture enables the viewer "to go to Vietnam," without of course ever actually going there, without, like Fonda, who did go there, having other or more than an American's or European's understanding of the place and people who live there. We see the "tragic face of the [American] actress," but can we believe in what it shows and tells us in this real-world moment?[32]

Godard and Gorin's analysis is provocative and interesting, but it is also exploitive. Fonda is damned for trying to listen, scrutinized and ridiculed for trying to understand Vietnam when few in France or the United States were so inclined. The left can be awfully hard on its own.

After her encounter with Godard, Fonda moved back to L.A. for good and strategically committed herself to progressive-themed Hollywood moviemaking. Off-screen, she reconnected with the Panthers, thanks to introductions made by the former blacklistee and erstwhile Hollywood Communist Dalton Trumbo. Fonda's name became a popular one to drop among the various factions of the West Coast left. And Fonda could drop some names as well, adding to her left-wing inner circle the campus activist and civil rights provocateur Angela Davis. Fonda was no longer bicontinental or even bicoastal, but still quite split between the film career and political engagement. And she had plenty of energy for both. It was while she was working on the latter that she met and fell in love with one of the anti-war movement's architects, the former Students for a Democratic Society (SDS) president and Chicago Seven coconspirator Tom Hayden, whom Fonda, anticipating the birth of a child together, married four days before the cease-fire agreement in Vietnam in January 1973.

We can't presume to know the truth about their relationship and marriage. When the TV journalist Barbara Walters asked Hayden, "What is the hardest part about living with Jane Fonda?" he replied quickly and candidly: "The attention. No one person deserves that much attention."[33] Was he making a comment on celebrity in general or his wife in particular? Or in some more ordinary way wondering why someone with his bona fides was somehow playing second fiddle?

There were plenty of doubters and critics, especially among those inclined to share Wolfe's notion of radical chic. Some suspected that Hayden was using Fonda for publicity. Gore Vidal summarized that view when he remarked to the press: "Tom Hayden gives opportunism a bad name." Others assumed it was the other way around—that Fonda was using Hayden to convince her critics that she was not a dilettante. Vadim, jealously perhaps, dismissed the relationship as a media stunt: "The whole thing was like a movie and Jane was living it.... She was acting the part of Jane Fonda in a big adventure and Tom was the hero of her movie."

Bosworth seems to share Vadim's cynicism as she writes candidly and not so flatteringly about the "Tom and Jane, celebrity revolutionaries" scenario: "Every morning [Fonda] and Hayden checked their battered Volvo for bombs. The couple did have grandiose fantasies about themselves. Tom wanted to be president. Jane sometimes saw herself as a martyr. [She once remarked:] 'If it had been the 1950s I would have been electrocuted like the Rosenbergs.'"[34] The outsized attention and criticism persisted throughout their seventeen-year marriage. But so did their efforts on behalf of progressive causes.

Fonda survived the counterculture. And as we've seen so far, that was something. And she survived Hollywood. In 2020 her career entered its seventh decade; and she was still a working actor. For over half a century she has engaged counterculture politics full on, and for her trouble she has been ridiculed by the left and pilloried by the right. She was certainly gray-listed (as she claims) after the North Vietnam trip. And over the years, she has lost parts to less talented, less controversial actors as movie executives, producers, directors, and costars had to consider what it might mean (careerwise, PR-wise) to work with Jane Fonda.

In 2014 Fonda received a Life Achievement Award from the American Film Institute (AFI). She ended her acceptance speech with a telling note of self-deprecation. The modesty seems today at once honest and instructive. As we assess Fonda's personal and professional life—which has been at once fervent and disorganized, meaningful and sometimes hard to pin down—best to take her at her word: "It is better to be interested than interesting."[35]

Dolores Hart Doesn't Want to Be Movie Star; She Wants to Be a Nun

Dolores Hicks, later Dolores Hart, was never counterculture—at least not in the way the term is generally used. She was quite literally a convent girl when she was discovered, a wholesome, blonde L.A. teenager who, like plenty of her peers, dreamed someday she'd be an actor and a movie star. But when she got precisely what she thought she wanted, she decided she wanted something else, something that had been available to her, waiting for her all along. Dolores Hicks, Catholic college coed, was discovered just before New Year's Day 1957. Just over six years later, Dolores Hart, the Hollywood movie star, decided to do something else, something very different with the rest of her life.

Hicks was, as the Hollywood press reported, in the middle of charm class at Marymount College in Rancho Palos Verdes, California, when a phone call came in from Hal Wallis's assistant to come to the Paramount lot for a screen test.[36] Her classroom teacher told her she'd never make the grade. But Mother Gabriel, Marymount's dean of girls, stopped by while Hicks waited for a friend to drive her to the lot, to offer encouragement: "Kids in drama school want an opportunity like what you're going for. Dolores, this is the big one. Go for it!"

When Wallis asked at the audition what she wanted to do with the rest of her life, Hicks answered without hesitation: "I want to be an actress." In short order, that dream came true. Dolores Hicks became Dolores Hart. And Dolores Hart became a movie star.

By the time winter term exam week arrived, Hart was a welcomed new face on the Paramount lot meeting with the legendary

FIGURE 27. Left to right: Dolores Hart, Elvis Presley, and Lizabeth Scott on the set of *Loving You* (Hal Kantner) in 1957 (Everett Collection).

Edith Head, being fitted for costumes for her screen debut opposite the biggest pop star on the planet, Elvis Presley, in *Loving You* (Hal Kanter, 1957). She was living the life of an overnight sensation, quite suddenly the lead in a fan magazine story of Hollywood discovery—a scenario so many young American women had at one time or another dreamed about.

Hart was typecast in the film: the good girl opposite Presley's bad boy. She was nervous of course, but hit her marks and held her own, which got her cast in a similar, bigger part in Presley's *King Creole*, released the following year. *King Creole* was directed by Michael Curtiz—the same Michael Curtiz who had directed *The Adventures of Robin Hood* (1938) and *Casablanca* (1942).

Hart and Presley hit it off. If she was leery of his reputation, and who could have blamed her if she was, she needn't have been. "He was quite a gentleman," Hart recalled years later, well past a time

[198] FOUR WOMEN IN HOLLYWOOD

when she needed to be careful what she said, "[with] a quality of simplicity, humor, and shyness." Hart got to know Presley well during the New Orleans shoot of *King Creole*. His outsized celebrity made moving around town impossible, and thus isolated them together in their hotel rooms after work on the set. Hart and Presley found it easy to kill time together. "Elvis would open the Gideon Bible," Hart recalled, "and whatever passage he'd open to, we would talk about it."

After the two films with Presley, Hart left Hollywood for Broadway, where she again found success, receiving a Tony nomination for her performance in the 1959 production of Samuel Taylor's *The Pleasure of His Company*. The nomination offered Hart a useful bona fide; it proved she was more than just that fresh-faced California girl who had costarred in a couple of Elvis pictures. The success didn't go to her head—in part because she was already drifting. Like a lot of young people at the time, she was searching for something else, something more.

A chance encounter during the New York run of the play proved in the end a lot more meaningful than the Tony nomination. After a performance, a friend came backstage and offered to introduce Hart to a couple of nuns from Regina Laudis, a Benedictine monastery in Bethlehem, Connecticut. Hart wasn't much interested: "NUNS! [her caps] I don't want to meet nuns." She eventually gave in and accompanied her friend to the monastery where, much to her surprise, she felt quite completely at home.

Hart returned to Regina Laudis several times during the play's run. Just before heading back to Hollywood, Hart asked the Reverend Mother if she thought she had a vocation. "No," the Reverend Mother replied, "Go back and do your movie thing. You're too young." Hart took her advice and accepted an offer for a part in *Where the Boys Are* (Levin, 1960), a studio film about young college men and women on spring break in Fort Lauderdale testing the waters of the sexual revolution.

Where the Boys Are marked MGM's attempt to follow up on Columbia's hit of the previous year, *Gidget* (Paul Wendkos), the story of a young woman—Francis Lawrence, a.k.a. Gidget (i.e., *girl* plus *midget*)—who falls in with the aimless surfer crowd. *Gidget* made Sandra Dee a movie star. And Hart had every reason to believe *Where the Boys Are* would do the same for her.

Where the Boys Are opens in a classroom on a snowy college campus just before spring break. Merritt (Hart) engages one of her professors in a debate about "random dating" and "premature emotional involvement." The conversation gets heated and Merritt invokes Kinsey. The class is suddenly hushed. Aghast, the professor admonishes Merritt: "We are not here to talk about Dr. Kinsey. We are discussing interpersonal relationships." The irony is lost on the teacher.

In Fort Lauderdale, Merritt meets Ryder (George Hamilton) and a romance blossoms. But the interpersonal relationship is complicated by what Kinsey has done to interpersonal relationships, to American culture. Ryder tells Merritt that she's a good kisser, but her reply stops him in his tracks: "No girl likes to be considered promiscuous." "You're a strong girl," he says, shifting gears, hoping to flatter her. But she contradicts him again: "No girl is, when it comes to love." His head is spinning. And thanks to Kinsey, so is hers.

In the film's third act, Merritt's resistance weakens. But just in time to protect her faltering chastity, a friend stumbles upon the couple with some terrible news: Merritt's classmate Melanie (Yvette Mimieux) has been date-raped. (We have in a previous scene seen the encounter, and it's astonishingly frank for a 1960 film.) By the time Merritt and Ryder find Melanie, she is wandering the strip and is in bad shape. Cut to the local hospital where Melanie is convalescing. Ryder tries to console Merritt, but she pushes him away. "Are you going to blame me for something someone else did?" he asks. Merritt's reply again surprises him: "I blame all of you who think of a girl as something cheap and common put here for your personal kicks."

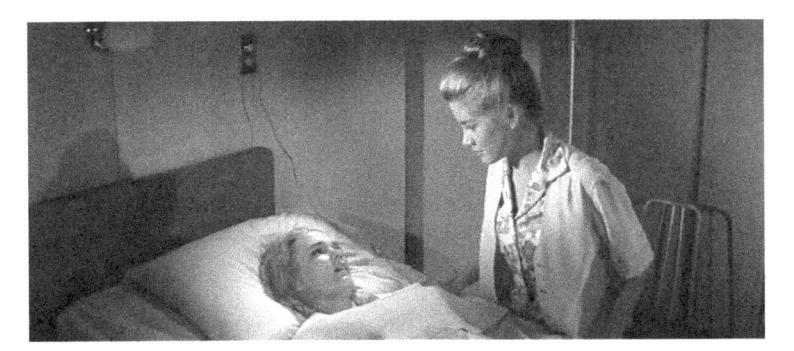

FIGURE 28. Dolores Hart (right) as Merritt trying to console her friend Melanie (Yvette Mimieux) after Melanie's rape in *Where the Boys Are* (Henry Levin, 1961, MGM). The film ran on the tagline: "The hilarious inside story of those rip-roaring spring vacations." But the film's final act rather doted on the vacation's sobering consequences.

Merritt then repairs to Melanie's hospital room to console her friend. The exchange is sobering—especially for a film that ran on the tagline: "The hilarious inside story of those rip-roaring spring vacations." Melanie greets Merritt: "I goofed up. I should have died. Why didn't I die?" Merritt is crying too as she tries to get her friend to look to the future: "Everything's gonna be all right. . . . As soon as you get back to school." Melanie sobs. Merritt says, "It's not the end of the world." But it is the end of the world, because things will never be all right for Melanie, and we know why; Kinsey or no, she is now and will forever be considered, "damaged goods." Merritt tries again to reassure her friend—"You'll meet somebody—some nice boy back home." But Melanie gets the last word, and Mimieux does well to step on Hart's line in the process: "Some nice boy? And I'll tell him all about my wonderful spring vacation. He'd like to hear that."

Hart quickly landed another lead role, Clare Offreduccio, later St. Clare (Santa Clara), in the Twentieth Century Fox biopic *Francis of Assisi* (Curtiz, 1961). The shoot took Hart to Italy, where, at a publicity event, she got to meet Pope John XXIII. Hart introduced herself: "I am Dolores Hart, an actress portraying Clara." The pope replied, "Tu sei Chiara [You are Clara]." Hart figured something was lost in translation, so she tried again; making clear that she was just an actress playing a part. But the pope had understood her the first time. He was rather making a point. Looking Hart square in the eye, he repeated "No. Tu sei Chiara." The former convent girl couldn't shake the encounter.

In January 1963, as Hart's career seemed on the ascent, Cal York, writing for *Photoplay*, penned a short gossip entry about an impending marriage: "Dolores Hart says her friends had her all pegged for a shelf in the old maid's home, but she's fooled them. She'll marry [the Los Angeles businessman] Don Robinson soon—either February or March. She's known the guy for three years."[37] In the subsequent issue, Hedda Hopper added her two cents, claiming to have the inside scoop on a supposed rivalry for Hart's affection between Robinson, whom Hart seemed to favor, and the actor Stephen Boyd. "As to who's consoling Steve," Hopper reassured her readers, "you can bet he's not weeping alone."[38] The romantic triangle was utter nonsense—Hopper's stock-in-trade.

Before film fans had time to digest Hopper's item, Hart called off the wedding. Hopper kept spinning: "Dolores Hart is still paying bills for the wedding she didn't have." The gossip columnist then added a neat detail: that the wedding dress designed by Edith Head had been put in storage, awaiting another lucky bride.[39] Two months later, Hopper linked Hart with the actor Gary Clarke, whom, the columnist claimed, was "in a spin" over Hart. Hopper added that Clarke might have to wait his turn, as Hart had been seen dallying with "a local doctor named Mitchell Covell."[40]

But in September, Hopper's runaway bride story hit an iceberg. In an issue touting the usual fan magazine nonsense—"What Burton does to Liz that no other man dared!" "Debbie [Reynolds] Loses 2nd Baby! Will She Have Another?" "Christine Keeler: Her Naked

Life"—*Photoplay* ran a feature story on Hart under the terse headline, "Dolores Hart Becomes a Nun!"[41]

The feature is a masterwork of industry self-congratulation and PR. Wallis went first: "In our business you don't find many girls [like Hart] who blush." Hart, Wallis noted, reminded him of Grace Kelly (who had abandoned Hollywood to become a princess in 1956)—and Hart, like Kelly "got a much better offer" than he or any other Hollywood executive could ever hope to make. The *Photoplay* reporter Michael Joya dutifully canvassed Hollywood's eligible bachelors, *not* in search of gossip but instead to portray Hart's "conversion" as always somehow "in the cards." It was essential for everyone involved to show respect for the Church. Presley: "She had every virtue—kindness, charity, good breeding, there was not one mean bone in her body." The actor, Ty Hardin: "I used to date Dolores. . . . She sure is one of the nicest people I've ever known." Vince Edwards, the star of TV's hit drama "Ben Casey": "I have never known any other girl in my life as wholesome and honest as Dolores." Even Don Robinson offered his best wishes for the future: "I know Dolores is very happy [now]. And I am happy for her." (Robinson would never marry. He remained devoted to Hart until his death in 2011.)

Hart, the *Photoplay* feature suggests, had everything: talent, good looks, ambition, a strong work ethic. She just wanted something more, something else. Joya made clear (on behalf of the industry he served) that it was not the sordid subculture of Hollywood that drove Hart away. It was instead something inside her, something that was already there before Wallis's assistant made that first, fateful call.

Joya got a great quote from a nun who had taught Hart in high school, which did well to support his story-line: "She always wanted to play good girls on the screen. She considered it a challenge because she felt it was much harder to portray a nice girl—and much harder to live like one off-screen. She used to say that a good girl has much more old-fashioned guts, if I may use the vulgarism, than her opposite. And she's right."

A letter from a faithful *Photoplay* reader (one Louisa Cristol of Los Angeles, California) printed in the November issue made clear that Joya's feature had hit its target. "Although I will miss Dolores Hart, it was inspiring to read about her beautiful faith. What makes it more wonderful is that a girl, who had everything we teenagers dream of, gave it all up for something more precious. It is such stories that make the world a tolerable place to live in."[42] The letter offered a particular brand of conservative reassurance that had come to characterize the gossip narrative at the time. It seemed to say that, despite so many news stories to the contrary, (at least some of) the kids were all right.

When the November issue arrived on newsstands none of *Photoplay*'s readers could have guessed at how swiftly things were about to change—how soon that "tolerable place to live in" would become a good deal less tolerable. On the twenty-second day of that month, John F. Kennedy's visit to Dallas would end in tragedy. Reassuring stories like Hart's, especially for the younger generation, would be in short supply after that.

Hart has led a monastic life since her arrival at Regina Laudis in 1963, serving Jesus and her community. In 2012, after over fifty years away from the business, Hart made a rare public appearance on (of all places) the red carpet at the Oscars in support of a documentary short film about her, neatly titled: *God Is the Bigger Elvis* (Julie Anderson and Rebecca Cammisa). The film was timed nicely to support the publication of Hart's memoir *The Ear of the Heart*, in which she addressed on the record the behind-the-scenes pressures she endured when she walked away from the movie business.

Hart's version of her final days in Hollywood differed from *Photoplay*'s. According to Hart, when the news of her Hollywood exit broke in 1963, *The National Enquirer* ran with the headline: "Star

Driven into Nunnery by Her Love for Elvis." It was nonsense, of course—and easily laughed off. But behind the scenes, things were not so rosy as *Photoplay* had suggested they were, in part because she had become by then and for a lot of people in the business, a valuable asset. God might be bigger than Elvis, but was God bigger than Hollywood?

Hollywood executives are a peculiar bunch. They figure everyone is more or less like them: greedy, amoral, kind of stupid. Hart was from start to end of her career in the movie business, none of those things. To deal with the pressures of her new career, Hart, at the time still a teenager, sought counsel from a handful of veteran actors, all of them politically and socially conservative. This cadre of smart, older, Catholic women included Irene Dunne, Loretta Young, Patricia Neal, and June Haver.

Haver had the most profound influence on Hart. Billed as "the pocket [Betty] Grable" (she was five feet, one inch tall) when she first hit the scene in the early 1940s, Haver's career seemed on a steady ascent when quite out of the blue in 1953 she announced her intention to quit the business to take vows as a postulant nun at the Sisters of Charity in Leavenworth, Kansas. After eight months at the convent, Haver discovered she did not have a calling. So she returned to Hollywood, but not to resume acting for a living. She wanted a husband and children—in that order. And with Fred MacMurray, she got both and settled down. In a 2013 interview, Hart reflected on her friendship with Haver: "I could perceive the depth of goodness [in Haver] and that she had struggled a great deal. She was very honest and never claimed what wasn't true. She was a great lesson to me."[43]

Photoplay's sunny retrospective in 1963 suggested everyone in the business respected and admired Hart's decision. The facts of the matter were different. Hal Wallis told *Photoplay* he was happy for Hart and wished her only the best for her future. But he was, Hart contends, in fact furious with her for breaking her contract, and he made clear to Hart in a private conversation "not to bother coming back to work with him." Hart's agent, Harry Bernson, sent her a note asking if she "had swallowed razor blades," as in his view she "had committed suicide." For these men there was nothing beyond or better than Hollywood, nothing of value that didn't have an apparent value to them. Hart knew better and got out of their world before it got anything else or more out of her.

It may seem counterintuitive to insist here that Hart was ahead of her time. During her brief career in Hollywood, she sought out the company of older colleagues, resisting the party scene the younger celebrity crowd indulged in. She was very much her own woman—in her way, a feminist, a trailblazer, a spiritual seeker who, like many of her counterculture peers (who arrived just after she left) found Hollywood celebrity empty and unsatisfying. She didn't need to go to India or study Zen or join a cult or take LSD, but she did need to get out. So she sought refuge at the convent—like Dorothy after Oz, she discovered her own private Kansas, a place she'd been before, a place she had been too caught up in being a teenager to appreciate. At the risk of indulging a sixties cliché: in 1963, Dolores Hart *found* herself. And once she did, she settled in to a life of duty and devotion—a perpetual, spiritual journey she felt sure she was always destined and meant to take.

Auteur Boys Club: Barbara Loden Does Everything Right and Then Does Everything Wrong

In the summer of 1966, Barbara Loden arrived in Hollywood on the arm of a famous director, Elia Kazan. A reputation preceded her: a stint at the Actors Studio, a Tony Award-winning performance on Broadway in an Arthur Miller play. She was in 1966 too old (she had just turned thirty-four) to be considered a starlet or an ingénue. And given the company she kept, and the reputation she brought with her from New York, it is hard to imagine anyone disrespecting her so. Loden was pretty, talented and (for Hollywood, worryingly) smart. She was also ambitious, but not in a way the studio suits were ever going to understand.

The ingredients were there for a solid career; and by most any measure, Loden had by that time already paid her dues. But things didn't work out—things didn't work out at all. She could have been successful. The reasons why she wasn't reveal a lot about what it was like to be a smart, talented, independent, thirty-something woman in Hollywood in the counterculture era.

Barbara Loden was barely out of her teens when she left a troubled home life in North Carolina for New York to work as a model. She got a few assignments and moonlighted as a dancer at the Copacabana. These early gigs got her noticed—that was what the gigs were for. She had her eye on other and better work in show business. She was ambitious—for the moment, in a good (as in, for the times culturally acceptable) way.

The acting career got off to a solid start in 1957 with a small part in a Broadway production of *Compulsion*, Meyer Levin's adaptation of the Leopold and Loeb story. A series of supporting roles followed with Loden appearing opposite a fellow up-and-comer, Robert Redford and the intense Method actor, Ben Gazzara. She seemed from the start to have a knack for comedy, which got her cast as a regular on the popular Ernie Kovacs TV show, where Loden became the ditzy brunt of the showrunner's jokes.

While getting paid to take pratfalls for Kovacs, Loden auditioned and secured a place at the Actors Studio. It was there she met Kazan, who recognized her talent and cast her in two films, as Montgomery Clift's secretary in *Wild River* (1960) and as Warren Beatty's sister in *Splendor in the Grass* (1961). Then, Kazan presented Loden with a first big break, cast as Maggie, the lead, in the first Broadway run of *After the Fall*, Arthur Miller's heartbreaking play about a difficult and suicidal actress based on the playwright's marriage to the difficult and suicidal Marilyn Monroe. Loden received a Tony for her performance and won the Outer Circle Award from theater critics nationwide assigned to the Broadway beat. On February 1, 1964, barely half a decade after signing on to be Kovacs's anonymous foil, Loden found herself on the cover of the *Saturday Evening Post*.

After the Broadway run ended, Loden ventured to Hollywood, cast in a featured role in the film adaptation of John Cheever's "The Swimmer," a 1964 short story about an upper-class suburbanite's existential despair at losing his job and with that misfortune, his family, his friends, his savings, and his mind. Burt Lancaster was cast to play Ned, the film's shattered hero, Loden his disillusioned former mistress, Shirley. A friend of Loden's from the Actors Studio, Frank Perry was hired to direct.

But then, quite suddenly, Loden's luck changed for the worse. Perry's relationship with the film's producer Sam Spiegel soured, and midway through production, Spiegel fired Perry—citing "creative differences"—and replaced him with Sydney Pollack.[44] One of the creative differences apparently involved Loden, so Pollack fired Loden and reshot all of Shirley's scenes with another actress, Janice Rule.

We can only guess at precisely why Loden got fired.[45] Rumors have circulated that Loden's performance was so good it overshadowed Lancaster's; so *he* engineered her ouster. Lancaster no doubt had a big ego, but it is hard to believe he would have felt much threatened by someone with such a small part in the film. More likely, Spiegel and Lancaster viewed Loden as an ally of Perry's, so they sent her packing to ease and/or mark the transition to Pollack. (To be fair, Rule's performance in the film is terrific. She is today the best reason to see the film.)

It was a setback, but nothing out of the ordinary, really. Actors get fired. It's a fact of life in Hollywood. But Loden never bounced

FIGURE 29. All that's left of Barbara Loden's performance in *The Swimmer* (Frank Perry, 1968) is a few still photographs taken on the set, including this one with the film's star Burt Lancaster. When Perry was fired and replaced by Sydney Pollack, Loden was fired as well and her part was given to another actor, Janice Rule (Everett Collection).

back. After *The Swimmer*, she would make only one more film, *Wanda* (1970), which she wrote and directed.

Loden and Kazan became romantically involved shortly after her matriculation at the Actors Studio (around 1957) and they married (in 1967) just as *The Swimmer* shoot went south. Kazan helped Loden a lot early on but not so much, maybe not at all, after she left New York for Hollywood.

Kazan remained defensive about his role in Loden's failure. He claimed she never sought and never listened to his advice. He couldn't control her because she wasn't controllable. That may be the truth. Let's be frank: Kazan was never a good guy. There is little debate about that. But to assume he sabotaged her career is to discredit Loden, who wanted for a lot of reasons, including the persistent rumors about Kazan's role in her success, to make it (or fail trying) on her own.

For the industry reporters who attended Loden's career, Kazan was always "the elephant in the room." When they wrote about her, they always wrote about her relationship with him.[46] For example: a 1969 *Variety* feature published during the production of *Wanda*. The reporter observes Loden as she sets up a shot, then spies and corners Kazan. "I'm just around to run errands," Kazan tells him, "It's Barbara's project."[47] The rest of the feature seems to very much doubt that fact. Even after the film was screened for reviewers, Kazan, the self-described errand boy, was still the subject at hand. Writing for the *New York Times*, Vincent Canby: "I suppose it's impossible not to wonder about any aid she might have received from her husband, but *Wanda* does not have the look of a Kazan film. It looks like an original."[48]

The Loden/Kazan relationship was complicated. When Kazan first met her, he had just turned forty-eight. She was twenty-five. By his own accounting, he was stuck in the doldrums of midlife crisis and exhausted from postproduction work on *A Face in the Crowd* (1957)—a film he loved but feared audiences and critics might not get. Kazan regarded Loden at first as just another pretty young conquest, one among many such conquests recounted casually and unpleasantly in his autobiography. Kazan flippantly describes their early encounters as a mere matter of animal attraction: "At first our affair was nothing more than dog and bitch." But things rather developed from there. And Kazan is anxious to explain why: "I'd never encountered anyone like this girl, anyone who'd uncover what is generally kept discreet with such candor.... Barbara Loden was born anti-respectable.... She observed none of the conventional middle-class boundaries.... [She was] not in awe of my reputation. . . . [She was] a roulette wheel that didn't stop turning."[49]

When Kazan cast Loden, then an unknown, as Maggie in Miller's play, he made clear the respect he had for her talent: "I hadn't needed anyone to tell me she fitted the role [as Maggie, Miller's reimagined Monroe]." The two women, Monroe and Loden, were in Kazan's view, quite similar; they were "floaters"—that is, they seemed aloof and ethereal, but appearing so was for both women more a defense than a philosophy. Both "had almost identical [which is to say awful] childhood experiences, which left them neurotic . . . desperate." That experience, that desperation and the coping mechanisms that evolved organically as a result, had fueled talents on stage and screen that were instinctive, deeply personal, idiosyncratic. Loden's Maggie was by most accounts a revelation. As Kazan describes it: "There was a naked truth in her acting that we rarely see." Good thing for Kazan, as he had a lot riding on the play and on Loden at the time.

After the Fall is a difficult play, a work tormented by Miller's still unresolved feelings for its central character (Maggie) and complicated by the audience's inevitably complicated feelings about the recently departed Monroe (feelings further complicated by Miller's seeming penchant for speaking ill of the dead). Kazan was at the time struggling with late-maybe-end-of-career doubts. The offer to direct *After the Fall* had to feel a bit like a last best chance.

Raising the stakes even further was that this latest big chance had come from Miller, a man of real status in American theater with whom Kazan had a long and difficult history. The two men had worked well together: Kazan had directed the definitive New York run of *Death of a Salesman*. And Miller believed Kazan uniquely had the experience and sensitivity to handle *After the Fall*—this despite the fact that the two men had not spoken much since the director's shameful blacklist testimony.

Casting Loden made a complicated challenge even more complicated. Kazan's wife, Molly, had come to suspect that Kazan was sleeping with Loden. (He was.) She was not alone in her suspicions; most everyone in Kazan's inner circle had guessed at the relationship. And they were all quietly wondering: was Loden really a good enough actor to justify giving her Maggie—a role that plenty of more experienced actors would have killed for?[50] There was a whole lot of pressure on Loden to deliver. According to Kazan, according to audiences and critics, she did.

Why, then, after the triumph on Broadway, why, considering her talent as an actor embarking on a film career, did things go so badly for Loden in Hollywood? Kazan asks and then answers that question, positing Loden's desire to be taken seriously as an actress *and* to become a movie star, all the while "[despising] Hollywood and the films it turned out."[51] Succeeding in Hollywood—and he knew this firsthand—involved a degree of tact, it meant being careful around and with the powerful men who ran the industry. Loden, Kazan admiringly notes in the autobiography, was never tactful or careful. When, for example, a casting director casually remarked that Loden got cast as Maggie because she was sleeping with Kazan, Loden did not (as Kazan reports) "write a polite note on monogrammed paper." She instead physically assaulted the man on a busy New York street, and slapped him around until he took back what he had said about her.

Aspiring actresses have to be careful not to cultivate a reputation for being "difficult." Even Monroe could not survive that. Loden, Kazan affirms (admiringly, again), was always difficult. That's what made her so interesting. That's what made her such a terrific actor.

There are plenty of good actors in Hollywood. And yes, plenty of bad ones too. The movie business is not a meritocracy; and that takes some getting used to. Making it requires talent and a good bit of luck. Loden had talent, but she was really unlucky, at least at first, when behind the scenes stuff she likely had nothing to do with got her booted off *The Swimmer* set. After getting fired, the next job was always going to be really important. It is hard to imagine Loden didn't know that. So why, then, was her next move *Wanda*—a project with so little appeal at the box office?

Some ideas for a script about an aimless working-class woman who can't figure out what she wants out of life had been kicking around in Loden's head for a while. She had talked with Kazan about it a lot. And when she seemed dead set to make it, he encouraged her to play the character and direct as well, saying only she (being from that part of the country and social class and temperament) could fully understand the title character, only she could tell Wanda's story. It was in many ways a left-handed compliment.

As the film historian Molly Haskell describes her, Wanda—the character that is—is a "non-entity . . . neither role model, nor easily classifiable victim. . . . [She is] rather something far less sentimental." Hollywood narratives, Haskell affirms, are generally built upon lovable people—people we can root for. With her career on the line, Loden set out instead to make a film about an unlovable woman, a woman who abandons a child and a husband, who sleeps around, who thinks so little of herself that filmgoers couldn't care about her at all.

Wanda superficially fit a brief cycle or subgenre of "mad housewife" films—films that, per Haskell, "roughed up" female roles and in doing so moved away from the old-fashioned "wink-wink plots" characteristic of "the last wheezing gasp of the Production Code." The subgenre depicted women of a certain age tossing aside their old lives for new, women who were "allowed, expected, encouraged to be [their] own person."[52] Included among these films: Coppola's road picture, *The Rain People* (1969); Perry's genre-defining *Diary of Mad Housewife* (1970), the meandering movie-industry melodrama *Play It As It Lays* (also Perry, 1972); Irvin Kershner's star vehicle for Barbra Streisand, *Up the Sandbox* (1972); Scorsese's bittersweet single-mom road picture, *Alice Doesn't Live Here Anymore* (1974); and Paul Mazursky's sexual-revolution tearjerker, *An Unmarried Woman* (1978). *Wanda* has similar elements to all of these titles, but it resists as well much of what made these other films appealing to female filmgoers. Interesting then to add the obvious, here: *Wanda* is the one mad housewife film directed by a woman.

Wanda is paced slow and runs long. The characters Wanda encounters are gruff and unattractive. The milieu is unglamorous; from start to close we find ourselves watching poor people making poor decisions. Early in the film, Wanda walks into a courtroom, disheveled, rollers in her hair. Loden the former model and Copacabana dancer does her best to appear un-pretty and unstylish. She arrives at the courthouse late to respond to her husband's suit for custody of their child. The judge asks Wanda to speak for herself. She tells him that the child would be better off if the dad got custody. There's an element of Herman Melville's Bartleby to Wanda's rebellion; when she tells the judge the child would be better off without her, it is less a matter of gender-based rebellion than a statement of fact. She'd prefer not to be married; she'd prefer not to be a mother. And, no, she can't or won't explain why.[53] Her behavior in the courtroom is baffling *and* transgressive and for many filmgoers at the time, unforgivable—a daring narrative gambit on Loden's part to be sure.

Wanda then takes us on a road trip—it's a trope, of course in the counterculture era and more narrowly in several mad housewife films—but hers covers little geographical or emotional distance. Her escape from housewifery stalls at a series of grubby local bars where she stops to offer sex for booze, a meal, and a safe place to sleep off the night. The sex Wanda so casually offers as currency isn't much fun for her or for her partners. And Loden's unselfconscious on-screen nudity in these encounters is by intention and design a lot more startling than the airbrushed, mainstream alternative. Loden's *Wanda* seems somehow more *naked* in the many ways we might want to use the term.

Wanda's life briefly changes, and not necessarily for the better, when she meets a gruff bank robber named Mr. Dennis (Michael Higgins) with whom she forges a sort of relationship. Everything with Wanda is always only "sort-of." They sleep and eat together. He buys her some clothes. And then he elicits her help in a caper—a bad idea, it turns out, because Wanda is a lousy accomplice. She gets delayed by a chatty cop and arrives late for the getaway ride. Mr. Dennis gets caught and the film ends with Wanda alone again, baffled by events that have moved too quickly for her.

Wanda won a Best Foreign Film Award at the Venice Film Festival and it got screened at Cannes. In 1970 such prestige showcases did well to impress one's colleagues and friends, but did little to boost a film's chances in the North American box office. In fact, *Wanda* failed after the festival playoffs to attract a single American distributor. Harry Shuster, a wildlife park entrepreneur who financed the production, in the eleventh hour created a new company, Bardene International just to book the film. *Wanda* cost Shuster between $75,000 and $160,000 to produce. (Estimates vary.) And even at the low end of such a paltry production and distribution budget, the film still lost money.

Loden was a terrific actor and promising director, but a lousy promoter—not quite so obstinate and obtuse as Mark Frechette, but close. Just as the film was about to open theatrically, she told interviewers precisely what she was thinking . . . about her movie, about movies in general, about Hollywood and America. She effectively if unintentionally "positioned" her film as a New Wave art project, a counterculture, counter-Hollywood film. She might as well have told the Hollywood establishment to get lost and everyday filmgoers not to see her film.

FIGURE 30. Barbara Loden in *Wanda* (1970, Bardene International), a film she also wrote and directed.

In an interview with McLandish Phillips for the *New York Times*, Loden remarked: "I really hate slick pictures. They're too perfect to be believable. . . . The slicker the technique is, the slicker the content becomes, until everything turns into Formica, including the people."[54] Talking with Kevin Thomas of the *Los Angeles Times*, Loden spoke admiringly of the crude New York underground films produced by Andy Warhol—films she said offered inspiration for *Wanda*.[55] Loden described *Wanda* to Rex Reed as an "anti-movie," in which she endeavored "to present the story without manipulating the audience and telling them what their responses should be."[56] Reed had no idea what she was talking about. And he wasn't alone.

On February 15, 1972, well after the film's first run was complete, Loden did a guest spot on daytime TV's *"Mike Douglas Show,"* cohosted that week by John Lennon and Yoko Ono. The conversation with Loden quickly veers, with all eyes on Ono, to what it might be like to have a really famous husband. Kazan's name, maybe by advance agreement, is never mentioned. Loden refers to him only as "my husband." But everyone on the dais knows who they are talking about. She and Kazan live separate lives, she tells Douglas, they have separate interests. Loden then comments admiringly at John and Yoko's amiable collaboration, their "togetherness." Lennon quips, "There are two angles to having a famous husband." The remark dangles. Everyone on the dais nods; of all the people in the world in 1972, Lennon and Ono should know.

Later in the spot, mostly because Douglas doesn't seem to know who Loden is, Ono asks Loden to recount the *Wanda* development backstory. Loden talks about how she did not intend to direct *Wanda* herself; she figured she'd hand it off to someone else, a man most likely. Ono nods. Her husband (Kazan, unidentified) encouraged her to direct because he figured someone else, a man most likely, would ruin it. "There are," as Lennon has just reminded us, "two angles to having a famous husband."

Douglas was an amiable lightweight; quite unlike today's snarky talk show hosts, he had little or no personality. Whatever his guests tell him seems quite like news to him. At one point, Douglas asks Loden if she ever appears in her films. The actress politely reminds him that she played the lead in *Wanda*, which is why she's on the show. Douglas dumbly confesses he's not seen the film, then finally takes a look up at the cue cards, which—we can fairly imagine the bold capital letters and exclamation points—bring him back on message, prompting him to ask Loden to talk about *Wanda*.

Douglas asks: "So what's it about?" The question takes Loden somehow by surprise. She collects her thoughts and offers a rambling pitch. Wanda, the character, "doesn't know what she wants. She just knows what she doesn't want. She is trying to get out of this very ugly type of existence, but she doesn't have the equipment. . . .

She doesn't know how to get out of her problem. . . . She can't get a job, she doesn't know how to take care of children, life is a mystery to her . . . [so she] 'drops out.'" Douglas has no idea what to ask to follow-up, so Loden fills the silence. Wanda is "passive, like a lot of people in society today." She lets everyone "walk over her." Wanda is a mad housewife. But she has no idea why.

Few in the live or home audience ever got an opportunity to see the film—its first run had by the show's airing ended, and given the nudity and oddball content it is hard to imagine *Wanda* airing on network TV. Still, Douglas cues a clip. The chosen clip—the courtroom custody scene—seems hardly a teaser for a movie anyone in Douglas's orbit might actually want to see. The audience applauds respectfully—it's that kind of show—and Douglas cuts to commercial.

When the show comes back on the air, Douglas stumbles over an introduction of Lennon's band: he calls it the Plastic Ono Band and then Elephants Memory—two different outfits, but it's all beyond him. Yoko fronts the group and sings "Shake." Lennon seems somehow interested, amused maybe—it's heartbreaking, really, for anyone who has ever heard of the Beatles. Loden joins the band and quite out of time plays a conga drum, thankfully un-miked. It has been among the worst ten minutes in TV history and it will be one of her last public appearances.

Assuming Loden was realistic about *Wanda*'s limited potential at the box office, the critical reception of the film (in the United States at least) still had to be disappointing. Several reviewers failed to distinguish between Loden the bright creative artist and the white trash loser she plays in the film. The character is a dumb blonde, they observed, so Loden (a blonde) must be dumb too. Judith Crist and Pauline Kael—two women Loden might have expected or hoped to be sympathetic—judged the director and the character she played just as harshly. Kael opened her *New Yorker* review by asserting, "There is much to praise" in *Wanda*. And then went about killing the film. Loden, Kael writes condescendingly, is "a beginner.... There's nothing coy or facile in her approach, she's doing things the hard way." What Kael really wants is a different film about a different (sort of) woman: "[Wanda is] an attractive girl but such a sad, ignorant slut, there is nowhere for her or the picture to go but down."[57]

Loden never wrote, directed, or acted in another feature film—but not for want of trying. Several projects stalled in development, starting with another mad housewife film. It was to be titled (with a wink at *Love Story*, the popular novel and 1970 film): *Love Means Always Having to Say You're Sorry* and it was to be about a married woman involved with three men at the same time. Loden planned to cast Joe Dallesandro, an actor with deep ties to Warhol and the New York underground, as one of the men. Financing never materialized. Packaging the project with Dallesandro, a fascinating albeit underground talent, didn't help.

In 1973, there was a mooted development deal with the producer Ray Stark and Columbia. It too fell through. A year later, Loden's name appeared alongside Hopper's, Scorsese's, and Nicholson's as part of the producer Bert Schneider's and the filmmaker Henry Jaglom's HHH Rainbow Productions.[58] Among the titles optioned by HHH were four novels by Anais Nin;[59] we can today only imagine what Loden would have done with any of them. According to Kazan, after HHH Rainbow came to nothing, Loden began working on an adaptation of Kate Chopin's *The Awakening*. That project stalled when Loden was diagnosed with advanced-stage breast cancer. She died a few years later, in 1980, age forty-eight, with pretty much nothing to show for nearly a decade of hustling in the development hell reserved for talented Hollywood women.

Wanda has become for art-filmgoers and cine-scholars a hallmark of feminist filmmaking—a mad housewife film of a different stripe, if you will, about a woman whose inarticulate rebellion evinced the peculiar predicament of working-class women in rustbelt America.

Sadly, *Wanda* was *not* embraced by seventies feminists. As Loden mused in a 1974 interview, "A lot of women are insulted by *Wanda* because they think it shows women in a bad way. . . . But women like Wanda are out there, and need to be heard. . . . The whole point of why I wanted to make the film was that these women never get a chance; nobody knows about their existence." Ignoring "a human being like Wanda who was unfortunate enough to be born into that kind of life," Loden remarked, was downright disrespectful.

Loden knew plenty of women like Wanda when she was growing up. Once upon a time she was quite like her, and but for a little luck, but for her good looks and talent, she could have ended up like Wanda, stuck in some awful relationship, some awful predicament with some awful guy, in some awful nowheresville, just like her film counterpart.

Loden was by nature bashful. (A lot of actors are.) She was much more likely in interviews to talk about the French New Wave or the New York cine-underground than her own work. She would have never been so pretentious as to compare herself to Truffaut or Godard, but it's hard to miss that the ending of *Wanda*, a freeze-frame, alludes to Truffaut's *The 400 Blows* and Godard's *Breathless*. When asked about her influences, in addition to Godard Loden cited two, neither American: Satyajit Ray and Luis Buñuel. Loden said she could watch Ray's *Pather Panchali* "over and over," then added: "My favorite film is Buñuel's *Los Olvidados*," the Spanish-born auteur's neorealist film about desperate street kids in Mexico City's slums, released in the United States under the title, *The Young and the Damned*.[60]

Realism may well be the common thread here among Loden's faves and her *Wanda*, and for good reason. Loden based *Wanda* on a true story—a back-page item she read in the *New York Daily News* about a woman sentenced to twenty years as an accomplice in a failed bank robbery. After receiving such a stiff sentence, the woman was offered an opportunity to speak to the court. Rather than plead for mercy or blame the men who got her into such a fix, she thanked the judge. She later told a *Daily News* reporter, simply: the judge seemed "nice."[61] Wanda was developed out of that story—a minor news story about an unremarkable person left baffled, like Wanda, at what all has happened around and to her.

After watching Loden's mash-up of New Wave cinema and dumb-ass American true crime, we can safely conclude she not only knew what she was doing, she made the film she wanted to make the way she wanted to make it. "There was just myself, a cameraman, a sound man, and a fellow who ran errands," she remarked in a 1974 interview. "I like working this way instead of having other people do these things for me." It was a hands-on, stripped-down production—a key to the New Wave/direct cinema realist style she was after. She delegated very little, but when she did, her choices were spot on. The cinematographer Nick Proferes in particular seems smartly chosen; he had shot *Monterey Pop*, a landmark direct-cinema title, for D. A. Pennebaker three years earlier. Using a documentary film cameraman was a tactic Godard would have surely appreciated.

There are today some famous fans of the film and its director, including the National Book Award winning novelist Don DeLillo, who has published a remarkable essay about the film. For DeLillo, Loden's title character is "a lost soul," a woman whose sad life Loden smartly "doesn't attempt to enlarge." Wanda is so odd and invisible; she just has to be real. Channeling his inner film critic, DeLillo writes astutely: "[*Wanda*] does not belong to the neorealist tradition. There is no social commentary: only a woman of shriveled perspective. [*Wanda*] is not film noir. There is no mingling of atmospheric suspense and fateful resolution. The bank robbery is not paced differently from the rest of the film. It is ordinary: with guns. [*Wanda*] is the dark side of the moon of *Bonnie and Clyde*, flat, scratchy, skewed without choreographed affect but not without feeling."[62]

The comparison to *Bonnie and Clyde* is apt. The similarities and differences are telling. Penn's film opens with Bonnie naked and alone in her room. All she really wants is out of that house, out of West Texas. She leaps at a chance to run off with Clyde, the handsome young man she spies fixing to steal her mother's car. *Wanda* stages a low-rent, low-octane version of the same basic setup. Like Bonnie, Wanda wants out of her life and figures a new man may be her best shot at escape. She dumps her husband and child, and then drifts into the lives of a series of barely interested and mostly unattractive would-be Clyde Barrows. Faye Dunaway's Bonnie gets Warren Beatty. Wanda attracts a series of balding barflies who with one exception stick around only long enough to get what they want from her. And with regard to the lone exception, Mr. Dennis, the one guy who sticks around: with all due respect, Michael Higgins is not Warren Beatty.

Bonnie transforms Clyde into a colorful, political criminal and a decent lover. She is the brains in the partnership. Wanda is by contrast never more than a passive accomplice. She makes little impact on any of her one-night stands, except for Mr. Dennis. If Loden was intentionally rebooting Penn's *Bonnie and Clyde*, she seemed determined to cut everything from that film that made it popular and successful.

Loden did not live to see the rediscovery of *Wanda*. And that's too bad. The film has lately earned a degree of appreciation if not, still, a very big audience, thanks to a Criterion Edition DVD, recent art museum and art house screenings of an excellent UCLA Film Archive restored print, and endorsements from a handful of influential women artists and scholars: the film's fans include the actress Isabelle Huppert, the writer Marguerite Duras, and the scholar-curator Nathalie Leger.[63] The current regard for the film reveals just how well Loden and her work have traveled through time—and that is not something you can say about a lot of films of the counterculture era.

Wanda's current *importance* far exceeds its cultural significance or impact back in 1970. And there are some good reasons why. Wanda was never *about* the counterculture. It was instead, in and of itself, counterculture—well ahead yet also very much of its time. Wanda is one of a kind. So was its director. Hollywood had no idea what to do with either of them.

Parting Glances

There were reasons—a lot of reasons it turns out, why things turned out the way they did for the four Hollywood women discussed here. All four women arrived at a particularly volatile time, a time when the film colony seemed pulled and drawn in several directions at once: politics, drugs, cults; the Panthers and Hoover; North Vietnam and Beverly Hills; God and Elvis; Antonioni, Godard, and Warhol.

Seberg arrived in Hollywood a white Midwestern teenager with a keen interest in doing more with the money she made than just buying a neat house. With her first paycheck she bought uniforms for Native American school kids. She later gravitated to the Hollywood progressive crowd and fell in with some charismatic Black men soliciting funds and attention from them. Growing up in Iowa, Seberg dreamed of joining the NAACP. A few years later, she was palling around with the Panthers, pissing off J. Edgar Hoover, a nasty and powerful man who chased her out of Hollywood and then out of her life.

Jane Fonda arrived with a lot more in her pocket, so to speak, enviable advantages that in the end made success all but unpreventable: a famous father and brother, plenty of connections (Strasberg, Logan, the weight of the Actors Studio), and let's face it, a boatload of talent as an actor (watch closely her jittery performance in *Klute* and you'll see). Fonda fully lived the late twentieth century, dallying along the way with a trio of powerful and interesting and very different men—the romantic fantasist Vadim, the activist intellectual Hayden, the iconoclastic media mogul Ted Turner. All three were always in the end *her husband*; such was the force of her personality, her talent, her commitment.

Hart's discovery narrative began like (of all the unlikely people) Lana Turner's—a schoolgirl discovered and suddenly vaulted to stardom. But with Hart we get a very different variation on that theme. Plenty of starlets dig being a starlet: the money, the men (or/and women), the adulation. Plenty seek the company of others quite like them—other celebrities in the throes of the same exciting narrative. Not Hart. She knew her mind, and she knew better.

Hart dated a handful of eligible men, some of them mid-level TV and movie stars, but it never seemed to go anywhere. She told Hedda Hopper she feared she was destined to be an old maid. And she didn't know why. To manage the business of being a celebrity, Hart sought the company of Hollywood women twice her age—women with lots of talent and experience. She was for a while Hal Wallis's protégé. He was a tough character with lots of power in the industry. Walking away from him could not have been easy. But Hart knew her mind. She got out before Hollywood got to her.

Loden was not so lucky. Whatever happened on the set of *The Swimmer* was bad luck and bad career strategy; it was Lancaster's film, and she should have known that—and she should have behaved accordingly. But she was not the sort of woman to behave for men. Her notion of a New American Cinema was a mix of Warhol, Pennebaker, and Godard—a neat recipe, but not one geared at profit. She got her hands on a hundred grand or so and made a little feminist movie, which did not exactly set the course for future ventures (for her or for more films like it). Seventies feminists found Wanda (the Bartleby barfly who, as Loden told John and Yoko on the *Mike Douglas Show*, knows only what she doesn't want) as baffling as my twenty-first-century students do.

Barbara Loden wasn't so much crushed as brushed aside by Hollywood. She could have been a movie star. She maybe could have been a New Hollywood auteur as well, though the odds were steeper there. Instead, she became just another sad story in a town quite teeming with sad stories—and a minor-case casualty at that, as absent were the dizzying heights from which to fall. It's a shame really; she had that gift from the fairies and, at first, decent timing. An object lesson then: the odds are always long, the road trip particularly tough for women in Hollywood.

4   *Charles Manson's Hollywood*

Los Angeles, outskirts of, early summer 1969. Charles Manson is for the moment just another anonymous, albeit colorful edge-city character manning the supply chain of drugs and sexually willing young women serving the boundless appetite of L.A.'s spoiled-brat celebrity subculture. Some of those who do business with him know about his alternative lifestyle; they know that he has decamped with a couple dozen scruffy kids—his "Family"—at a decommissioned movie ranch in nearby Chatsworth (just north and west of Hollywood). Others don't know anything about him. And they don't much care. Manson is like a lot of people in their lives. He provides a service. He's the help.

On August 8, a particularly grisly multiple murder takes place at 10050 Cielo Drive in the tony Benedict Canyon neighborhood. Found dead at the site: an heiress and her jet-setter boyfriend, a celebrity hairdresser (i.e., a man who cuts the hair of famous movie stars), a pregnant young actress, and a teenager in the wrong place at the wrong time. Two nights later, in the Los Feliz neighborhood due east of Cielo Drive: another home invasion and two more killings. The two murder scenes are related. But the cops don't know that yet.

In early December, police investigators finally catch a break. They stumble upon the perpetrators of the crimes. The mastermind of the murders is "a self-styled hippie guru"—"self-styled," as Manson is in fact neither a hippie nor a guru. The newspapers make the most of the Family's unconventional, counterculture lifestyle and depict Manson as a cult leader. But plenty of people in Hollywood know better. At least they know something else, too: that Tex Watson, Manson's right-hand man who participated in both sets of murders, had been in the past year a frequent houseguest at 10050 Cielo Drive; he was in fact a regular on the counterculture Hollywood party circuit. No one knows much about him; few ever bothered to ask for his name. But no one needed to be told why he was always around, "what he brought to the party" so to speak.

For months, the murders were assumed to be random and motiveless. The truth—that the killers had (albeit in an oblique, truly crazy way) targeted the city's rich and ridiculous—would be, in so many ways, worse.

The Manson Family story began in the Haight-Ashbury neighborhood in San Francisco during the "Summer of Love." Manson was in full improvisation mode after yet another stint in prison, subtly and serially tweaking a well-honed "pimp riff" with the "hippie free-love-riff" he picked up on the streets there. When they decided to hit the road, he and his new entourage headed south. Everyone was hitting the road back then, with the destination not necessarily the key to the trip.

At the time, Manson figured he was doing all right. He had a handful of sexually willing young women devoted to and dependent upon him; he and they were living rough, but free. They ended up on the outskirts of Los Angeles—at the Spahn Movie Ranch in Chatsworth, north-northwest of Santa Monica. Fame and celebrity were not initially on the agenda, but both became part of the story soon enough. First Manson got lucky—really lucky. And then just as suddenly his luck ran out. In some ways, his L.A. story wasn't so unique. In others...

One fateful day, two of his "girls" (as most everyone back then referred to them, *girls* was certainly the word Manson would have used at the time) were out hitchhiking. A for-real rock star—the Beach Boys' Dennis Wilson—stopped to pick them up. The girls introduced Wilson to Manson. Wilson then introduced Manson to Terry Melcher, a successful music industry executive.

In Hollywood, the odds are always against you. Few "make it," and among the few who do, even fewer hang on for very long. Patience may well be a virtue, but it's not indulged much in L.A.

After a few months, Wilson and Melcher got bored with and maybe a little spooked by Manson. So they moved on. Manson's long shot at a recording career disappeared along with them. For most any other aspiring musician trying and failing in Los Angeles, that would have been that. But Manson was not most any musician. And he was not so easily set back.

The murders on August 8 and 10 proved to be a moment of truth for a lot of Los Angelinos, many of whom depended upon Manson or some other guy quite like him—some guy who got illegal things or did dirty jobs for them. Being counterculture in Hollywood meant one thing before August 1969 and something else again afterward. It would be foolish to argue otherwise.

In the weeks and months after the murders, movie and music industry people in the celebrity party scene were wont to say that what happened to Sharon Tate, the ill-fated movie star on Cielo Drive, could have easily happened to them. And there was none of the usual Hollywood bluster in saying so. They were right: it could have. The murders did not mark the end of the Hollywood counterculture. But they did mark its nadir, its most terrifying antiestablishment, antisocial climax.

The Outskirts

The Manson murders were awful, unbelievable, but not wholly unprecedented. There have always been shady and dangerous characters loitering on the margins of Hollywood scene. And every once in a while, one of these characters surfaces to make their mark—if only to remind everyone else they're there. Manson was not the first or last lost, crazy lunatic to crash the L.A. party. He did, however, give the familiar story line a counterculture vibe, a counterculture spin.

Movie and music industry celebrities have always had money and lots of free time. Many of them have over the years engaged in a range of risky diversions. Dating as far back as the 1910s, movie industry celebrities have flirted with countercultural, subcultural tastes: illicit drugs, unconventional sexual practices and arrangements. In doing so they have encountered the difficult and dangerous people such proclivities require and involve. There have been as a consequence of these encounters, a fair share of Southland tragedies: suicides, murders, drug busts, deaths by misadventure.

Among the first: the still unsolved murder of the movie actor and director William Desmond Taylor, shot in the back at his home in the posh Westlake District of Los Angeles in February 1922.[1] The murder was initially thought to be drug related, a retaliation, or so the studio spun things, for Taylor's work combatting drug traffickers preying upon the Hollywood movie colony. The story, as it began to unfold, and then unfold some more, proved to be more complicated than the studio public relations team let on. Turns out, there was no shortage of shady suspects who may well have wanted Taylor dead.

Even a quick survey of the several suspects in the Taylor case revealed a web of intersecting subcultures and unsavory subplots—a sordid picture of the movie colony circa 1922. The authorities' first suspect was Taylor's African American chauffeur, Henry Peavy. He was the only Black man in Taylor's orbit, so no surprise he was a person of interest. In addition to Peavy, law enforcement looked at Taylor's former servant Edward Sands—a lifelong criminal. Sands had split town before the murders and (as it was later revealed) he had been forging checks against Taylor's account for a while. Sands never resurfaced. People in L.A. disappear all the time, especially guys like Sands. So the cops collectively shrugged, and moved on.

Of interest as well were the movie stars Mabel Normand (whose love letters were found on the premises) and Mary Miles Minter (who left behind monogrammed underwear). Many internet Taylorologists (it's still a thing) contend that the Normand and Minter souvenirs were planted in Taylor's bungalow.[2] Studio emissaries, they say, had an hour to sort through and plant evidence at the crime scene before the authorities arrived.

Normand was a talented comedienne—a former Chaplin costar. There were rumors that she was also a habitual cocaine user and (rumor had it), with Taylor, into wild, kinky sex. She and Taylor were rumored to have been members of the sex-magic satanic cult, *Ordo Templis Orientis*, organized by the notorious Aleister Crowley. Suffice to say: Normand and Taylor got around.

Minter was never really a suspect, but her mother, Charlotte Shelby, was. Taylor was thirty years older than Minter. Allegations that he deflowered the young actress and that Shelby killed him for harming her child (and diminishing the value of her meal ticket) seemed to the press and the cops at the time quite irresistible.

A late addition to the suspect list was an actress named Margaret Gibson, who had appeared with Taylor in four films in 1914. A few months after the murder, Gibson was arrested for vagrancy (most likely, prostitution), blackmail, and opium trafficking. The charges were eventually dropped after she made the necessary payoff with money supplied most likely by the clients she was blackmailing, clients who figured a quiet end to the matter benefitted everyone. In 1964, Gibson confessed to the crime on her deathbed.

Gibson's was not the only deathbed confession. According to the film historian Simon Louvish, the film producer Mack Sennett, for whom Normand worked for a while, confessed on *his* deathbed that he decided to kill Taylor, "for being queer," and for giving Normand drugs.[3] The possibility that Taylor was not fighting drug traffickers but was instead profitably involved in the drug business remains a point of contention. That Taylor might have been a closeted gay man did not circulate widely in 1922. It may, though, explain the letters and underwear planted by the studio at the scene of the crime; "evidence" that incriminated Normand and Minter and made Taylor out to be a ladies (and not a gay) man. The possibility that Taylor was gay helps explain why Peavy, dubbed by the press a "flashy character" (newspaper code for gay in those days) was so quickly released after police questioning. Stories have surfaced that the cops released Peavy because he had an alibi—he was, this story goes, at the time of the murder in Griffith Park procuring young male "talent" for his boss. At the behest of the studio, that alibi was not shared with the press.

We will never know for sure who killed Taylor, but the identity of the killer is, with due apologies to the avid true crime detectives on the internet, beside the point here. The key to the Taylor story, and to its relationship to the Manson story, is the array of associations between Taylor, the celebrity victim, and the many unsavory characters in his daily orbit, characters making their living feeding (and feeding off of) the Hollywood movie colony. Peavy and Sands and Gibson and Normand and Crowley—all of them had ties to the illegal drug trade, to Satanic cults, to (for the times) unconventional sexual appetites and tastes. And Taylor knew all of them.

Living among such a colorful cast of characters, Taylor was himself living a secret life. Taylor, it turns out, was not Taylor; he was William

Cunningham Deane-Tanner. And Deane-Tanner had deserted a wife and child on the east coast in 1908. Sometime between leaving New York and arriving in L.A. he changed his name and concocted a new biography. Taylor was for the duration of his career in the movie business, living life on a knife's edge, living in fear of being unmasked. That he took a bullet in the back one day for doing or saying something, for being found out, for getting involved with someone with a short fuse or a grudge was no surprise to anyone who knew him. And the murder was no surprise to anyone who knew 1920s Hollywood. Something bad was bound to happen to someone.

For counterculture-era Los Angelinos who'd been around through the postwar boom, the murders perpetrated by Manson surely harkened back to another seemingly random and savage crime: the January 15, 1947, murder of Elizabeth Short, a.k.a. the Black Dahlia.[4] It too was the sort of crime folks were not likely to forget; most anyone around L.A. and the industry at the time could tell you where they were when they heard the news, when the local papers ran with the story about a young woman discovered dead in a vacant lot on the edge of town.

The details of the Black Dahlia story were horrifying: Short was murdered, her body drained of its blood, cut in half, then driven from the scene of the crime and dumped by the side of the road. A sketchy biography emerged in the newspapers. Short was a naive Hollywood wannabe, an innocent, an out-of-towner, a good girl gone bad in the city's depraved bar scene. She was—and not so uniquely—well poised to be somebody's victim.

Manson was a very different sort of Hollywood wannabe. And he arrived in town with a very different resume: ex-con, thief, pimp, con man, would-be hippie guru. No one had ever told him, as so many had told Short, that he should be in pictures; no one had ever told him he had any talent at all.

FIGURE 31. The Beach Boys' Dennis Wilson photographed in 1977 for the cover of his first solo album, *Pacific Ocean Blue*. (Creative Commons: "wilson, dennis-pacific ocean blue" by cdrummbks is licensed with CC BY 2.0. To view a copy of this license, visit https://creativecommons.org/licenses/by/2.0/).

Early in the summer of 1968, when Dennis Wilson picked up the hippie-girl hitchhikers Patricia Krenwinkel and Ella Jo Bailey, it set in motion a fateful sequence of events. Krenwinkel and Bailey introduced Wilson to Manson. The rock star opened his house to the three of them. In Hollywood in those days, people picked up hitchhikers; they invited total strangers into their homes. After August 1969, such a social fluidity would quite abruptly end.

Wilson later introduced Manson to Melcher. He told his friend that Manson "had something. . . . Charlie's real cosmic, man. He's deep. He listens to Beatles records and gets messages from them about what to do next." Little did he know. For a while, Manson and his scruffy entourage lived with Wilson rent-free. They got to drive the musician's car, which they used, among other errands, to go dumpster diving. Melcher stupidly dangled a recording contract, a tactic he'd used before to get in on the action. The tactic was in play at Wilson's and it gave Melcher access to Manson's girls and dope.

To be clear, Manson was not talentless. In fact, Wilson liked one of Manson's songs enough to steal it. (OK, Wilson didn't exactly *steal* it; in the most repeated version of the story, Wilson acquired the publication rights for a very modest up-front cash payoff and a BSA motorcycle.) Wilson subtly revised Manson's "Cease to Exist" without Manson's permission. He retitled the song "Never Learn Not to Love" and recorded it with the Beach Boys. Wilson took sole credit as the song's composer. The Beach Boys released "Never Learn Not to Love" as a single on the B-side of "Bluebirds over the Mountain," which charted modestly at number sixty-one and then included the song on "20/20," an album released in February 1969.

Soon after "Never Learn Not to Love" was pressed, Wilson found a bullet neatly placed on his bed. "I gave him a bullet," Manson later explained, "because he changed the words to my song."[5]

At the time Manson encountered Wilson, the musician was neck deep in the sex, drugs, and rock-and-roll world that seemed daily to be magically presenting itself to him. Manson was just another in what had become by then a long list of lively procurers of young, sexually available women and mind-altering substances. When Melcher carelessly discussed the possibility of making a record together, Manson took the prospect seriously. Manson later discovered that Melcher was never really serious, so he decided to send the Hollywood hot shot and by extension the celebrity subculture in which

Melcher prospered a message: Charles Manson was not to be fucked with. Unlike the Dahlia, unlike Taylor, Manson was never going to be anybody's victim.

A Simple Jailhouse Logic

Manson auditioned for Melcher twice, not at a recording studio with a band of studio musicians but instead alone and on the outskirts of the city, in a steep gully at the Spahn Movie Ranch. For those less limber and not used to the locale, and that included Melcher and the recording industry hangers-on he brought with him, there was a rope to ease the descent. The symbolism, months later, would not be lost on Melcher; he was that day in fact descending into an underworld he was too stupid to recognize.

There were, as Melcher had hoped, some of Manson's girls in the pit. Some sang along with Manson as he performed his songs. Others tapped in time. It was not really what Melcher was used to. And it was surely not a professional audition. But Manson was not to know that.

Failure is built into the celebrity bargain. And the frequency of failure in its way justifies the many and astonishing perks of success. Some folks are born lucky, like Melcher, whose mother was the Hollywood recording and movie star Doris Day. He, to be fair, had a talent for music management. The Byrds, his most successful band, were pretty terrific and successful in their prime. But talent was for him beside the point; it was always going to be easy for Terry Melcher to get by in the business, to meet people willing and anxious to help his career.

In 1969, when Melcher met Manson, he had a reputation as a swinger. He hung out a lot with Wilson, and the two young men called themselves, without the slightest hint of embarrassment, "the golden penetrators."[6] The free love thing was a pretty good

FIGURE 32. The Family posed in the gully where Charles Manson auditioned for Terry Melcher and Gregg Jakobson (*Six Degrees of Helter Skelter*, Mike Dorsey, 2009, Mance Media).

deal for guys like them—not always so good for the women in their lives, as Karina Longworth, the auteur/host of the podcast "You Must Remember This," reports: "The secret history of [the counterculture Hollywood] story seemed to be the stories of women.... It would become gruesomely clear to me that the era of free love didn't leave every woman who was expecting to participate in it feeling more free."[7]

I suppose some might say Melcher got what he deserved—for promising Manson something he never intended to deliver, for exploiting and probably abusing young women, for being a selfish prick—that it was somehow karmic justice that he would become forever known as the guy Manson wanted dead on August 8, 1969, when he sent Susan Atkins, Linda Kasabian, Krenwinkel, and Watson to 10050 Cielo Drive. Manson knew Melcher was no longer living in the rented house, which poses an even grislier scenario, if such a thing is possible: Manson ordered Atkins et al. to kill whoever they stumbled upon there, a bunch of people none of them knew: the actress Sharon Tate (and her unborn child), the coffee heiress Abigail Folger, Folger's boyfriend Wojciech Frykowski, the hairdresser-to-the-stars Jay Sebring, and Steven Parent (an unlucky bystander with no relation to the celebrity occupants of the house). He meant only to send Melcher a message. A well-honed jailhouse logic held that living with others' blood on his hands would be worse for Melcher than being dead. Manson may well have been right about that.

Melcher got to tell his version of his encounter with Manson on August 23, 1971, when the L.A. district attorney and soon to be celebrity true crime author Vincent Bugliosi called Melcher to the stand as a state's witness in *The People of the State of California vs. Charles Denton [Tex] Watson*. Two years had passed since the awful events of August 1969 and Bugliosi was working his way through Manson's accomplices. Melcher's testimony was revealing if not entirely honest. It was the story he'd been telling since his name had come up in connection with the murder spree, a story in which he came off as an unlucky victim. And that was never the truth.[8]

Bugliosi opened the questioning by establishing a time line starting with Melcher's two-and-a-half-year tenancy at 10050 Cielo Drive—from the early summer of 1966 through the summer of 1968, nearly a full year before the murders. The DA then tracked Melcher's several encounters with Manson, all the way back to when Manson was crashing at Wilson's home and Melcher was living on Cielo Drive. "The day I met [Manson] he was playing songs," Melcher recalled. When it was time for him to head home, Melcher asked Wilson to drive him. And yes, "Manson was in the car" too. The line of questioning established that Manson knew where Melcher lived (in the summer of 1968, at least)—for Bugliosi, an important stipulation.

Bugliosi then moved on to a subsequent encounter, nearly a year later, in May 1969 at the Spahn Movie Ranch. Melcher recalled driving to the Ranch with one of Wilson's friends, a songwriter named Gregg Jakobson, on the pretense of listening to Manson play his songs. Bugliosi: "You went to the Spahn Ranch to audition someone?" Melcher: "That is right." Bugliosi: "Mr. Manson?" Melcher: "That is right." Later, Bugliosi: "Did Mr. Manson in fact perform for you?" Melcher: "Yes, he did." Bugliosi: "How long did this audition take place?" Melcher: "Perhaps an hour." With this line of questioning, Bugliosi established motive: revenge for a failed and, by implication, insincere audition—both scenarios an L.A. jury could easily understand.

Asked to describe the Ranch, Melcher noted: "The buildings weren't really inhabitable, they were mostly living outside." As to the site of the audition: "It was in a, I suppose you might call it, a gully." After Manson played his songs, the two men spoke, "briefly." Manson registered, according to Melcher, "a keen desire to record." Melcher offered instead some constructive suggestions and then asked Manson if he was a member of the AFL or AFTRA musicians' unions. He was not. Melcher realized then that even if he had liked what he saw and heard, Manson would not be able to record with him. Melcher ran a union shop. Melcher tried to explain this to Manson—imagine that conversation, if you will; the jury certainly did. Baffled by what he dumbly disregarded as red tape that would not have anything to do with him, Manson ended the conversation by boasting that *he* wasn't interested in joining a guild. In doing so he gave Melcher an easy out.

Bugliosi moved on to another line of questioning: "Did you give Mr. Manson any money." "Yes," Melcher replied; he gave Manson $50. Bugliosi: "Why?" Melcher: "Well, they all seemed to be hungry." A subsequent snapshot of life at the Ranch followed. Melcher told Bugliosi that he observed fifty or so hippies living rough, hungry, broke, desperate. The description helped Bugliosi explain to the jury how and why once decent kids (now living rough, hungry, broke, desperate) might be willing to commit murder at Manson's behest.

Bugliosi then asked Melcher to recount his return to the Ranch a week later, with Jakobson and a fellow recording industry exec named Mike Dacy. This time, Melcher brought portable recording equipment with him, which got Manson thinking he was being seriously considered for a contract. An obvious question Bugliosi never asked: Why did Melcher go back if he wasn't interested in (and knew, because of the union situation, would not be) recording Manson? Bugliosi certainly knew the answer. And he didn't want it on the record; he didn't want it confusing the story he was telling.

Bugliosi segued from Manson's second audition at the Ranch to Melcher's multiple encounters with Watson, the defendant in the case. Melcher testified that Watson made "approximately six" visits to the house on Cielo Drive he had rented from Rudy Altobelli. Bugliosi asked why had Watson visited? Melcher replied: "Watson was a friend of Wilson's and Jakobson's and was often tagging around with either or both of those men." Melcher then added that in the fall of 1968 he went to Europe to supervise a recording session and Jakobson housesat for him. During that time, Melcher surmised to Bugliosi, Watson likely paid Jakobson a visit or two. Bugliosi's examination of Melcher convinced the jury that Watson, Manson's right-hand man, had been to the Cielo Drive house on several occasions and knew the layout. But the DA did not want the jury to think so much about why. Throughout his questioning of Melcher, Bugliosi tiptoed around the drug culture subtext to Watson's role in the music executive's life—a subcultural connection about which he was certainly aware. Bugliosi knew that Watson was never, in any way the jury might use the term, Jakobson's "friend."

Watson's attorney Maxwell Keith handled the cross-examination. He was never getting Watson off, he knew that; but he nonetheless tried to get the jury to think a bit more about Melcher's relationship with Watson, considering how Watson looked, how he lived, and who he lived with in the summer of 1969. Keith asked Melcher if Watson was a hippie. Melcher replied that he didn't use or like the term. Did Manson or "his girls" wear blue jeans or love beads? Melcher couldn't recall. Did Watson have long hair in the summers of 1968 and 1969? Maybe. The questions seemed designed to highlight the difference between Melcher's and Manson/Watson's entourages. How might a "dirty hippie" like Watson find himself a welcomed guest... at least six times!... at Doris Day's son's home?

Invoking the term *hippie* was strategic. While we might use the term today more casually to refer to someone living a free-spirited lifestyle, someone perhaps stuck in the sixties, it was used back then to mark certain generational and ideological differences. The jury did not look kindly upon "long hairs." In his cross-examination of Melcher, Keith wanted the jury to imagine Watson as he might have looked back in 1968 and 1969; he wanted the jury to imagine why Melcher and by extension Wilson felt comfortable hanging out with a guy like Watson, a dirty hippie who lived on a commune and did drugs and engaged in wild, promiscuous sex—the sort of guy who would become Manson's right-hand man.

A second line of Keith's questioning focused on the auditions. First, there was the unlikely setting: the gully. Second, the very different way Melcher and Manson seemed to view the performances. Keith got Melcher to admit he wasn't at the time interested in recording "a new singer." He had returned for a second audition less than a week after the first as "a favor to Mr. Jakobson," which was, let's face it, nonsense. Melcher went on to describe Manson's second performance as "rehearsed" and "staged," which is to say Manson took this second encounter really seriously, because he didn't know (yet) that he was being played.

Keith pressed and Melcher eventually confessed that he had indulged aspiring musicians lots of times and was always careful

FIGURE 33. The music producer Terry Melcher with the actress Candice Bergen at the Whiskey a Go Go in 1967. Melcher and Bergen lived together at 10050 Cielo Drive (Everett Collection).

not to let on what he was thinking. Looking back on the first audition, Melcher opined: "If one is in the business of recording people, auditioning them, both vocally and as a composer, you learn to adapt a certain amount of . . . " Keith completed the sentence for him, "diplomacy . . ." to which Melcher replied, "Yes." For emphasis, Keith suggested that it was often a matter of, "Don't call me, I'll call you." Melcher ignored the question and dissembled, saying he left the Ranch after telling Manson that "[he] would be in touch with him through Mr. Jakobson." Melcher had, of course, no intention of doing any such thing.

As to how and why Watson had become part of Melcher's social circle, the last of the three parts of his cross, Keith asked Melcher if Watson had attended parties at his Cielo Drive home, and if he had ever been an invited guest. Melcher again dissembled. He recalled

Watson only vaguely. He never got to know Watson, never talked with him for more than a minute at any one time. Watson was Jakobson's friend; he was Wilson's friend. He was part of someone else's entourage.

Watson was in fact a drug connection—a connection to Manson's entourage, so a sex connection as well. But neither Keith nor Bugliosi got Melcher to say so in court. The jury likely took Melcher at his word. But plenty of the celebrities around town knew what Watson was doing on Cielo Drive in the months before the murders. And that's what made August 8-10, 1969, so important in Hollywood history. Many of these celebrities had been to Cielo Drive once or twice for a party; they, as Keith's cross-examination of Melcher implied, had been to parties where Watson or someone quite like him—some hippie drug or sex connection—was usefully hanging around.

How much Manson believed or had invested in his own talent is today hard to gauge. We know he used his songs to assemble and entertain his flock. And his music was a big part of daily, Family life at the Ranch. But impressing Melcher was a whole different sort of challenge. We know that Manson rehearsed for the second audition, which explains why Manson got angry with Melcher when he realized the auditions were a hoax, and that the executive and his wealthy friends had made a fool of him. After the second audition, Melcher gave Manson $50 because the Family "looked hungry." The money struck Manson as a kiss-off, a tip (and a shitty one at that).

Manson told his followers that the murders would kick-start Helter Skelter, his apocalyptic vision of an impending race war. Bugliosi focused a lot on Helter Skelter at Manson's trial; but the DA was only doing his job, establishing one of several possible motives.

From stories told by his followers, we know that Helter Skelter was in fact something Manson talked a lot about. And we can trace its origins to Manson's Appalachian roots and to his experiences behind bars as a young man—that is, to the pervasive racism of his poor white-trash upbringing (it was his fundamentalist Christian grandmother who taught him about a forthcoming Rapture, as foretold in the Book of Revelations), and to the segregated societies he had witnessed and participated in at Boys Town, juvenile hall, and prison. Helter Skelter was a pathological vision to be sure, but not impossible to appreciate and understand given the subcultures Manson had emerged out of.

A quick summary: at the outset of Helter Skelter, Manson and his followers would assemble together in a pit (precise site and depth, TBA) where they would wait out a race war. Black Americans would win the initial conflict, and for a while the Family would remain underground, going about the business of increasing their numbers and further purifying the white race. The physical superiority that had allowed the Blacks to be victorious would be followed, in Manson's fantasy, by their realization that they were not intellectually equipped to maintain order and power. When the Family's numbers reached 144,000—a number specified in *Revelations 14:3*—Manson and his followers would (quite literally) resurface. The Blacks would acknowledge Manson as the reincarnation of Jesus (risen and born again, from the pit) and he would take his rightful place atop the post-race war world.

According to the cultural historian Dan Sinykin, the rhetoric of Helter Skelter underpins many of the apocalyptic pseudo-Christian white power subcultures that have taken shape in contemporary America. Such is Manson's legacy at its most troublesome and influential: "If we read Manson allegorically, we must read him not only as representing the violent end of the 60s, but as the warning shot, the start of a white apocalypticism that was to emerge from the disappointments and dislocations of the long downturn. He wasn't a hippie or a radical, even if at times he appropriated that language. He was a poor Appalachian aspirant to an American dream."[9]

Manson may have believed in Helter Skelter. Or he may have simply used it as a means to an end. He said a lot of different things to different people. He was in fact expert at telling people what they wanted to hear, preying on their insecurities. As the poet/singer/activist Ed Sanders wrote (and without the benefit of years of hindsight) in his 1971 book *The Family*, the key to Manson's ideology, if that's really the right term for the crazy stuff he told his fellow travelers, was that it was so malleable. The prophecy of Helter Skelter was serially and necessarily tweaked to mean whatever the available audience wanted or needed it to mean. "There was something in it for everybody," Sanders writes, "those who had creepy childhoods looked upon Helter Skelter as a means for saving the children. Others had a more racist point of view in that Charlie put up a picture of a white elite ultimately ruling over a black population. People who liked violence looked upon Helter Skelter as a chance to engage in warfare. People into robbery and chase dug it for its plunder and looting. End of the world freaks could really rejoice in Helter Skelter."[10]

Manson's apocalyptic, megalomaniacal fantasies—his pathological and narcissistic aspirations—were serially frustrated by his mother and his wives (that is, the women who abandoned him), by Wilson and Melcher, by internal struggles within the Family. He turned to Revelations though he was never in any real way religious, and the Beatles, who could never have imagined their music might be part of such an annihilating vision. Manson said as much on the stand. He knew the Beatles' record (the so-called "White Album") really well, which is something Wilson had remarked upon when he introduced Manson to Melcher. And the lyrics really did speak to him, directly and personally, operating in concert with the sprawling and crazy apocalyptic scenario he shared with the Family.

"I am only what you made me," Manson remarked during the trial, "I am only a reflection of you.... You made your children what they are ... these children who come at you with their knives, they are your children. You taught them. I didn't teach them . . . [and] as for Helter Skelter. Helter Skelter is confusion. Confusion is [and here he quotes Lennon and McCartney] coming down fast. . . . Why blame it on me? I didn't write the music."[11]

Manson was a manipulative psychopath and didn't have to believe in what he was saying to run with what seemed a persuasive riff. He was an unhappy product of his upbringing and of prison culture; he had seen enough pain and violence to believe in Armageddon. And he was for sure enough of a narcissist to believe it would all be about him.

Crucially, on the nights of August 8 and 10, 1969, I don't believe a race war was much on his mind. Instead, a fairly simple jailhouse logic prevailed. Here, we'd do well to take Manson at his word, taken verbatim from his testimony in court:

> I never went to school, so I never growed up to read or write so good. So I have stayed in jail and I have stayed stupid and I have stayed a child while I watched the rest of the world grow up and then I look at the things you do and don't understand. My father is the jailhouse, my father is your system. . . . I have done my best to get along in your world and now you want to kill me? Ha! I'm already dead. Have been all my life. I've spent 23 years in tombs you've built.[12]

Wilson and Melcher had no idea who or what they were dealing with. Neither did Tate and her privileged entourage, who could have hardly seen Manson coming. Neither did the whole entitled celebrity subculture. Being involved in the clandestine drug scene must have *felt* counterculture. It must have been exciting and a little bit *real* to defy convention (and federal drug laws)—not like all that play-acting in the movies. But it was also dangerous in a way these celebrities never stopped to consider—that is, until the second weekend of August 1969 rather scared them straight.

Who Was Charlie Manson?

Charles Manson was born on November 12, 1934, in Cincinnati, Ohio, the illegitimate son of sixteen-year-old Kathleen Maddox.[13] Manson grew up believing his birthday was the day before; Maddox, a drunk and petty criminal, only vaguely remembered he was born sometime around Veterans Day.[14] During Charles's early childhood, Maddox lived with a succession of men, one of whom, William Manson, married Maddox when she was pregnant with Charles and hung around just long enough to give her son his last name. After three years, William Manson secured a divorce, citing "gross neglect of duty." Charles was left with Kathleen.

So far as we can tell from the public record, the biological father was Colonel (his given name, not his military rank) Walker Henderson Scott, an occasional mill worker and (by local reputation) petty con artist. Scott left town well before the child's birth, setting in motion a trend that would characterize Charles Manson's life, at least the parts of that life spent outside prison.

In 1939, the same year Kathleen and William Manson broke up, Kathleen was arrested for robbery. Charles, then five years old, was sent to live with his aunt and uncle in West Virginia. When Kathleen was released from prison, she reclaimed her son and eventually they moved to Indianapolis. But motherhood was still beyond her. After several attempts to place her son in a foster home, she got some money together and sent him to the Gibault School in Terre Haute, a Catholic boarding school for boys. Charles was briefly happy there, but Kathleen could not keep up with the tuition and the boy was asked to move on. Rather than move back in with his mother, Charles, then only fourteen, emancipated. He made ends meet doing odd jobs and stealing things from local stores. Kathleen was anxious about the new arrangement, so she turned her son in to the juvenile authorities who ferried the teenager off to Boys Town in Omaha, Nebraska, over six hundred miles away.

In a feature piece written for the New York Times Magazine in anticipation of the July 1970 murder trial, a full four years before District Attorney Vincent Bugliosi's true crime best seller *Helter Skelter* brought the scale and scope of the Manson story to light, Steven Roberts opened his capsule biography with what now still seems a telling setup: "[Manson's] life stands as a monument to parental neglect and the failure of the public correctional system." For those inclined to (try to) understand Charles Manson, Roberts could have ended the article there.

Manson lasted all of three days at Boys Town before running away with a new buddy, the colorfully named Blackie Nielson. A petty crime spree followed. They got caught robbing a grocery store and Manson, still a minor, got sent to the Indiana Boys School in Plainfield. According to Roberts, Manson ran away from (and was summarily returned to) the school eighteen times. His nineteenth adventure on the lam climaxed with the theft of a car in Beaver City, Utah, after which he was sent back east for a stint at the National Training School for Boys in Washington, D.C.

By the time he secured release from the D.C. facility, Manson was twenty years old. Fully on his own for the first time, he returned to West Virginia. There, he met and within a few months married Rosalie Willis. She became pregnant. He resumed stealing cars. By the time the baby was born, he was again in jail, this time in L.A. Rosalie, the baby, and quite astonishingly, Kathleen traveled to California to be near him. But by the time Manson secured release, they were all gone.

Abandoned again, Manson resumed his criminal career. After brief stints behind bars for car theft and pimping, a 1960 conviction for forging government checks landed him at McNeil Island

Penitentiary in Washington State with a stiff ten-year sentence. Manson would serve seven years at McNeil, and his stay there proved formative.

Among other things: it was at McNeil that he learned to play guitar and wrote his first few songs. He learned a thing or two about adult life there as well, adult prison life that is—lessons learned and most certainly not forgotten upon his release in 1967. As one of Manson's (as Roberts quaintly calls them) "acquaintances" at McNeil opined in 1970, "Doing time strengthens you, you know. You learn how much you can take and how much you can give."

Another "acquaintance" added, "Inside you have to be aware of everything." Manson would make the most of that disposition, that talent as well. Soon after his release in 1967, Manson drifted to the Haight in San Francisco. The district had become the West Coast capital of the hippie subculture. There were plenty of charismatic characters there plying their riffs on the streets, and Manson, by then a charismatic sociopath with a guitar slung over his shoulder and a ready smile on his face, blended in. He was operating—and that's the right word here for sure—with, as his former cellmate suggested, an awareness that the many amiable hippies he encountered could never hope to match or understand. In short order, he assembled a following—a dozen or so lonely seekers, all of them looking to drop out of lives that for them seemed emptied of meaning.

In the spring of 1968, Manson commandeered a converted school bus and with his entourage (composed of nine young women and five young men) drove south. They got only as far as Oxnard in Ventura County before running afoul of the law, as the group's clothing-optional vibe did not sit well with the locals. The charges in Oxnard were eventually dropped, and they moved on to the Topanga Canyon home of Gary Hinman, a professional musician. Hinman had an open-door policy, and Manson's ragged crew exploited the hospitality.

FIGURE 34. The Spahn Movie Ranch in Chatsworth, California, where Charles Manson and the Family resided in the summer of 1969 (*Six Degrees of Helter Skelter*, Mike Dorsey, 2009, Mance Media).

(For his generosity, a year later and a few weeks before the Tate and La Bianca murders, Manson acolyte Robert "Bobby" Beausoleil, with Susan Atkins and Mary Brunner by his side, murdered Hinman in cold blood. Beausoleil would later say he killed Hinman because the drugs Hinman manufactured in his basement and sold to Beausoleil were not up to the quality his customers [a biker gang loosely affiliated with Manson] wanted. The murder of Hinman, as Manson's celebrity clients would soon discover, was just something that happened every now and then in the drug business. Somewhere in the illegal drugs supply chain in 1969 one always found an amiable hippie like Hinman. Elsewhere in that same supply chain one might encounter instead or as well a career criminal like Manson.)

After leaving Topanga, Manson et al. encamped briefly at Wilson's posh home in the Pacific Palisades and then moved on to Spahn's Movie Ranch in the remote Simi Hills just above Chatsworth in northwest L.A. County. The Ranch was little used by then. Westerns had gone out of fashion. But its founder, the eighty-three-year-old George Spahn, still lived there. Manson knew how to play the old man—that is, he left Spahn to "the girls."

The Family lived at the ranch from the summer of 1968 until the fall of 1969, when a series of raids by the Los Angeles Sherriff's Department, pursuant to reports of stolen cars on the premises, pushed the group farther out into the desert. Among the first to get pinched was Susan Atkins, who foolishly boasted to a cellmate about the murders. The cellmate snitched, and on December 1 arrest warrants for Kasabian, Krenwinkel, and Watson were issued and carried out. A week later, Manson and Leslie Van Houten joined them behind bars.[15]

Early coverage of the Tate murders had highlighted the Hollywood angle. And in that coverage, Polanski, standing in for a decadent and careless celebrity subculture, came off looking pretty bad in the process. Roberts thought Polanski's press conference stunk of Hollywood grandiosity: "Screen director Roman Polanski, Miss Tate's husband [bet that rankled], called a press conference to defend his wife's reputation and say that her unborn baby 'had been her best picture.' Before leaving he found time to pose for magazine photographs in their blood-stained living room." In Hollywood, was everything, even mass murder, spun as PR?

To be fair, Polanski was not himself that day. He hardly had time to process what had happened before the cameras and microphones were thrust in his direction. Rumor has it he at first suspected that John Phillips (of the Mamas and the Papas) was somehow involved. But even if he harbored such a suspicion, in an early interview with the police, Polanski advised thinking outside the normal frames of reference to find the killers, who, he surmised, might not have had a rational motive for the crime.

After the arrests, Polanski was no longer the focal point of the story; he would be upstaged by, in Roberts's words, "the roving 'family' of young people, mostly middle- or upper-middle-class backgrounds, slavishly devoted to a bearded guru." Roberts's *youth counterculture gone wild* story proved fascinating *and* to an extent true. And in that story, Atkins became for Roberts something of an unofficial spokesperson. (Manson would hardly need a mouthpiece once he took center stage, but he wasn't there yet.) Atkins took some pleasure in fueling the panic, insisting to Roberts that the murders were "arbitrary, random." She coined a phrase Roberts couldn't resist repeating as he endeavored to characterize and contextualize the crime: "Live freaky, die freaky." Atkins was referring to the Family's freakiness. But Roberts used the phrase to touch upon something else and something more: the Hollywood colony's freakiness, its evocation of a generation's collective freakiness.[16]

Roberts and other journalists trying to make sense of Manson at the time had lots of questions and few answers. What put Manson and his followers in the same orbit? And what put the killers in the same room as a movie star and an heiress? Were the killings some random thing (as Atkins claimed), something that could have happened to anyone, anywhere in America? It was important to most everyone not living in L.A. that the answer to this last question was: "no." The murders seemed to be (they just had to be) peculiar to L.A., peculiar to the wild and shameful lives lived by folks in the movie, TV, and music industries. To sleep at night, the through line in this Hollywood story was clear: the celebrities had brought this upon themselves.

All the Lonely People . . .

In her 1979 essay, "The White Album," Joan Didion recalled what it was like to be in L.A. when the news of the murders broke. Like a lot of people, she remembered vividly where she was and what she was doing: "I was sitting in the shallow end of my sister-in-law's swimming pool in Beverly Hills." And how she felt: "I remember all of the day's misinformation very clearly, and I also remember this, and I wish I did not: *I remember that no one was surprised.*"[17]

In August 1969, Didion lived with her husband, the writer John Gregory Dunne, and their preschool-age daughter Quintana in a sprawling, down-on-its luck house on Franklin Avenue, just west of La Brea. (The house has been beautifully restored and is now the HQ for the Shumei America Hollywood Center, a new age spiritual retreat.) Back then there were always people driving by, turning up unannounced, and sometimes uninvited. The neighborhood was pretty rough; it had been, several decades earlier, far trendier; it had been where movie stars lived. But in the sixties, rock bands and their sprawling entourages moved in, and by the end of the decade, there were plenty of freaks and druggies, as well as the houseless and worryingly crazy.

Something was in the air, Didion recalled, and had been for a while. "There were rumors. There were stories. Everything was unmentionable but nothing was unimaginable. This mystical flirtation with the idea of 'sin'—this sense that it was possible to go too far." To illustrate this observation, Didion mused on a news item from the year before; the October 30, 1968, murder of the former silent film star Ramon Novarro at his home in the trendy Laurel Canyon subdivision, less than three miles away from her Franklin Avenue house. The killers were two brothers: Paul and Thomas Ferguson, aged seventeen and twenty-two. The crime was vicious and seemed senseless—a harbinger of Manson. During the trial—which was by no means a trial of the century, as Manson's would be—neither brother had much to say to help the jury make sense of the crime. A horrific bottom line prevailed; two guys from the outskirts had come to town, happened upon a house, and then ...

What little sense Didion could make of the Novarro killing was culled from two small and disconnected comments, the first from a psychiatrist who noted that the brothers had (living on the near outskirts of L.A.) become accustomed to "a world of people moved by strange, conflicted, poorly comprehended and, above all, devious motivations." The second, more worrying, Didion found in the testimony of the elder brother, Paul. Rambling on the witness stand about what it takes to be a successful hustler, he paused, as if considering for the first time why he and his brother had killed Novarro: "There are a lot of lonely people in this town, man."[18]

Not So Easy Riders (Anymore)

In his New Hollywood history *Easy Riders, Raging Bulls*, Peter Biskind alludes to Didion as he assesses the impact of the Tate murders on the complexly interconnected communities working in and for the entertainment industries at the time: "The murders hit home. No one was untouched. Everybody knew [the victims]. They had their hair done by Sebring, like [Warren] Beatty and [the screenwriter, Robert] Towne, or had been invited up that night and begged off because they were too tired, too stoned, or had something better to do, like [the film producer] Bob Evans. The sense that 'it could have been me' haunted the [Hollywood] hills." The news about the murders on Cielo Drive was always going to be all about them, the celebrities that is. Hollywood's that kind of place.

The production designer Richard Sylbert wryly observed that after the news broke about the murders: "All over town, you could hear toilets flushing." The very real dangers of the drug counterculture for the many celebrities and industry players who partook had rather suddenly and simultaneously come clear. The screenwriter Buck Henry—whose counterculture credits include the screenplays for *The Graduate*, *Candy*, and *Catch-22*—offered a more nuanced view, cannily observing how the murders prompted a certain self-loathing uniquely suited to Hollywood: "Everybody who was anybody had been about to visit the Polanski home the night of the murders. It was as if people wanted to be part of the slaughter, like animals for some dark purpose of their own. . . . Manson was the essence of the 1960s. If Hollywood was the forbidden planet, he was the monster of the id. It was 'I'm famous. I'm a celebrity. I don't deserve it. Someone is going to kill me and my family.'"

After his arrest, Manson reveled in his sudden celebrity: while awaiting trial, he began in earnest developing a Charles Manson biopic, imagining first and foremost whom he might cast to play his film's eponymous lead. According to Biskind, Manson's first choice for the role was Dennis Hopper. *Easy Rider* was that summer season's surprise hit, and Hopper seemed just the right combination of charismatic and crazy. And he still had the scruffy beard he'd grown to play Billy in *Easy Rider*.

Hopper was suitably leery about taking a meeting with Manson; there were lots of reasons to beg off. He had been one of Sebring's many celebrity clients, and they were friends. But Hopper could not resist the proposition, so he took the meeting. "I walked up to the courthouse," Hopper recalled, "where [Manson] was in a cell, and the little girls [Hopper tellingly added the diminutive] were camping in tents outside. . . . [Manson had] cut himself, a cross on his forehead. I asked him why. 'Don't you read the newspapers, man, all my followers have cut themselves like this so when the black revolution comes, they'll know which ones are mine.'" Hopper figured Manson had summoned him because he'd seen *Easy Rider*. But Manson wasn't going to the movies much in the summer of 1969. He was thinking instead about another, less well-known role. "He'd seen me on a TV show, *The Defenders*," Hopper later recalled, "[an episode in which] I killed my father."[19]

The *Defenders* episode had stayed with Manson. Of course it did. But like a lot of development deals, the biopic never got off the ground—at least not right away, and not with Manson's input. Manson was about to learn for a second time that deals fall apart all the time in Hollywood. Best not to take it personally.

The Road to Romance and Ruin: Charles Manson Blows Our Minds

One of the most pressing questions about the murders involved the Family, especially the young women who had been and, in many cases, remained for years hopelessly devoted to Manson. What got them hooked? How did Manson get these otherwise unremarkable people to follow his lead, to behave with such savagery?

As Roberts reported in 1970, several of Manson's female followers were in important ways quite like him, wounded survivors of desperately failed family lives. Atkins's mother died when she was fifteen. Her father was emotionally incapable of dealing with her grief; he had never been able to deal with her growing up. There was a run-in with the cops, but as a once-proper middle-class white girl, Atkins got off—in her father's view, too easy. He carped afterward that the courts had become too lenient on youth offenders, falling easily into the role of the Nixon-Republican patriarch baffled by his unaccountably wayward, hippie daughter. "She once did some beautiful things," he told the press. "But that was a long time ago. I don't know what went wrong."

Patricia Krenwinkel, who participated in the murders at both the Tate and La Bianca residences, struggled as well through a difficult adolescence. She wasn't pretty or popular, and after a brief flirtation with a life devoted to the Church, she fell in with her older half-sister and her wild drug-addled crowd. She was twenty when she first met Manson, and it was love at first sight, mostly because he was the first guy to pay attention to her.

Linda Kasabian grew up in Milford, New Hampshire. In the fifteen years she spent under her mother's roof, she met her father only twice. After she hit puberty, she became determined to get right what her mother and father got wrong. It was a bad idea, and she failed miserably. She tried her hand at marriage early and often—tying the knot for the first time at sixteen. She divorced a couple of months later, then married again—less than a year later, had a child, and moved west. Husband number two abandoned her soon after their arrival in California. Barely twenty, she was pregnant with her second child in August 1969 when some of her new Family got arrested. Long absent from her life, Kasabian's mother turned up and stood by her. "There is no hate in her, at all," mom opined on her daughter's behalf. "She was searching, searching for love."

Lynette "Squeaky" Fromme was nineteen when she met Manson. Her father was an aeronautical engineer who, like Atkins's father found his daughter's adolescent rebellion impossible to understand or tolerate. Fromme's childhood had been quite perfect; she performed with a popular dance troupe that appeared on *The Lawrence Welk Show* and at the White House. But by age fifteen, Fromme was like a lot of girls her age: experimenting with drugs and alcohol and getting in trouble with boys. After showing little interest in classwork in high school, she enrolled at El Camino College, mostly to make her father happy. But college wasn't for her. When she dropped out of college (during her first term), Fromme's father threw her out of the house. She was on her own and on the streets when she met Manson, sitting at a bus stop in Venice, California. Manson saw her sitting on the curb and said, "Your parents threw you out, didn't they?" It was a reasonable bit of deduction. But Fromme viewed the remark as clairvoyant.

After Manson's conviction, Fromme became one of his emissaries on the outside. In 1972 she got mixed up, most likely on Manson's behalf, with the Aryan Brotherhood and a murder in Stockton,

California. And three years after that, she was front-page news after attempting to assassinate President Gerald Ford.

Sandra Good came from a wealthy family in San Diego. Her father left her mother when she was two. From that point forward, Good became an impediment to her mother's social ambitions. So she was shipped off to boarding school and after that briefly stayed with her father and his new wife. By the time she met Manson she had drifted into and out of three universities. She had at one point declared her major: marine biology, but the discipline of college work was never for her. Like Kasabian, she was pregnant when the sheriff's department raided the Spahn Movie Ranch in the late summer of 1969.

After Manson was convicted, Good and Fromme lived together in a run-down attic flat near Folsom Prison—so they could be near *him*. Both women remained devoted to Manson until his death in November 2017.

When Roberts interviewed Good, she insisted that she and the rest of the girls had been not so long ago quite typical and normal American youths. (The past tense was important to the argument. She was never saying they were typical any longer.) Van Houten, Good told Roberts, had been a high school homecoming princess. And when Mary Brunner met Manson in San Francisco in 1967, she was gainfully employed at the University of California, Berkeley library. Good's bio sketches for Roberts led inexorably to an otherwise frightening point, expressed by Good in what can only be termed a payoff line: "You can't categorize us. We're going to blow people's minds."[20]

Once he was caught, Manson would be plenty interested in blowing people's minds. He was never going to beat this latest rap; he knew that. And he was never going to get out of prison again. He had engineered a terrifyingly violent crime to settle a comparatively minor score (with Melcher) and a less specific score to settle with

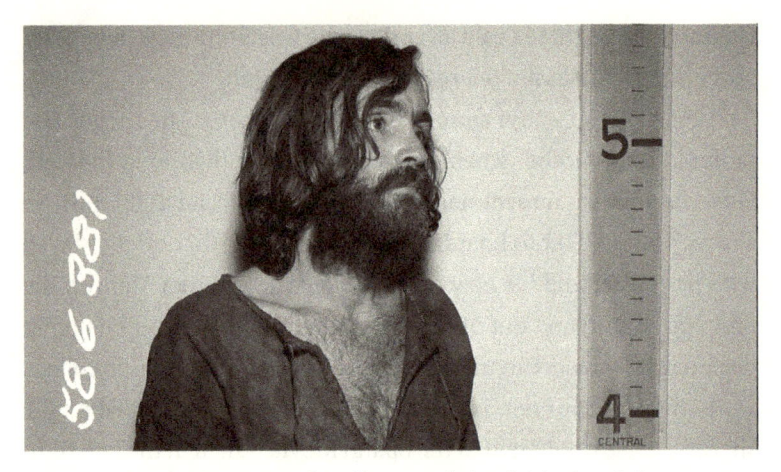

FIGURE 35. Charles Manson in police custody (again) (*Helter Skelter: An American Myth*, episode 5: "Some Bad Mistakes," Lesley Chilcott, 2020, Epix/MGM).

the rest of the world, a world that had never been much interested in what he thought or said. Quite suddenly he had everyone's attention. And he took full advantage of the opportunity: "Mr. and Mrs. America—you are wrong. I am not the King of the Jews nor am I a hippie cult leader. . . . I am what you made of me and the mad dog devil killer fiend leper is a reflection of your society. Whatever the outcome of this madness that you call a fair trial or Christian justice, you can know this: In my mind's eye my thoughts light fires in your cities."[21]

Making Meaning of Manson

Manson initiated relationships with Family recruits by intuiting their needs and then saying whatever they needed or wanted to hear. Krenwinkle was waiting for someone to tell her she was pretty. So he told her she was pretty. Fromme was waiting for someone to recognize her predicament; her father never understood her and had thrown her out onto the streets. (Who did her father think she would meet there?) Manson knew what it was like to be abandoned, to feel unwanted and unloved; he knew what it felt like to be alone and desperate, willing to do most anything to get by.

There is in all of these quasi-street corner pickups an element of the con: Manson was only ever playing the part of the hippie guru. He told these lonely young women that he knew what made them tick, that he had a solution to their problems. But he was not ever in any normal way interested in them or their problems. He was by instinct or habit, a pimp—an exploiter, a sexual predator. He caught just enough of the subcultural drift in San Francisco and L.A. to mildly tweak his grooming enterprise. And he was enough of a sociopath to use his skill as a pimp for his own personal benefit, to satisfy his own increasingly pathological narcissism. Manson was counterculture so long as it kept him safe from the cops, so long as it got him laid.

The early party line on Manson—that his followers had been drugged and duped, that he had some sort of hypnotic power over them, that the Family was a hippie death cult and Manson its deranged guru—was less terrifying to most Americans than the more simple and obvious truth: that whatever he had on offer was to his followers preferable to social convention. Manson offered a different sort of life on the metaphorical and actual outskirts of conventional society. He gave the Family a sense of belonging, no small thing for a group of social rejects. All he asked for in return was devotion and love—at least at first.

In the summer of 1969, Manson felt the community beginning to fracture. Or maybe he was just getting impatient with such a ragtag hippie entourage; they had settled into something at the Movie Ranch and maybe it didn't feel like it was all about him anymore. So, and not for the first time, Manson improvised. The criminal enterprise began with the evening adventures dubbed "creepy crawling"—prowling outside posh houses, breaking and entering, stealing small, useless things, moving stuff around so the owners knew they had been there, inside. It seemed at first just fun and games.

These early and tame criminal excursions doubled as hazing rituals, like those routinely indulged by fraternities, sororities, and sports teams. The rituals in this case of course extended beyond mere team building; they bound the Family in collective criminality, they implicated the Family in everything that followed. Manson knew a lot of gangsters and bikers from his prison days, so he tweaked his hazing rituals accordingly. If you want to be accepted as a member of a biker gang, you may well be asked to harm someone—someone you might not know—to express your loyalty. "You make your bones by burning your bridges," the cultural commentator Adam Gopnik notes; after all, "the fanatic leader convinces his adherents not that [murder] is the only way forward but that [after committing the crime] there is no way of turning back."[22] Whether or not Manson had it together enough to understand or plan such a strategy is beside the point. Once the family started killing people, there would be no route back to the rest of the world. There would be, after the crimes, only Charlie Manson. And *his* counterculture.

All cons finesse the distance between appearance and reality, between the bait and the switch. Accepting that, we can see that Manson's pitch was for the times not so extraordinary. Free love, communal living, and (at first playful) lawlessness were all well within the bounds of a lot of the alternative living experiments underway at the time, as was the authoritarian bent—the charismatic, exploitive leader and his flock. Inherent and intrinsic to these sixties experiments (for many of those who fell into the alternative lifestyle) was, counterintuitively, a search for authority, different from the authority of old boyfriends and heartless right-wing dads, from teachers and preachers and other adults in general—a search for someone to tell them what to do. Manson's authoritarianism gave the abandoned and discarded youths he encountered someone new and different to belong to.[23]

Dr. Joel Hochman, a psychiatrist called in to examine Susan Atkins during her trial, tried to make sense of Manson's impact on her: "She is suffering from a condition of *folie a famille*, a kind of shared madness in a group situation."[24] After observing Atkins on the stand, the *Los Angeles Times* reporter David Smith added: "Watching her behavior—bold and actressy in court, cute and mincing when making eye play with someone, a little haunted when no one pays attention—I get the feeling one day she might start screaming and never stop."[25] Manson asked his followers to "cease to resist," and in doing so, to "cease to exist"—and not just in a manner of speaking,

Half-a-century has passed since those fateful nights in August 1969, and we now can safely spend a little time with a onetime "Manson girl," in Olivia Klaus's 2014 short film, *Life after Manson*, which focuses on Patricia Krenwinkel. Klaus meets up with Krenwinkel after years of jailhouse therapy have done a job on her—a good job mostly; she is a model prison citizen, a mentor, and role model. Klaus asks us to consider Krenwinkel's apparent rehabilitation, to consider in this most extreme of situations the possibility of forgiveness. It's not an easy ask.

Krenwinkel looks straight into the camera and tells us that, thanks to all the years of therapy, she has come to believe that she was always only a victim: of what a society demands of young women (to be attractive but chaste, to be defined by the approval of men but to be careful how far you go to secure that approval), of drug addiction, of misfortune (in encountering a manipulative psychopath). At one point in the film, Klaus asks Krenwinkel to talk about her life with the Family. Tellingly, she recalls a day not long before the murders, sitting in a car with Manson, speeding down the road. Manson intuits her unease—he is thinking she may want to leave the Ranch.

"If you want out," Manson tells her, "you can always jump out of the car." A metaphor, perhaps—or quite precisely what he meant at that moment. What Krenwinkel doesn't recall to Klaus is the night in August 1969 when she repeatedly stabbed Abigail Folger, at one point chasing Folger out of the house and onto the lawn.

During her trial, Krenwinkel's attorney offered the ridiculous fiction that his client had been an invited guest who had by chance and luck left the premises just before the killers arrived. At least that's how he tried to explain why his client's fingerprints were found at the crime scene. No one in the courtroom believed him; not even his client, who seemed quite blissfully uninterested in the proceedings, spending most of the trial doodling on a pad. At her first parole hearing nearly a decade after the murders, Krenwinkel was asked how it felt to have committed such a terrible crime. She replied: "Nothing, I mean, what is there to describe? It was just there, and it was right." She was still one of "Charlie's girls."

Klaus's documentary climaxes with a parole hearing, featuring an awkward and unforgettable guest spot from Debra Tate, Sharon's sister, who explains to the board why she has made the trip—why she makes an appearance at every relevant parole hearing. As if she had been watching the film along with us, Tate—and it is impossible not to notice the family resemblance—observes the new and improved version of Patricia Krenwinkel and doesn't buy any of it. She rejects Krenwinkel's claims to victimhood: "She has totally minimized her action and blamed everything on other people." Tate tells the board: Abigail Folger was a for-real victim. And so was her sister, Sharon. Krenwinkel on quite the other hand is a cold-blooded killer.

Tate completes her speech, and the board takes barely a minute to issue the predictable determination. Patricia Krenwinkel will never get out of prison. The film picks Krenwinkel up only to knock her down—though I don't think that was Klaus's intention.

So what got Krenwinkel into the car on August 8? What made her a party to brutal murders that night, and then got her back into the car two nights later for more of the same? There are explanations but no excuses. She may well have been Manson's victim—she was certainly groomed and recruited into the fold. And she may have come to appreciate from the Family's mischievous, innocuous, funny little acts of vandalism and theft (the "creepy crawling"), that delinquency could be fun—could *feel* revolutionary. If petty theft and mischief was a kick, imagine what the big-time felt like?

Consider an argument posed in Travis Hirschi's monograph, *The Causes of Delinquency*, written just a year after the Manson trial. "Delinquency," Hirschi writes, "is not caused by beliefs that require delinquency, but rather is made possible by the absence of beliefs that forbid delinquency."[26] Hirschi's argument built upon a wave of 1960s-era scholarship that focused on postwar teen alienation and delinquency, work like Kenneth Keniston's *The Uncommitted: Alienated Youth in America*, which blamed delinquency on "incomplete socialization," on a "failure of acculturation."[27] Relevant here as well, the work of the psychologist Bruno Bettelheim, who focused as well on incomplete socialization, specifically on the breakdown of generational norms and values.[28] And Erik Erikson, whose work formed the foundation for modern adolescent psychology, who argued that deviance and delinquency were social (and not necessarily psychological) problems. "It is the young," Erikson posited, "who by their responses and actions, tell the old whether life represented by the old and presented to the young has meaning."[29] Working from Erikson's formula, in an address the membership of the American Academy of Child and Adolescent Psychiatry, John Schowalter seemed to have someone quite like Manson in mind when he said: "When there's turmoil and social change, teenagers have a tendency to follow each other more. The leadership of adults is splintered and they're more on their own—like *Lord of the Flies*."[30]

If delinquency is a rejection of adult life as it is presented by the old to the young, what then might we make of the Family's interactions with industry celebrities—people whose lives were so clearly and materially different from their own? Manson's encounter with Wilson, Watson's with the Cielo Drive crowd—these encounters only exacerbated their alienation. The Hollywood entertainment community smacked of entitlement, of conspicuous consumption. Meantime, the Family was living rough on the city's outskirts, eating garbage out of dumpsters. The rich and entitled among the Hollywood entertainment community, starting but not ending with Wilson and Melcher, had no comprehension of and frankly no interest in the social forces they were engaging when they interacted with the Family, the sort of people they were letting into their pampered and ridiculous lives. And they rather paid the price for their arrogance, for their ignorance.

The Manson Family members commissioned on August 8 and then again on August 10, 1969, did not need to understand the psychology or sociology of their alienation to be fairly easily pointed in the direction of a radical deviance and delinquency. When playful plunder escalated into planned slaughter, they were willing and able. So deep was their alienation, so profound was their commitment to antisocial behavior, so blind was their devotion to Charles Manson—the man who had delivered them from the society they rejected, the society that had rejected them.

Once Upon a Time in Hollywood

The "Manson murders" have become part of American folklore; the awful crimes and the arch-villain who planned them endlessly analyzed and fetishized online, researched and rehashed in academic, literary, musical, and cinematic works. The books and films range widely in taste, quality, and historical accuracy. None of them offer anything like the last words on the subject—bad news for anyone who'd like to be finally done with Charles Manson.[31]

In November 2017 Manson finally shuffled off this mortal coil. But his death has done little to diminish the action. To mix Shakespearean metaphors, the evil in Manson has surely lived on after him. With every August anniversary comes another "collective deep breath," as the cultural historian Jeffrey Melnick has recently noted, an annual invite to reconsider the vast trove of Manson folklore.

The murders remain emblematic for a certain style or mode of outrageous and quasi-random American violence. And the mostly nonsensical prophecy of Helter Skelter continues to resonate with the far (and far-out) Right.[32] Manson was at once monstrous *and* quintessentially American. To understand him—to understand what he did and what he tapped into: the rage, the alienation, the generation and gender gaps—is to understand the freaky core of the American sixties. And it is not a pretty picture.

In August 2019, Melnick, writing for the *New Yorker*, marked a collective intake of breath: the fiftieth anniversary of the murders. Hollywood was hardly going to let such a moment go by without comment, without content. First into theaters: Mary Harron's *Charlie Says*. Harron was a rising star on the indie circuit in the late nineties and though she has since faded from that limelight (and into prestige TV along with so many other talented women directors), she came to *her* Manson project with unique bona fides, having directed two notorious, and notoriously grisly indies about maniac killers: *I Shot Andy Warhol* in 1996 and *American Psycho* in 2000.

Her film premiered at the Venice Film Festival in September 2018, then opened in a limited release in US theaters on May 1, 2019, quietly anticipating the start of the blockbuster summer season and roughly marking the anniversary of the terrifying crimes. A far more widely advertised Manson film directed by Quentin Tarantino, *Once Upon a Time in Hollywood* debuted at Cannes twenty days after Harron's film, and went into a saturation, blockbuster-style release in the United States on July 24 (tastefully eschewing a perfectly timed/dated release as well).

Comparisons between the two films were inevitable but also unfair, as Harron's film was always operating at a disadvantage. The production budget and subsequent theatrical play off of Harron's film was by most any measure small to the point of insignificance. *Charlie Says* earned less than $100,000 after limited runs—on average, a-week-and-a-half—in less than forty theaters nationwide. The film then quietly disappeared onto premium cable. Tarantino's star-studded $90 million epic opened in nearly thirty-seven hundred theaters and grossed $140 million domestically, nearly $375 million worldwide.

Charlie Says focuses on three Manson girls: Atkins, Krenwinkel, and van Houten, all of whom became the subjects of a prison research project coordinated by the sociologist Karlene Faith in the early 1970s. In the film, Harron has Faith (played by Merritt Wever) guide us into the lives of the three, in the researcher's words, "unexpectedly endearing and vulnerable women." Harron tells Atkins's, Krenwinkel's, and van Houten's stories one a time in the film. Manson is a character in their stories, and not the other way around.

When Faith first meets Atkins, Krenwinkel, and van Houten (played, respectively by Marianne Rendon, Sosie Bacon, and Hannah Murray) in Harron's film they are sequestered from the general population at the California Institution for Women, housed in a Special Security Unit. They live there in a perpetual limbo, ostensibly on death row in a state that no longer performs executions. There's a palpable "lost boys" vibe in their continued isolation; they live in a Never-Never Land that encourages and enables them to, per *Peter Pan*, never grow up.

In three sequential flashback narratives Harron recounts each woman's story, tracking, one at a time, how they met Manson, what got them involved with the Family, what role they played in the evolution of life at Spahn Ranch, and then what they did or didn't do in August 1969. Because Harron depicts Atkins, Krenwinkel, and van Houten as variations on a single theme, a lot of attention in the flashbacks is paid to their sexual awakening. There is as a result a lot of simulated sex and nudity in the film. The women are objectified visually, much as we assume they were in the patriarchal structure of Manson's L.A. commune. It's a risky strategy for Harron, especially in the #MeToo culture of 2019, but it is at once necessary and necessarily contextualized by Faith's study and Harron's identity politics.

Manson (played by Matt Smith) takes center stage only once, in van Houten's story, when we see his audition for Melcher.[33] The music producer arrives in a Jaguar convertible. Manson performs a competent but relatively tame roots rock number as a few of the "girls" go-go dance topless. The taste level is off-kilter; the casual, pointless nudity and out-of-time dancing makes clear Manson's cluelessness about what Melcher, what anyone in the legit music world might want or expect to see in an audition. When the song ends, Melcher and Manson talk briefly, out of van Houten's (and our) earshot. As Melcher exits, we watch Manson's reaction from a distance, again from van Houten's point-of-view. He is alone in a place—a barn—where he is used to holding court, where we have earlier seen him orchestrate an orgy. Like a spoiled child, he throws a tantrum. Van Houten doesn't know what Melcher has said to set Manson off, so neither do we. The particulars of what it is his followers are asked to avenge on August 8, 1969, is, as far as we can tell, never articulated. And to get them to kill, the particulars were never really necessary, which is really chilling.

When Harron takes us to the Tate and La Bianca crime scenes, she doesn't hold back. She shows Watson slashing Tate's throat and later, Watson suffocating Leno La Bianca. Horrifying stuff, but it is a third and final bit of violence that lingers longer. At the La Biancas, we watch Watson from van Houten's point of view. She is, like us, at first a bystander to the chaos. But then Krenwinkel hands her a knife and tells her to have at it. Van Houten's eyes go wild and she repeatedly stabs La Bianca's already dead body. Her rage is unmistakable, if also quite clearly misplaced.

We segue from van Houten's face splashed with blood to the film's "once upon a time" coda. A handsome biker arrives at the Ranch, some time before Manson orders the murders. He has come to rescue van Houten from Manson. He tells her he just wants to help, and that he wants nothing in return. Manson and van Houten exchange looks. Manson waves goodbye, feigning disinterest in the encounter. We have seen this scene before, during van Houten's flashback. The first time, van Houten declines the biker's offer (as, had such a confrontation happened in real life, she would have) and decides to stay. But in the film's whimsical coda, in this second staging of the same scene, she defies Manson, mounts the bike, and rides off, forever safe and free. If only.

Tarantino has a more ridiculous "once upon a time" moment up his sleeve, and he makes us wait well over two hours to get to it. The fateful night of August 8 begins for Tate, Sebring, Folger, and Frykowski with dinner at the El Coyote, a Mexican restaurant on Beverly, just west of La Brea. The stunt man Randy Miller (Kurt Russell) narrates the scene, though he is neither in attendance nor relevant to what we (think we) know is about to happen. Tate (Margot Robbie), he tells us, is "melancholy." She's got a bad feeling about something she can't quite put her finger on. We cut to the TV actor Rick Dalton and his stunt double Cliff Booth (Leonardo DiCaprio and Brad Pitt) at another Mexican restaurant in the Valley and then to Rick's house, where Cliff's dog Brandy prowls the living room as Rick's new wife Francesca (Lorenza Izzo) sleeps off jet lag in the bedroom.

Tate and her houseguests arrive back at 10050 Cielo Drive at the 129-minute mark.[34] Duration is important because Tarantino has made a meal of making us wait; and he isn't nearly done yet. We see Folger at the piano as she performs a song for her friends. A sound bridge takes us to Folger later in the evening, in bed smoking a joint, reading *Madame Bovary*. It is 11:04 p.m. on August 8. Nearly, finally, time.

We cut to a TV as a B-horror picture gives way to a TV host, who intones: "Now it's time for what I know you've all been waiting for. A little fanfare please." Metafiction. We see Frykowski reading the TV guide. A title supers: 11:45. Cut to Rick and Cliff arriving at Rick's house, next-door to Tate's, in a yellow cab. Inside, Rick makes frozen margaritas. Cliff leashes up Brandy and decides to smoke an LSD-laced cigarette he bought off "a hippie girl" for fifty cents. "Tonight's the night?" he asks Brandy. Of course it is.

Back to Tate's as Sebring cues up the Mamas and the Papas on the turntable. (Remember, Polanski initially suspected John Phillips. Tarantino, who certainly knows that story, is just having some fun.) Stacked in plain view: an album by Paul Revere and the Raiders—a Terry Melcher group popular at the time. Here again, Tarantino is good with details, even when he's being bad with history. Cliff and Brandy head down the street. Will they miss the action? A stationary camera shows Cliff and Brandy as they disappear into the night. The long take continues as a car rumbles past him up the road and toward the camera, stopping near Tate's gate. Tex is behind the wheel.

Cut to Rick manning the blender. He stops mixing and hears the car. "Fucking private road," he mutters to himself. Blender full of drinks in hand, he waddles out onto the street. "Goddamn fucking hippies." Uh-oh—he's going to confront Tex Watson: "Who are you?" Tex replies: "Nobody, sir." The scene is played for comedy. Like a grumpy grandpa, Rick chases the hippies off his street, pausing comically for a drink straight out of the blender. He embodies the very Hollywood sort of piggy entitlement Manson endeavored to snuff out. Tex touches his gun, then thinks better of it. From Rick's eyeline and subjective point-of-view we see Katie (Patricia Krenwinkel, played by Madisen Beaty); there's murder in her eyes. Rick is drunk. He says: "What are you lookin' at, you ginger-haired fucker?" Are the five dead bodies we know about not enough of a climax for Tarantino?

Tex backs down the street; 137 minutes in. Tex reminds Katie, Sadie (Susan Atkins, played by Mikey Madison), and Flower Child (Linda Kasabian, played by Maya Hawke) what they've been sent to do—to kill everyone at Melcher's house, and to "make it witchy." Melcher isn't going to be there, and they know that—a brief encounter with Manson earlier in the film showed him strolling up to the gate at 10050 Cielo Drive, engaging in polite conversation with Tate, who tells him that Melcher has moved out.

At the bottom of Cielo Drive Katie figures out why the guy who yelled at them seemed familiar: "That was Rick Dalton," she says, which prompts a conversation with Tex about *Bounty Law*, Rick's fifties-TV show. Tex says he had a *Bounty Law* lunchbox. The show was his favorite. Sadie misses their point; she muses off-topic on the violent impact of violent TV. "Every show on TV that wasn't *I Love Lucy* was about murder," she says; and already getting their destination wrong: "We [have been sent to] kill the people [like Rick?] who taught us to kill." It's utter nonsense. But it's also like the "Royale with cheese" riff in *Pulp Fiction*; time, in Tarantino's films, is there to be wasted, especially when you've got characters sent someplace with murderous intent.

At the 138-minute mark, Tex says the words we've all been waiting for: "You two ready to kill some people?" It seems at first an innocuous slip of the tongue, as there is a third person in the car. To be fair, Flower Child (Kasabian) seems a lot less in the moment than Tex, Katie, and Sadie. All four leave the noisy car at the bottom of the Drive and walk up the street. He is self-referencing here—to the opening of *Reservoir Dogs*. This time, the long walk is in silhouette.

Flower Child stops half way up the road; she's forgotten her knife. Is this another stall? The scene has by now taken on an almost Monty Python vibe, a gag that is funny because you can't believe how long it's been going on. Tex tosses Flower Child his keys; he's locked the car. (Who'd steal *that* car? In *that* neighborhood?) At 139 minutes in: Flower Child drives off. This is not how it really went down. Kasabian was the lookout and the get-away driver; she didn't kill anyone, but she dutifully waited outside at 10050 Cielo Drive from start to finish.

Meantime Cliff gets back to Rick's place. By then, the LSD-laced cigarette has taken effect. Tarantino stalls for another comedy bit as Cliff negotiates the can opener and then samples Brandy's food. Cut to Tex and the gang. Cut to Rick on a float in the pool listening to music in wrap-around headphones, still drinking. Wow, it's a really long walk up the road.

The pace of the editing finally picks up. Cliff, Francesca, Rick, Tex with Katie, Sadie walking around the house, we gather heading to the back door. It's been a while since we've seen anyone in Tate's house. We're about to discover why.

Tarantino cues the Vanilla Fudge: "You Keep Me Hanging On." Another joke. "Hanging on" is what we've been doing for a while now. Low-angle shot of Tex and Katie. Finally,143 minutes in: it's the wrong house. A very wrong house, as Cliff is there, a guy who can leap from ground to roof in a couple of bounds. We've seen Cliff knock Bruce Lee on his ass. And Cliff is Brad Pitt. We've seen those abs a couple of times already and in a number of other films, enough to know.

For anyone still worrying what Tarantino was going to do when he got to Cielo Drive, the answer—not just after two-and-a-half hours, but after nearly a year waiting for the film—has finally arrived. Bait and switch—ultra violence and utter nonsense. A made-up stunt man and a made-up TV star (armed with his trusty flamethrower), a

FIGURE 36. Damon Herriman as Charles Manson—little more than a cameo in Quentin Tarantino's fractured fairy tale *Once Upon a Time in Hollywood* (2019, Sony Pictures).

pit bull terrier, and the TV star's "pissed-off-after-being-woken-up-from-her-nap" wife make brutal work of the would-be killers. Tate and her houseguests live to see another day . . . once upon a time.

Manson gets very little screen time in *Once Upon a Time in Hollywood*. He is talked about a lot and in the long final scene his name is invoked and his plans briefly elaborated. The film focuses instead on Rick and Cliff, fictional characters. In an interview published on the website *Bustle.com*, Tarantino described Rick as a mash-up of several popular sixties TV actors: George Maharis (who starred in *Route 66*), Edd Byrnes (Kookie in *77 Sunset Strip*), Vince Edwards (who starred in the medical melodrama, *Ben Casey*), and Ty Hardin (the lead in a popular TV western, *Bronco*). In mind as well, or so he has said, were two clean-cut, late-fifties/early-sixties celebrity heartthrobs: Tab Hunter and Fabian Forte, both of whom would have been in 1969, like Rick, well past it.

Cliff, like Rick, is a composite. And since we seldom learn the names of stunt people in Hollywood, it maybe doesn't matter so much who he's patterned after. A name that comes up a lot on the Web is Hal Needham, who worked with Burt Reynolds. Tarantino

[272] CHARLES MANSON'S HOLLYWOOD

has used Rick and Cliff to highlight a generational rift in late-sixties Hollywood, during which, in Tarantino's words, "a certain kind of leading man . . . handsome and most of them kind of rugged" went out of style, replaced "all of a sudden . . . [by] these long shaggy haired androgynous types."[35]

Rick struggles with this very transition—his slow and steady fall from show runner to character actor, from hero to heavy. The "you're too hip baby" TV director asks Rick to give him "evil sexy Hamlet."[36] Rick can't believe what's become of his business—the business of being a TV star, that is. As Tarantino puts it: "If Rick's going to get a part in a movie with [the shaggy haired androgynous types] he's probably going to be the cop that's busting them."[37] That's why he introduces Marvin Schwarz (Al Pacino), an industry player who books Rick a couple of B-list spaghetti westerns. The reference to Clint Eastwood is tough to miss here; Eastwood was once upon a time quite like Rick, a TV western star in the United States (for Eastwood, it was *Rawhide*) who moved on to the widescreen in Italy.

Rick will not get Eastwood's remarkable second and third acts as a movie star and auteur. And as Tarantino makes explicitly clear, he is not Steve McQueen either—though, again a parallel is apparent. McQueen played a bounty hunter on a TV series (*Wanted Dead or Alive*) early in his career, before he became a movie star. More than once in the film, Rick repeats the story that he was once upon a time up for the Virgil Hilts role in *The Great Escape* (1963), the role that made McQueen a star. The lost opportunity rankles; it marks the moment McQueen's career went one way, his another. Tarantino has some fun at Rick's expense as he shows us Rick daydreaming about starring in the film. Credit to DiCaprio: a really good actor convincingly playing a bad actor trying to be good.

In one of several "dark nights of the soul" moments, Rick admits he was never close to getting the role; he is not so stuck on himself to think he was ever in McQueen's league. The "real" McQueen, played by Damien Lewis, shows up in the film to eye Tate at a party and to wonder aloud how on earth wimpy shrimps like Sebring and Polanski got her into bed, and he couldn't. It's hard to tell what Tarantino is up to with McQueen; he seems another sixties detail that, thanks to Lewis, he gets right.

Unlike Rick, who is an anxious narcissist, Cliff is from start to end an old-school tough guy, a for-real rugged strong and silent type. That is why Tarantino has Cliff take us to the Spahn Movie Ranch. Once upon a time Cliff shot westerns there and we see the place in August 1969 much as he does, as a shabby remnant of better days.

Tarantino gets the vibe of Family life at the Ranch absolutely right. He captures the hardscrabble conditions, the underlying creepiness of life there. To get Cliff to the Ranch, Tarantino introduces a composite: Pussycat (Margaret Qualley), a beautiful teenage hitchhiker who thinks everyone, including Cliff, would dig Manson if they only got to meet him. The hitchhiking scheme recalls the Dennis Wilson/Patricia Krenwinkel/Ella Jo Baily story, but unlike the pop musician, Cliff isn't much interested in the sex that's on offer.

Structurally in the film, Pussycat doubles Tate as well; they are both pretty, wide-eyed innocents full-on engaged in Southland cults—respectively, Manson's Family and the Hollywood movie colony.[38] During the drive to the Ranch, Pussycat unwinds and puts her bare and dirty feet up against the dash. When Tate goes to Westwood to watch *The Wrecking Crew* (Phil Carlson, 1968) at the Bruin Theater, she puts her feet up on the seat in front of her; bare, dirty feet again. Tarantino seems to be making a point—and not just about beautiful women's feet.[39]

Our first look at life on the Ranch is in a crowded interior as Clem and five women relax in front of a TV set. Their repose is interrupted by the sound of Cliff and Pussycat's arrival. Snake (a.k.a. Dianne Lake, played by Sydney Sweeney) checks them out.[40] It is "a bitchin' yellow Coupe de Ville," she tells her friends. The car coasts to a stop.

Snake describes Cliff to her comrades: "Some old-looking dude in a Hawaiian shirt."

Pussycat leads Cliff by the hand into the compound and introduces him to Gypsy (a.k.a. Catherine Share, played by Lena Dunham). Tarantino shoots the Ranch exteriors much as old-time westerns would have been shot there; long takes held in long and extreme long shots. We then meet Tex (Austin Butler), and Tarantino holds on him in a medium shot, canted just so. Tex is dispatched to check Cliff out, and Tarantino can't resist an Ennio Morricone (who famously composed music for spaghetti westerns) quotation on the music track as the camera follows Tex's slow ride into the scene.

The edge-city weirdness hardly fazes Cliff. He sizes up Tex and figures he can take him. (In another film this would be a mistake; but, not in Tarantino's old Hollywood macho fantasy. The Manson crew are poseurs. Cliff is the real thing.) Cliff has a throwaway line about two weeks on a chain gang in Houston. That satisfies Tex, and he rides off. Pussycat finds Cliff handsome, cool. Gypsy is not so sure, especially when Cliff starts asking questions about George. "So, George gave you all permission to be here?" he drawls. Dunham's line delivery in reply seems off, which works: "Of course he did." Tarantino cuts to a reaction shot of Cliff, eyes obscured behind his aviators (like a highway cop); in the background, we see a beat-up old school bus (is it the one they used on the drive down from the Haight?) and four more hippies (three women, one man). Cliff should be afraid—this is the hideout for the Manson gang—but he isn't. Out in the sun in the center of the street, Cliff is still the old Hollywood cowboy.

A reverse angle shot from out of George's cabin frames Cliff again in the foreground, the lone gunslinger unwelcome in the dusty western town. The set has been decorated and dressed with busted, half disassembled cars—a reminder this isn't a movie ranch anymore. Cliff walks over to George's cabin and eyes Squeaky (Dakota

Fanning): "You the mama bear?" It's a rhetorical question. A Dutch-angled close-up frames Cliff: "I used to shoot westerns here at the Ranch." Cliff makes clear he won't leave before he's sure George, who is even older old Hollywood, is all right.

A series of shot/reverse shot setups (unusual in the film, and used here self-consciously) track the conversation, as Cliff makes clear to Squeaky that she can't stop him. "Suit yourself," she says finally, and flips the latch on the screen door. A low-angle medium close-up shows Cliff looking for the first time a little worried—but not about himself; he's worried about George. He pauses at the door and from his eye-line we scan the faces of the lost boys and girls. Tarantino lingers in close-up on Pussycat, biting her lip. This isn't exactly what she hoped or thought would happen when she brought Cliff to the Ranch.

Cliff's encounter with George (Bruce Dern) is played for laughs—two really good actors at the top of their games. Here again Tarantino is playing with time, and tone. The faces, the eerie underscoring music, Squeaky's attitude all speak to what we know about the Family and what they are about to do back in town. But Tarantino and Cliff focus in the meantime on George. "It's Cliff Booth. Just stopped in to say hello . . . to see how you're doing." The name doesn't ring a bell. "John Wilkes? . . ." (Booth—Lincoln's assassin, and an actor.) Cliff mentions Rick, whom George mistakes for a Dalton brother (from the outlaw gang, also from the previous century). George says he is OK—getting old, losing his eyesight. Just one thing makes him happy: Squeaky. "So, suck on that," he says to Cliff. George cuts short the encounter to go back to sleep. Just as Squeaky had told Cliff earlier, George needs a nap so he won't fall asleep watching "The FBI" on TV with her later that night.

Cliff begins the long walk to his car. The street's quiet: as they say in westerns, "too quiet." He walks past Pussycat. The camera tilts up, taking her in from behind, head to toe. Tarantino crudely sizes her up. But not because Cliff is much interested. Back to Cliff as the long walk becomes a gauntlet of sorts composed of hippies shouting at him. He gets to his car and there's a knife in one of his tires. It's flat. He arrived at the Ranch an old-Hollywood tough guy and he intends to exit as one. He assumes Clem (a.k.a. Steven Grogan, played by James Landry Hébert) has stabbed the tire, so he beats Clem in front of the Family and forces him to change it.[41]

We cut to Tate outside the Bruin Theater in Westwood. She is happy—we figure, not for long. It's dusk in Hollywood as Cliff and Rick drive by the Pantages Theater. On the marquee: Christopher Jones in *3 in the Attic*. When Cliff and Rick arrive at Rick's house, they settle in to watch *The FBI* on TV. Just like Squeaky and George.

Once Upon a Time in Hollywood was by most every industry marker a success: a Palme d'Or at Cannes, ten Oscar nominations, and two well-deserved wins: Pitt for Supporting Actor and Barbara Ling and Nancy Haigh for their spot-on Production Design. Box office home and away (domestic and overseas) exceeded expectations. Some of the critics were a bit less enthusiastic, and their complaints were predictable. And frankly, wearying. The problem with movie reviewers is they have to see films they don't want to see. The problem (for reviewers) with moviemakers is they make the movies *they* want to make—movies that often are not what the reviewers want from them, or from anyone. *Once Upon a Time in Hollywood* is the Manson film Tarantino was always going to make: a nostalgic macho star vehicle. They don't make them like that anymore, and, as a number of critics added, there are reasons why—though I hasten to add, none of those reasons are particularly useful or good.[42]

A consistent compliant among critics and on filmgoers' online forums focused on Tarantino's "use" of Margot Robbie, her limited screen time, and his seeming limited interest in Tate, whom she portrays in the film. No doubt Tarantino was more comfortable writing for Rick and Cliff, his made-up male heroes, than Tate, a real-life

FIGURE 37. Margot Robbie as Sharon Tate, for the moment in a happy place in her life and career in *Once Upon a Time in Hollywood* (Quentin Tarantino, 2019, Sony Pictures).

victim. But then again, Tate gets to live in his version. Tarantino gives us enough of Tate (and Robbie) in the film to really like her, then doesn't have the heart to kill her. In *Once Upon a Time in Hollywood*, Tate is a good-natured actor in a happy place in her life and career—a late sixties Hollywood aspirant, still jazzed enough by the absurdity of her success to be impressed by it (the scene at the Bruin Theater attests to that), a nice kid who should have lived longer. And she does (live longer) in Tarantino's fractured fairy tale.

Manson isn't given much to do in the film—a surprise to anyone previously worried about what Tarantino might do with the story. It was a smart move. Tarantino had the good sense (when was the last time a sentence began with those words?) and taste (ditto) to make Manson a bit player, to depict him as the small-time loser he really was in real life. The defense rests.

Epilogue

Joan Didion famously wrote that for folks in Los Angeles, "the sixties ended abruptly on August 9, 1969, ended at the exact moment when word of the murders on Cielo Drive traveled like brushfire through the community." Turns out, there was still more to come. For the counterculture, it would be a bumpy ride to the finish.

Just a few weeks after the murders, Woodstock brought some much-needed good news. Peace, love, music. A little rain never hurt anyone. A hit movie and multi-LP album followed soon after the event, and that was a good thing (as we would need reminding). In the years and decades to follow, we'd refer to a "Woodstock generation." But that was always an incomplete and convenient fiction.

The euphoria of Woodstock lasted barely four months; it surrendered to and was supplanted by a badly planned copycat event staged at a racetrack in Altamont, California—a music festival climaxed by a fatal stabbing. Mick Jagger's face, bewildered and crestfallen, captured in freeze frame at the end of the film about the event (*Gimme Shelter*, directed by Albert and David Maysles and Charlotte Zwerin, and released in 1970), would tell us all we needed to know about—to loosely paraphrase Joyce Carol Oates—where we had been and where we seemed to be going.[1] Peace and love had given way to bad mojo and pointless violence; violence that had been in the air was also in the world. Again.

Roads to Nowhere

Mark Frechette was once upon a time just another complicated young man hanging out on the streets of Boston. He was minding his own business when he was quite suddenly plucked from what Hollywood deems "obscurity"—that is anywhere that is not Hollywood—and signed to make a movie for MGM. Stardom would be there for the taking, but Frechette opted instead for a communal life in a rugged part of Boston, devoting his few remaining years to a former musician turned spiritual guru. A series of odd jobs and roles followed: bank robber, inmate stage director, murder victim.

Before he made *Easy Rider*, Dennis Hopper had been hanging around Hollywood for over a decade. The film made him popular and famous, admired even. He followed up on his long-awaited success with the surefire career suicide of *The Last Movie*, released the following year. The supposed counterculture western was precisely that, for him—his last movie for a decade.

Daria Halprin, Frechette's costar in *Zabriskie Point*, dated Frechette and then married Hopper, and then went on a spiritual journey that took her well and safely far from Hollywood, far from Frechette and Hopper and men like either of them.

In the space of a year or so, Christopher Jones went from working with David Lean in Ireland to sleeping rough, strung out on the streets of Hollywood, his physical decline a rejection of his *moneymaker*—his resemblance to James Dean. Jones's disappearing act was also an affirmation of the many pressures at the office, his unhappy discovery that being a professional actor might actually be, for a hip sixties celebrity like him, kind of a drag.

Dolores Hart thought she wanted Hollywood stardom, then changed her mind and devoted her life to God. She dropped out (of Hollywood) leaving behind a world in which she never quite fit. Barbara Loden wanted something else as well—to be an artist; but that is seldom an option in Hollywood. The available alternatives, the Hollywood movie star thing, the Hollywood wife thing were for her untenable, especially given the sorts of films she'd have to make, especially given the character of the man in her life.

To compensate for their good fortune—their Hollywood celebrity and privilege—Jean Seberg and Jane Fonda tried to do some of the right things: they rallied to stop the war, they raised money to defend the downtrodden and oppressed. For her efforts, Seberg was nudged closer and closer to the ledge by some very powerful and awful people, until she finally jumped.

Fonda was made of sterner stuff. And she has proved indomitable. Nearly fifty years after her visit to North Vietnam, hecklers are still calling her "Hanoi Jane." Most of them don't know why; they weren't around in 1972. Fonda has moved on; at least she's she tried to. Thick red coat in hand, celebrating a recent birthday with another night in jail, protesting yet another matter of political stupidity, she is counterculture Hollywood's enduring survivor, this book's lone start to finish success story.

If not for a terrible set of circumstances—the very bad luck of renting a house previously occupied by a creep like Terry Melcher—Sharon Tate would have survived the sixties. At the time of her death, she was just twenty-six years old. Her career trajectory evinced a fairly modest ascent and followed a familiar pattern. Her first credited roles were on episodic TV, beginning with guest spots on *Mister Ed* and, like Christopher Jones, *The Man from U.N.C.L.E.* Steady work followed, including a recurring part in a multi-episode arc on *The Beverly Hillbillies*. In 1967, Tate graduated from the small to big screen with featured roles in three mid-budget films: the occult

FIGURE 38. Sharon Tate (foreground) with costars Patty Duke (left) and Barbara Parkins in a publicity photo for the 1967 Hollywood melodrama *Valley of the Dolls* (Mark Robson) (Everett Collection).

thriller *Eye of the Devil*, directed by J. Lee Thompson, with David Niven; *Don't Make Waves*, a light comedy directed by Alexander Mackendrick, opposite Tony Curtis; and the New Wave comedy-horror mash-up *The Fearless Vampire Killers*, directed by her future husband, Roman Polanski.

Slightly bigger roles in films no one would or should call good followed. Tate played one of the ambitious starlets in Mark Robson's tawdry, campy adaptation of Jacqueline Susann's tawdry, campy Hollywood potboiler *Valley of the Dolls* and then did a comic turn on the Bond-girl thing in the Dean Martin/Matt Helm spy farce *The Wrecking Crew* (both in 1969). Her final film, the counterculture comedy *12+1* (a.k.a. *13 Chairs*) was released in the United States after her death, and its light comic tone seemed, as most any film starring Tate would have at the time, disrespectful and in bad taste. *Variety* aptly summarized its appeal in the first line of its December 31, 1969, review: "mainly of interest as being the last of the tragically fated Sharon Tate."[2] There was little else or more to say.

It has become fashionable to argue that Tate was on the verge of becoming a movie star, that she was terrifically talented and it was just a matter of time before she got the right part in the right film. Putting sentiment aside, it is just as possible that the right part in the right film might never have turned up for her, and that she would have been eye candy in tawdry melodramas, spy farces, and low-budget comedies until she wasn't eye candy in anything anymore. We'll never know. She will be forever the era's most famous victim, counterculture Hollywood's enduring martyr.

This Is the End . . .

One last vignette: In "The White Album," Didion briefly indulges a rock and roll anecdote, but it is not the obvious one. It's not her take on "The Beatles" (the actual title of their "White Album," so named because it had a white jacket) but, instead, an account of an L.A. recording session with the Doors—a recollection that allows Didion to obsess on Jim Morrison in his black vinyl pants and no underwear. Didion tells us in the essay that she had beforehand listened some to the Doors' music and couldn't shake its effect. She dubs the band, "missionaries of apocalyptic sex." She digs the Doors' music, and she for sure digs Morrison.

"The Doors music insisted that love was sex and sex was death and therein lay salvation," Didion mused. She was at the time of the session in her mid-thirties—not exactly a fan girl and not part of the counterculture, but nonetheless grooving on Morrison's nihilist persona, his avowed interest in (and here, Didion is quoting Morrison) "anything about revolt, disorder, chaos."

Didion was following her instincts with the Doors and Morrison, a 1965 UCLA film school grad whom she recognized as a keen fellow observer of the Southland scene. The lyrics Morrison wrote for the Doors got under her skin. And she was not the only one. The Doors' 1967 song, "The End" got under Francis Coppola's skin as well, so much so, the director, who was at UCLA just a few years before Morrison, opened his 1979 film *Apocalypse Now* with the number, boosting in the sound mix Morrison's vocals and the song's lyrics.

According to Morrison, "The End" was really or at least initially about a broken-up love affair. But the imagery and the song's dramatic performance seem more portentous, more ominous than that. "There's a danger on the edge of town," Morrison tells us. (Manson isn't due for another two years, but still, plenty of guys like him were already there.) Morrison then screams "Fuck" into the microphone seven times, "Fuck me baby," then "fuck" three more times, then "yeah," "whoah," and "baby," then "kill, kill, kill, kill, kill, kill." The one word repeated six times. "Fuck" and "kill"—rage and frustration—repeated for effect. The final stanza gestures at abdication: "It hurts to set you free / But you'll never follow me," and then

FIGURE 39. Jim Morrison of the Doors: poet, rock star, counterculture casualty (Everett Collection).

ends with a harbinger, a warning: "The end of laughter and soft lies / The end of nights we tried to die / This is the end."

Counterculture to his core, Morrison engaged, as Didion observed, "the range of the possible just beyond a suicide pact."[3] Hard to imagine being in or getting to such a place, but wherever Morrison's head was at, wherever he seemed to be going in 1969, pop celebrity was already too much for him to bear. His former Chateau Marmont neighbor Christopher Jones would succumb to the same pressures and self-destructive impulses.

Morrison was all of twenty-seven years old in 1971 when he was found dead in a bathtub in Paris. There was by then an ocean between himself and whatever spooked him back in L.A. (and on the outskirts of that town)—the beautiful people *and* the many unlovely and lonely as well, who are always already there. He spent his last days mostly alone and anonymous, hiding out from what he once had been, from what most everyone else in America wished they could one day be: a rock star. Morrison's particular road trip took him from Florida (and then after several stops en route) to L.A. and then finally to Paris, which, like L.A., was in the end nowhere to him.

Notes

Introduction

1. Joan Didion, *The White Album* (New York: Farrar, Giroux, Strauss, 1979), 42. The italics are hers.

2. This is a story told elsewhere and often, well worth retelling here, as it neatly sets the stage for counterculture Hollywood. See Mark Harris, *Pictures at a Revolution: Five Movies and the Birth of a New Hollywood* (New York: Penguin, 2009); Louis Menand, "Paris Texas: How Hollywood brought the cinema back from France," *New Yorker*, February 17 and 24, 2003, 169-177; David Newman and Robert Benton, "Lightning in a Bottle," in Sandra Wake and Nicola Hayden (eds.) *The Bonnie and Clyde Book* (New York: Simon and Schuster, 1972), 13, 15, 23; and Richard Brody, *Everything Is Cinema: The Working Life of Jean-Luc Godard* (New York: Metropolitan Books, 2008), 220-222. The vignette is recalled as well in the introduction to a book I coedited with Jonathan Kirshner, *When the Movies Mattered: The New Hollywood Revisited* (Ithaca, NY: Cornell University Press, 2019), 2-3.

3. Bosley Crowther, "Shoot-Em-Up Film Opens World Fete; '*Bonnie and Clyde*' Cheered by Montreal First-Nighters," *New York Times* August 7, 1967, 32.

4. Joseph Morgenstern, "Two for a Tommy Gun," *Newsweek* August 21, 1967, 65.

5. Joseph Morgenstern, "The Thin Red Line," *Newsweek* August 28, 1967, 82, 95.

6. "The whole equation of pictures" was mooted first by F. Scott Fitzgerald in *The Loves of the Last Tycoon* (New York: Scribner, 1994), 3. The phrase continues to be relevant now, nearly a century later. See: David Thomson, *The Whole Equation:*

A Hollywood History (New York: Vintage, 2006) and Thomas Schatz, *The Genius of the System: Hollywood Filmmaking in the Studio Era* (New York: Metropolitan Books, 1996).

7. For (much) more on labor and race in Hollywood, see: Eithne Quinn, *A Piece of the Action: Race and Labor in Civil Rights Hollywood* (New York: Columbia University Press, 2019).

8. With Ruth Bernhard, van Peebles chronicled the cable-car experience in a book-length photo-essay: *The Big Heart* (San Francisco: Fearon Press, 1957).

9. Rick Setlowe, "Saga of a Negro Filmmaker: Van Peebles in Filmways Break," *Variety*, December 13, 1967, 7, 18.

10. Van Peebles directed an episode of Cosby's popular TV show in 1970. The two men seem today (given their profiles, given what we now know about both of them) unlikely partners.

11. The MPPA refused to grant the film an R in 1971, so in its first run *Sweetback* was distributed with an X rating. That rating was modified to an R in 1974 for the New World rerelease.

12. Roger Greenspun, "Screen Ideas for Cliches," *New York Times*, April 24, 1971, 17.

13. Clayton Riley, "What Makes Sweetback Run?" *New York Times*, May 9, 1971, D11.

14. Vincent Canby, "'*Sweetback*': Does It Exploit Injustice?," *New York Times*, May 9, 1971, D1, D18.

15. Accounts of the UCLA shootout vary wildly: See: Marina Dindjerski, *UCLA: The First Century* (Los Angeles: Third Millennium Press, 2012), 183-184 and Kathleen Cleaver and George Katsiaficas, *Liberation, Imagination, and the Back Panther Party* (New York: Routledge, 2001), 93-94.

16. See: Rick Perlstein, "Politics and Oscar Night," *The Nation*, February 25, 2013, https://www.thenation.com/article/politics-and-oscar-night/.

17. The "Cumulative Index" is available on line through the Hathi Trust Digital Library, https://catalog.hathitrust.org/Record/003964497.

18. Jon Wiener, "When Old Blue Eyes Was Red," *New Republic*, March 31, 1986, https://newrepublic.com/article/125328/old-blue-eyes-red.

19. "Sinatra Arrested after Attack on Film Editor Here," *Los Angeles Examiner*, April 10, 1947, 1.

20. Much of what follows about the last days at BBS and Blauner's unlikely friendship with Huey Newton is taken from Peter Biskind's wild and wonderful *Easy Riders, Raging Bulls* (New York: Simon and Shuster, 1998), 271-273.

21. Arthur Ross's credits include the script for B-horror classic *Creature from the Black Lagoon* (Jack Arnold, 1954), and the story (most likely for an early draft) for the Oscar-nominated *Brubaker* (Stuart Rosenberg, 1980).

22. Biskind, *Easy Riders, Raging Bulls*, 272.

23. Lanre Bakare, "How Hollywood Feted the Black Power Movement—and Fell Afoul of the FBI," *Guardian*, December 5, 2019, https://www.theguardian.com/film/2019/dec/05/how-hollywood-feted-the-black-power-movement-and-fell-foul-of-the-fbi.

24. See Ken Kelley, "Huey: I'll Never Forget," *East Bay Express*, September 14, 1989, https://archive.org/stream/Huey-Never-Forget-1989/1989-EBExpress-Cropped_djvu.txt.

25. For a comprehensive history of the Panthers, see: Joshua Bloom and Waldo E. Martin, *Black against Empire: The History and Politics of the Black Panther Party* (Berkeley: University of California Press, 2016).

26. "Arrest in Murder of Huey Newton," *New York Times*, August 26, 1989, https://www.nytimes.com/1989/08/26/us/arrest-in-murder-of-huey-newton.html.

27. See: Columbia Pictures Industries, Inc. v. Schneider, 435 F. Supp. 742—Dist. Court, SD New York 1977, https://scholar.google.com/scholar_case?case=10910068820884805445&hl=en&as_sdt=6&as_vis=1&oi=scholarr.

28. Rex Reed, "A Film Americans May Not See," *Independent Press Telegram*, August 18, 1974, https://www.presstelegram.com/.

29. Vincent Canby, "*Hearts and Minds*: A Film Study of Power," *New York Times*, March 24, 1975, https://www.nytimes.com/1975/03/24/archives/hearts-and-minds-a-film-study-of-power.html.

30. I saw *Hearts and Minds* when it came out; I was in college by then and had seen my number come up, so to speak. Briefly: my May 8, 1955, birthdate was entered into the draft lottery in 1974. My lottery number was 169, which meant I didn't have to get a physical, as my draft status designation was 1-H (for Holding). The war and with it the draft ended before I had to decide what to do. *Hearts and Minds* had a profound effect on me—on a lot of other young men like me. For sure: Floyd's monologue in the film deeply moved me.

31. Tom Wolfe, *Radical Chic and Mau-Mauing the Flak Catchers* (New York: Farrar, Strauss & Giroux, 1970).

32. See George Orwell's 1941 essay, "The Lion and the Unicorn: Socialism and the English Genius," https://www.orwellfoundation.com/the-orwell-foundation/orwell/essays-and-other-works/the-lion-and-the-unicorn-socialism-and-the-english-genius/.

Chapter 1. Road Trips to a New Hollywood

1. "Negative pickup" is an industry term referring to a film licensed for distribution *after* production is complete and paid for.

2. Andrew Sarris, "*Blow-Up*" (review), *Village Voice*, December 29, 1966, http://www.openculture.com/2017/08/read-1000-editions-of-the-the-village-voice-a-digital-archive-of-the-iconic-new-york-city-paper.html.

3. Bosley Crowther, "Screen: *Blow-Up* Arrives at Coronet; Hero Switches between Luxury and Squalor," *New York Times*, December 19, 1966, https://www.nytimes.com/1966/12/19/archives/screen-blowup-arrives-at-coronet-hero-switches-between-luxury-and.html.

4. *L'Avventura* opened in the United States in March 1961, one month before Fellini's *La Dolce Vita*. Jean-Luc Godard's *Breathless* reached American screens in February. It was a very good year.

5. Andrew Sarris, "Andrew Sarris Demands You See This," *Village Voice*, March 23, 1961, http://www.villagevoice.com/news/andrew-sarris-demands-you-see-this-6723489.

6. Stanley Kaufman, "Arrival of an Artist," *New Republic*, Aril 10, 1961, https://newrepublic.com/article/62856/arrival-artist-0.

7. "The *Sight and Sound* Top Ten Poll," *BFI Film Forever*, http://old.bfi.org.uk/sightandsound/polls/topten/1962/html.

8. Robert B. Frederick, "Valenti at Society of Mag Writers: Snobs Deify Foreign Film Directors Whose Name End with 'O' or 'I,'" *Variety*, September 18, 1968, 3, 17.

9. Frederick, 17.

10. The MPAA Production Code was written in 1930 by a Jesuit priest and a pro-censorship activist. By 1966 it was well out of fashion and out of date, but still retained absolute authority. The PCA, which enforced the MPAA censorship Code, gave films a seal of approval. Or they didn't. And if they didn't, theater owners booking such a film were left very much on their own, risking local boycotts, bans, and print seizures.

11. I make this argument at length elsewhere. See Jon Lewis, *Hollywood v. Hard Core: How the Struggle over Censorship saved the Modern Film Industry* (New York: New York University Press, 2000).

12. Ronald Gold, "Valenti Won't 'Blow-Up' Prod. Code for Status Films; No Church Push," *Variety*, January 11, 1967, 1, 78.

13. "'*Blow Up*' B.O. Comforts Metro," *Variety*, March 22, 1967, 6.

14. Pauline Kael, "Tourist in the City of Youth: *Blow Up!*" *New Republic*, February 7, 1967, https://scrapsfromtheloft.com/2018/07/17/blow-up-pauline-kael/.

15. Penelope Gilliat, "Into the Eye of the Storm," in *Film 69/70: An Anthology by the National Association of Film Critics*, edited by Joseph Morgenstern and Stefan Kanfer (New York: Simon and Shuster, 1970), 36.

16. See: Jon Lewis, *Whom God Wishes to Destroy . . . Francis Coppola and the New Hollywood* (Durham, NC: Duke University Press, 1995).

17. After over a decade at MCA, Tanen's Midas Touch continued at Paramount, supervising the production of *Ferris Bueller's Day Off* (Hughes, 1986), *Top Gun* (Tony Scott, 1986), and *Fatal Attraction* (Lyne, 1987).

18. Renata Adler, "The Screen: *Head*, Monkees movie for a Turned-On Audience," *New York Times*, November 7, 1968, 51.

19. Pauline Kael, "*Head*" (review), *New Yorker*, November 23, 1968, 202.

20. "Non-news Story of the Year Award," *Rolling Stone*, February 1, 1969, https://www.rollingstone.com/results/#?q=Head%20Non%20News%20story%20of%20the%20year%201969.

21. J. Hoberman, "One Big Real Place: BBS from Head to Hearts," *On Film*, November 28, 2010, https://www.criterion.com/current/posts/1671-one-big-real-place-bbs-from-head-to-hearts.

22. See: Jonathan Kirshner, "'Jason's No Businessman . . . I Think He's an Artist': BBS and the New Hollywood Dream," in *When the Movies Mattered: The New Hollywood Revisited*, edited by Kirshner and Jon Lewis (Ithaca, NY: Cornell University Press, 2019), 51–68. As Kirshner notes, Nicholson's role in *Easy Rider*—the role that made him a movie star—was originally contracted to Rip Torn. That actor's last-minute exit provided Nicholson with his big break.

23. After writing the novel, *Drive He Said*, Larner became a speechwriter for Eugene McCarthy, the Democratic Party "peace candidate" in the run-up to Hubert Humphrey's badly miscalculated run in 1968. Four years later, Larner would win a screenwriting Oscar for the cautionary political melodrama *The Candidate*.

24. Vincent Canby, "Nicholson's *Drive, He Said*; Movie Marks Actor's Debut as Director," *New York Times*, June 14, 1971, 49.

25. Paul Zimmerman, "The Streets of Anarene," *Newsweek*, October 11, 1971, 57.

26. Pauline Kael, "*The Last Picture Show*" (capsule review), https://www.newyorker.com/goings-on-about-town/movies/the-last-picture-show.

27. Roger Ebert, "An Interview with Michelangelo Antonioni," *Chicago Sun-Times*, June 19, 1969, http://www.rogerebert.com/interviews/interview-with-michelangelo-antonioni.

28. Charles Thomas Samuels, "Interview with Michelangelo Antonioni," https://scrapsfromtheloft.com/2017/10/11/interview-michelangelo-antonioni/. Among the influential underground artists, Antonioni singles out Andy Warhol: "His characters do and say what they want to and are, therefore, wholly original."

29. Ebert, "An interview with Michelangelo Antonioni."

30. Donato Totaro, "*Zabriskie Point* (1970, Antonioni): A Scene by Scene Analysis of a Troubled Masterpiece," *Offscreen*, 14:4, 2010, https://offscreen.com/view/zabriskie_point_1970.

31. Not long after the production wrapped, Kathleen Cleaver reunited with her husband in Algeria, where he had been living in exile. Together, they then moved to Paris and then back to the United States, where Eldridge Cleaver once again faced the American justice and penal system, as so vividly chronicled in his groundbreaking book, *Soul on Ice*. The couple eventually split, and Kathleen Cleaver went back to school, receiving a BA and then a JD at Yale University. She currently teaches law at Emory University in Atlanta.

32. George Pocari, "Antonioni's Orgy: Zabriskie Point," *Lightmonkey*, http://www.lightmonkey.net/antonionis-orgy.

33. Totaro, "*Zabriskie Point*."

34. Michelangelo Antonioni, "A Conversation about *Zabriskie Point*," in *The Architecture of Vision*, edited by Carlo di Carlo, Giorgio Tinazzi, and Marga Cottino-Jones (Chicago: Universality of Chicago Press, 1996), 94.

35. Murray Pomerance, *Michelangelo Red Antonioni Blue* (Berkeley: University of California Press, 2011), 170.

36. See: Beverly Walker, "Michelangelo and the Leviathan," *Film Comment*, September/October 1992, 36–49.

37. The "G," "M," and "R" classifications in place when Antonioni produced *Zabriskie Point* accommodated a wide range of on-screen content. Material deemed outside that range received no rating at all and had to be released without an MPAA seal. The "X" rating, which Valenti did not copyright because he felt that the studios should not get into the soft- or hard-core business, could be self-imposed but it lumped potentially serious adult-themed films with more purely prurient and exploitative pictures.

38. Pierre Billard, "An Interview with Michelangelo Antonioni," in *Michelangelo Antonioni Interviews*, ed. Bert Cardullo (Jackson: University of Mississippi Press, 2008), 55.

39. Liz Diamond, "Joseph Chaikin," *Bomb*, no. 68, July 1, 1999, https://bomb magazine.org/articles/joseph-chaikin/. *Zabriskie Point* scenarist Sam Shepard contributed to Chaikin and the Open Theater's final production, *Nightwalk* (1973), an exploration of levels of sleep and dreams, expressed through music, dance, and speech.

40. Pomerance, *Michelangelo Red Antonioni Blue*, 162–65.

41. For the record, my dad was an accountant for the Teamsters back in the 1970s. When I say that Antonioni was never going to get the Teamsters to do anything they didn't want to do, I say so acknowledging here that the Teamsters did right by my father, while also appreciating how the organization and its membership operate.

42. Guy Flatley, "Antonioni Defends '*Zabriskie Point*,'" *New York Times*, February 22, 1970, https://www.nytimes.com/1970/02/22/archives/antonioni-defends-zabriskie-point-i-love-this-country.html.

43. "Grand Jury Will Look Into '*Zabriskie*' Today," *Los Angeles Times*, May 28, 1969, D14.

44. Flatley, "Antonioni Defends '*Zabriskie Point*.'"

45. It was not until 1989 and the decision in *California v Freeman* that paid performance of sex acts in motion pictures *whether real or simulated* could not be construed as a mode of prostitution. For more on this fascinating case, see https://caselaw.findlaw.com/us-supreme-court/488/1311.html. As then California Supreme Court Justice Sandra Day O'Connor wrote at the time, since the ostensible reason for the sex act is to entertain and not to sexually arouse, paying actors to perform in a pornographic film (a category that *Zabriskie Point* in 1969 fell into, for some filmgoers and jurists) was not the same as paying a prostitute for sex.

46. Bryan Thomas, "*Zabriskie Point*: Young Love and Death in the Symbolic American Desert," *Night Flight*, July 16, 2015, http://nightflight.com/zabriskie-point-antonionis-countercultural-late-60s-look-at-young-love-and-death-in-the-symbolic-american-desert/.

47. Pomerance, *Michelangelo Red Antonioni Blue*, 175–76.

48. Flatley, "Antonioni Defends '*Zabriskie Point*.'"

49. Pomerance, *Michelangelo Red Antonioni Blue*, 187, 189.

50. Antonioni, "A Conversation about *Zabriskie Point*," 92.

51. Antonioni as cited by Beverly Walker, "Michelangelo and the Leviathan," 48.

52. While researching his book, *Michelangelo Red, Antonioni Blue*, Pomerance talked with Beverly Walker and several others who worked with Antonioni on

the film. Pomerance believes Aubrey was sincere in his admiration of the director and the film and that he tried his best to position and platform the film in the marketplace.

53. Joyce Haber, "'*Zabriskie Point*' Rescued by Aubrey," *Los Angeles Times*, December 2, 1969, G12.

54. Haber, G12.

55. A quick note on *Midnight Cowboy*: When the film was submitted to the MPAA, it received an R-rating. But United Artists' Arthur Krim decided to self-impose an "X" because he felt the film was so radically different from the other films distributed by the studio. He was right about that, of course; it was different, and that's in large part why it was so successful (winning a Best Picture Oscar, etc.). After the Oscar, United Artists resubmitted the film and its subsequent theatrical and home box office runs were with the R-rating.

56. Pauline Kael, "The Beauty of Destruction," *New Yorker*, February 21, 1970, 95–99.

57. Haber, "'*Zabriskie Point*' Rescued by Aubrey," G12.

58. Whatever Aubrey's true feelings were—that is, assuming film executives have true feelings—in the end, for sure, MGM did *not* give *Zabriskie Point* a wide release.

59. Vincent Canby, "Screen: Antonioni's *Zabriskie Point*," *New York Times*, February 10, 1970, http://www.nytimes.com/movie/review?res=9E04E2DB1F3FE034BC4852DFB466838B669EDE.

60. Charles Champlin, "Movie Review: Plight of U.S. Basis of Plot in '*Zabriskie*,'" *Los Angeles Times*, March 18, 1970, F1 and F13.

61. Cohen, as quoted by Flatley.

62. Roger Ebert, "*Zabriskie Point*" (review), *Chicago Sun-Times*, January 1, 1970, http://www.rogerebert.com/reviews/zabriskie-point-1970.

63. Michael Cimino's gorgeous and expensive *Heaven's Gate* cost around $44 million to produce and earned, even under the most generous estimations, under $4 million after a couple of poorly handled theatrical releases in 1980 and 1981. For most historians of the New Hollywood, *Heaven's Gate* marks the demise of the auteur renaissance, a brief era when the studios invested in the appeal and artistry of individual directors. There are lots of reasons why United Artists (UA) lost control of the production and then took a bath on *Heaven's Gate*. For more on the UA/*Heaven's Gate* story, see: Stephen Bach, *Final Cut: Art, Money, and Ego in the Making of "Heaven's Gate," the Film That Sank United Artists* (New York: Newmarket, 1999) and Jon Lewis, "The Auteur Renaissance: 1968-1980," in *Producing*, edited by Jon Lewis (New Brunswick, NJ: Rutgers University Press, 2016), 86–110.

64. "Antonioni Pleads Guilty to Pot Charge," *Los Angeles Times*, February 11, 1970, D12.

65. Dennison so admired Antonioni's work that she sought him out. After completing her internship on *Zabriskie Point*, she went on to a successful career as a casting agent. Dennison is credited on over forty films including *The China Syndrome* (James Bridges, 1979) and *Heathers* (Michael Lehmann, 1988).

66. Roos worked on the popular TV shows *I Spy* and *Mayberry RFD*. In 1971 he was hired by Paramount to cast (and would later receive a producer's credit for) *The Godfather*.

67. Sam Tweedle, "Return to *Zabriskie Point*: The Mark Frechette and Daria Halprin Story," *Confessions of a Pop Culture Addict* (blog), http://popcultureaddict.com/movies-2/zabriskiepoint-htm/.

68. Rasa Gustaitas, "Michelangelo, Mark and Daria," *Los Angeles Times*, May 11, 1969, M22.

69. Gustaitas, M22.

70. Ryan H. Walsh, *Astral Weeks: A Secret History of 1968* (New York: Penguin, 2018), 158.

71. Gustaitas, "Michelangelo, Mark and Daria," M23.

72. Gustaitas, M23.

73. Gustaitas, M23.

74. George McKinnon, "*Zabriskie Point*: Stars Rap Movie," *Boston Globe*, July 10, 1969, https://www.bostonglobe.com/.

75. Ebert, "An Interview with Michelangelo Antonioni."

76. Gustaitas, "Michelangelo, Mark and Daria,", M27.

77. Gustaitis, M27.

78. Much of what I have to say about Lyman is based on: Walsh, *Astral Weeks: A Secret History of 1968*; David Felton, "The Lyman Family's Holy Siege of America: Inside the Cult Led by Mel Lyman, the East Coast Charles Manson," *Rolling Stone*, December 23, 1971, http://www.rollingstone.com/culture/features/the-lyman-familys-holy-siege-of-america-19711223; and various postings on https://www.trussel.com/f_mel.htm, a site that aggregates published and posted material on Lyman and Fort Hill.

79. Walsh, *Astral Weeks*, 28–29.

80. David Felton and David Dalton, "Charles Manson: The Incredible Story of the Most Dangerous Man Alive," *Rolling Stone*, June 25, 1970, https://www.rollingstone.com/culture/culture-news/charles-manson-the-incredible-story-of-the-most-dangerous-man-alive-85235/.

81. Felton, "The Lyman Family's Holy Siege."

82. Alpert/Dass used the royalties earned from his books to support nonprofits focused on spiritual well-being—a detail often omitted in the critique.

83. In February 2017, *Boston* magazine ran a feature on Fort Hill, including an interview with Benton, who at the time was living at the Community's Martha's Vineyard property. See: Simon Van Zuylen-Wood, *Boston*, February 19, 2017, https://www.bostonmagazine.com/arts-entertainment/2017/02/19/counterculture/3/.

84. There is no death certificate on file for Lyman anywhere in the United States. The Community went public with news of his 1978 death in 1985. No investigation followed. See Walsh, *Astral Weeks*, 301–4. See: David Johnston, "Once Notorious '60s Commune Evolves into Respectability: After 19 Years the Lyman Family Prospers as Craftsmen and Farmers," *Los Angeles Times*, August 4, 1985, https://www.latimes.com/archives/la-xpm-1985-08-04-vw-4546-story.html.

85. Walsh, *Astral Weeks*, 242–43.

86. Hunter S. Thompson, *Fear and Loathing in Las Vegas* (New York: Vintage, 1971), 179. "Spirit and Flesh" likely refers to the Brotherhood of the Spirit, a cult assembled around Michael Metelica, sited in Warwick, Massachusetts, in 1970. The Brotherhood eschewed drugs and promiscuous sex and espoused spirituality through the medium of rock and roll music. Cult members produced a record album, titled "Spirit in Flesh," released by Multimedia Records and currently posted in its entirety on YouTube: https://www.youtube.com/watch?v=VjVOI8WVkbs. For more on Metelica and the Brotherhood, see: *Free Spirits*, a documentary directed by Bruce Geisler in 2007. Like Fort Hill, the Brotherhood, later renamed (less ominously) the Renaissance Community expanded in the early 1970s; at its peak, over four hundred followers lived at one of four different Massachusetts sites.

87. Dave O'Brian, "The Sorry Life and Death of Mark Frechette," *Rolling Stone*, November 6, 1975, 32

88. Thomas Moore, "Tom Benton, 83: Never Argue with Youth," *Life*, July 14, 1972, 73.

89. Charles Thomas Samuels, "Interview with Michelangelo Antonioni," interview conducted in 1969 while Antonioni was editing *Zabriskie Point*, https://scrapsfromtheloft.com/2017/10/11/interview-michelangelo-antonioni/.

90. Roger Ebert, "An Interview with Michelangelo Antonioni."

91. *Uomini contro* is currently available for streaming on YouTube: https://www.youtube.com/watch?v=jgYTQQNRBD4.

92. In a blog post for popcultureaddict.com, Sam Tweedle mentions a third film, *Man Against*, produced in Yugoslavia. The film is not listed on Frechette's IMDB page and there is no IMDB page for the film.

93. A. H. Weiler, "*The Jerusalem File* Arrives," *New York Times*, February 3, 1972, https://www.nytimes.com/1972/02/03/archives/the-jerusalem-file-arrives.html.

94. Daria Halprin, "My Esalen Story," https://www.esalen.org/page/daria-halprin-my-Esalen-story.

95. See: http://www.dariahalprin.org/.

96. Marin Hopper, "Destiny in Taos," the *New York Times Style Magazine*, September 9, 2014, https://tmagazine.blogs.nytimes.com/2014/09/09/dennis-hopper-taos-new-mexico/.

97. Hopper.

98. Walsh, *Astral Weeks*, 169–74.

99. Walsh, 173.

100. O'Brian, "The Sorry Life and Death of Mark Frechette," 32.

101. Flatley, "Antonioni Defends '*Zabriskie Point.*'"

102. Rumors persist about the Orbison song. I've encountered different and contradictory versions: (1) that Antonioni supervised the film's final music program in Italy (including "So Young,") with Aubrey and MGM's full support *and* (2) that this final song, which was written and performed by talent under contract at MGM, was added (most likely under Aubrey's direction) at the last minute (without Antonioni's approval) to make the film a bit more upbeat. We'll never know for sure.

103. William Hall, "Movies: Reality and Vision Meet," *Los Angeles Times*, December 30, 1973, H16.

Chapter 2. Christopher Jones Does Not Want to Be a Movie Star

1. The biography told here is compiled from a number of sources: Jan E. Morris's "Christopher Jones—Wild at Heart," *Cinetropic*, http://www.cinetropic.com/jones/bio.html, an online publication Morris developed with Jones's "personal approval"; Peter Winkler, "Whatever Happened to Christopher Jones? (Part One)" *World Cinema Paradise*, February 24, 2014, http://worldcinemaparadise.com/2014/02/24/whatever-happened-to-christopher-jones-part-1/, and Peter Winkler, "Whatever Happened to Christopher Jones? (Part Two)," *World Cinema Paradise*, February 27, 2014, http://worldcinemaparadise.com/2014/02/27/whatever-happened-to-christopher-jones-part-2/; "Friday Night Movie: *Three in the Attic* (1968) Christopher Jones Tribute," *Ouch! By Mr. E* (blogpost), https://3lawnview.blogspot.com/search?q=Christopher+Jones; Paul Vitello, "Christopher Jones, 72; walked away from movie stardom," *Boston Globe*, February 10, 2014, https://

www.bostonglobe.com/metro/obituaries/2014/02/10/christopher-jones-actor-who-walked-away-from-movie-stardom/xhiPHP9SCwvwp6cklfIO4K/story.html; Jack Croft, "Christopher Jones, Phil Ochs, and the Chords of Fame," *From a Pawned Smith Corona* (blogpost), August 18, 2016, https://jacroft3.com/2016/08/18/christopher-jones-phil-ochs-and-the-chords-of-fame/; Duke Haney, *Death Valley Superstars: Occasionally Fatal Adventures in Filmland* (Los Angeles: Delancey Street, 2018), 211–33; and Pamela Des Barres, "The Agony and the Ecstasy," *Movieline*, August 1996, 49–53, 79 86.

2. Morris, "Christopher Jones—Wild at Heart."

3. "Moody New Star: Hoosier James Dean Excites Hollywood," *Life*, March 7, 1955, 125–28. See also: Dennis Stock, *Dennis Stock: James Dean* (London: Thames and Hudson, 2015).

4. The real or historical Jesse James was no socialist outlaw, no progressive political avenger; he was instead a "bushwhacker," a Confederate sympathizer from southern Missouri and anti-abolitionist who likely rode with and certainly fought for the same cause as the Confederate terrorist William Quantrill. After the war, James continued his anti-Union, by then anti-American activities by robbing banks at gunpoint. For reasons that say more about the American psyche than they do about the facts of James's exploits, James became a cult hero—a status only enhanced by the betrayal of his former gang member Robert Ford, who famously shot James in the back on April 3, 1882. The rest (via Hollywood) is most certainly *not* history.

5. Howard Thompson, "Dracula Returns," *New York Times*, March 27, 1969, https://www.nytimes.com/1969/03/27/archives/dracula-returns.html.

6. See: https://www.driveinmovie.com/. Note: There are only three hundred such theaters in operation today, nationwide.

7. Samuel Arkoff with Richard Trubo, *Flying through Hollywood by the Seat of My Pants* (New York: Birch Lane Press, 1992), 165.

8. Arkoff, 241.

9. "Wild in the Streets," *Variety*, December 31, 1967, https://variety.com/1967/film/reviews/wild-in-the-streets-1200421455/.

10. Renata Adler, "Going 'Wild in the Streets,'" *New York Times*, June 16, 1968, https://www.nytimes.com/1968/06/16/archives/going-wild-in-the-streets-going-wild.html. Half the year had passed by the time Adler wrote the review, which is significant. That said, Adler qualified the praise later in the review by noting that 1968 had been, in her view, "the worst year in a long time for, among other things, movies."

11. "Bruce Dern," *WTF with Marc Maron* (podcast), episode 1052, September 9, 2019, http://www.wtfpod.com/podcast/episode-1052-bruce-dern.

12. Michael Schumacher, *There but for Fortune: The Life of Phil Ochs* (Westport, CT: Hyperion, 1996), 120-21.

13. Ochs's 1970 song The Chords of Fame" included the refrain: "God help the troubadour who tries to be a star."

14. See: Jack Croft, "Christopher Jones, Phil Ochs, and the Chords of Fame" (blog post) https://jacroft3.com/2016/08/18/christopher-jones-phil-ochs-and-the-chords-of-fame/. Ochs is maybe not so well known today, but he was famous enough, important enough, to have really interested the FBI, which assembled a five-hundred-page dossier tracking his counterculture activities. On April 29, 1976, the feminist and anti-war activist Congresswoman Bella Abzug read the following into the Congressional record:

> Mr. Speaker, a few weeks ago, a young folksinger whose music personified the protest mood of the 1960s took his own life. Phil Ochs—whose original compositions were compelling moral statements against the war in Southeast Asia—apparently felt that he had run out of words.
>
> While his tragic action was undoubtedly motivated by terrible personal despair, his death is a political as well as an artistic tragedy. I believe it is indicative of the despair many of the activists of the 1960s are experiencing as they perceive a government that continues the distortion of national priorities that is exemplified in the military budget we have before us.
>
> Phil Ochs's poetic pronouncements were part of a larger effort to galvanize his generation into taking action to prevent war, racism, and poverty. He left us a legacy of important songs that continue to be relevant in 1976—even though "the war is over".
>
> Just one year ago—during this week of the anniversary of the end of the Vietnam War—Phil recruited entertainers to appear at the "War is Over" celebration in Central Park, at which I spoke.
>
> It seems particularly appropriate that this week we should commemorate the contributions of this extraordinary young man.

15. In the early sixties Paul Jones was in a band with Elmo Lewis, who later went by the stage name Brian Jones. Legend has it that Lewis and his friend Keith Richards asked Paul Jones to front a group they were putting together, a group that would later become, of course, the Rolling Stones. Paul Jones turned them down.

16. See: Roger Ebert, "*Wild in the Streets*," https://www.rogerebert.com/reviews/wild-in-the-streets-1968 (review first published: May 20, 1968).

17. Paul Jones enjoyed similar crossover success with the songs he performed in *Privilege*. "I've Been a Bad, Bad Boy," sung by Jones as Steven Shorter, charted at number five in England in 1967. Four years later, Patti Smith covered "Set Me Free," another song from the film.

18. Jordan Runtaugh, "When John Lennon's 'More Popular Than Jesus Turned Ugly," *Rolling Stone*, July 29, 2016, https://www.rollingstone.com/music/music-features/when-john-lennons-more-popular-than-jesus-controversy-turned-ugly-106430/.

19. Johnny Whiteside, "What Were the 1966 Sunset Strip Riots Really Like? Eyewitnesses Look Back," *L.A. Weekly*, November 11, 2016, https://www.laweekly.com/what-were-the-1966-sunset-strip-riots-really-like-eyewitnesses-look-back/.

20. In a conference talk in 1961, the University of Chicago professor of educational psychology Bruno Bettelheim examined (and this was also the title of his talk), "the problem of generations." Absent "a pattern for the transition from young to old," Bettelheim posited, absent a discernible rite of passage into adulthood, a disconcerting competition emerges between the old and the young—a phenomenon that the media would soon dub, "the generation gap." Throughout history, the older generation had a stake in youth's rite of passage, "an emotional need to see its way of life continued by the coming generations." But instead of an "intimate feeling for their life's work," Bettelheim observed, the older generation had been exhibiting disillusionment and disaffection recently—an anomie that fifties cultural historians like David Riesman and C. Wright Mills had observed in the new American workplace.

21. Paul Goodman, *Growing Up Absurd* (New York: Random House, 1960), 11.

22. See: Alfred Kinsey, Wardell B. Pomeroy, and Clyde E. Martin, *Sexual Behavior in the Human Male* (Philadelphia: W.B. Saunders, 1948), Alfred Kinsey, Wardell B. Pomeroy, Clyde E. Martin, and Paul H. Gebhard, *Sexual Behavior in the Human Female* (Philadelphia: W.B. Saunders, 1953) and Vance Packard, *The Sexual Wilderness* (New York: David McKay, 1968). Also: William Masters and Virginia E. Johnson, *Human Sexual Response* (Boston: Little, Brown, 1966).

23. Vance Packard, *The Sexual Wilderness: The Contemporary Upheaval in Male-Female Relationships* (New York: McKay, 1968), 13–14.

24. Dixon v. Alabama State Board of Education, 186 F. Supp. 945 (M.D. Ala. 1960).

25. Vincent Canby, "Bye, Bye, Beach Bunnies: Bye, Bye, Beach Bunnies," *New York Times*, March 2, 1969, D1.The "neo-Simon and Garfunkel" was supplied by the pop duo Chad and Jeremy.

26. Howard Thompson, "*Looking Glass War*, a Le Carre Spy Story," *New York Times*, February 5, 1970, 33.

27. This is a frequently repeated story, but it's hard to believe, really. If indeed the dialogue was looped and provided by someone else, that "someone else" gets Jones's voice (timbre, tone, etc.) spot on and synchs/loops every syllable perfectly.

28. Sarah Miles, *Serves Me Right* (London: Orion, 1996), 332-33.

29. Vincent Canby, "Thoroughly Romantic Rosie," *New York Times*, November 22, 1970, https://www.nytimes.com/1970/11/22/archives/thoroughly-romantic-rosythoroughly-romantic-rosy.html

30. Pauline Kael, "The Current Cinema," *New Yorker*, November 21, 1970, 118, 124.

31. Melvyn Bragg interview with David Lean, https://www.youtube.com/watch?v=QvB-u7vVZus.

32. Des Barres, "The Agony and the Ecstasy," 53, 79.

33. Des Barres, 49.

34. For the record: Jones, Tate, and Morrison were all about the same age. Jones was born in 1941. Morrison and Tate in 1943.

35. Morris, "Christopher Jones—Wild at Heart."

36. Susan Strasberg, *Bittersweet* (New York: G. P. Putnam, 1980), 162.

37. See: Emily Crane, "Olivia Hussey Claims She was Raped by Ex at Sharon Tate's Home," *Daily Mail*, May 21, 2019, https://www.dailymail.co.uk/news/article-5992009/Olivia-Hussey-claims-raped-ex-Sharon-Tates-home.html. Susan Strasberg recounted Jones's violent streak as well to *People* magazine in 1980. See: Strasberg, "A Child Born under a Square," *People*, May 5, 1980, https://people.com/archive/a-child-born-under-a-square-vol-13-no-18/.

38. Olivia Hussey (with Alexander Martin), *The Girl on the Balcony: Olivia Hussey Finds Life after Romeo and Juliet* (London: Kensington Books, 2018).

39. Morris, "Christopher Jones—Wild at Heart."

40. Haney, *Death Valley Superstars*, 227.

41. Strasberg, *Bittersweet*, 11.

42. Haney, *Death Valley Superstars*, 213-14.

43. Haney, 212.

44. See the entry for Cabot on the *Glamour Girls of the Silver Screen* website: http://www.glamourgirlsofthesilverscreen.com/show/330/Susan+Cabot/index.html.

45. Skip E. Lowe Looks at Hollywood," https://www.youtube.com/watch?v=1oG7p-TSqNg.

46. After a bit of sleuthing, I tracked down a photograph of the actor John Drew Barrymore (who early in his acting career went by "John Barrymore Jr.") standing alongside "his half-brother John Perkins Barrymore." John Perkins (Barrymore), Jones's friend and the booked guest on Lowe's show, claimed throughout his odd "career" to be (and this is contested by the Barrymore family) the illegitimate son of John Barrymore, John Drew's father and Drew Barrymore's grandfather. John Drew Barrymore Jr.—and there is a physical resemblance between him and Perkins—was a working actor for three decades. He appeared in B-movies and got steady work on episodic TV. Among his many credits, most noteworthy are his Method performance as the momma's boy maniac killer in Fritz Lang's film noir, *While the City Sleeps* (1956) and a memorable turn as a juvenile delinquent delivering a jive version of *Romeo and Juliet* in Albert Zugsmith's wonderfully inane 1958 B-melodrama *High School Confidential*. John Perkins (Barrymore) tells Lowe he has a lot on his plate, but there is no available record of him ever having an acting or singing career.

47. Maggie Abbott started her career as a secretary at the William Morris Agency in Rome. She became an agent in the 1970s and represented a number of rock stars (Mick Jagger and David Bowie most famously), later adding the movie actors Martin Sheen, Robert Redford, Peter Sellers, and Raquel Welch. Why Abbott would waste her time on Jones in 1984 is tough to figure.

48. Des Barres, "The Agony and the Ecstasy," 86.

49. Haney, *Death Valley Superstars*, 238.

50. Jim Mueller. "Life after Fame," *Chicago Tribune*, January 26, 2000, https://www.chicagotribune.com/news/ct-xpm-2000-01-26-0001260275-story.html.

51. Des Barres, "The Agony and the Ecstasy," 50.

52. The New Left refrain was, of course: "Don't trust anyone over thirty." The slogan is generally attributed to Jack Weinberg, an activist at Berkeley in the mid-sixties. The black-comic coda in *Wild in the Streets*, punctuated by the exit line, "We're going to put everybody over ten out of business," refers to this epithet as well.

53. Kevin Thomas, "Chris Jones's Career: Even His Ex-Wife Is Enthused," *Los Angeles Times*, July 8, 1968, F1.

54. Thomas, F1, F17.

Chapter 3. Four Women in Hollywood

1. Tom Wolfe, *Radical Chic and Mau-Mauing the Flak Catchers* (New York: Farrar, Straus and Giroux, 1970).

2. Garry McGee, *Neutralized: The FBI vs Jean Seberg* (Albany, GA: BearManor, 2015).

3. Lanre Bakare, "How Hollywood Feted the Black Power Movement—and Fell Afoul of the FBI," *The Guardian*, December 5, 2019, https://www.theguardian.com/film/2019/dec/05/how-hollywood-feted-the-black-power-movement-and-fell-foul-of-the-fbi.

4. Brando's speech is currently available on line: https://www.youtube.com/watch?v=1g05Sb9CcnE.

5. Bakare, "How Hollywood Feted the Black Power Movement."

6. Taken from internal FBI documents accessed via the Freedom of Information Act scanned and posted on the "official" Jean Seberg website: http://www.saintjean.co.uk/menu2.htm.

7. Steve Wasserman, "Rage and Ruin: On the Black Panthers," *Nation*, June 24–July 1, 2013, https://www.thenation.com/article/rage-and-ruin-black-panthers/.

8. Taken from memos scanned and posted on the "official" Jean Seberg website: http://www.saintjean.co.uk/menu2.htm.

9. See: David Richards, *Played Out: The Jean Seberg Story* (New York: Random House, 1981), 234–53; Janet Maslin, "Star and Victim," *New York Times*, July 12, 1981, https://www.nytimes.com/1981/07/12/books/star-and-victim.html; and Paul Broder, *A Writer in the Cold War* (New York: Faber and Faber, 1997), 159–65.

10. In her 1974 interview with Bart Mills, Seberg states unequivocally: The baby was Romain Gary's. "A Show-Biz Saint Grows Up, or, Whatever Happened to Jean Seberg?" *New York Times*, June 16, 1974, 17.

11. "Seberg Awarded $20,000 in *Newsweek* Libel Suit," *Telegraph-Herald*, October 26, 1971, 18.

12. Bakare, "How Hollywood Feted the Black Power Movement."

13. Tony Pale, "*Bonjour Tristesse*: A Golden-Age Masterpiece Ripe for Rediscovery," *Guardian*, October 10, 2012, https://www.theguardian.com/film/filmblog/2012/oct/10/bonjour-tristesse-masterpiece-ripe-rediscovery.

14. Laura Mulvey, "Visual Pleasure and Narrative Cinema," *Screen*, 16, no. 3 (1975), 6–18.

15. Mills, "A Show-Biz Saint Grows Up," 17, 34.

16. Ryan Parker, "Jane Fonda Arrested a Fifth Time While Protesting in Washington, D.C.," *Hollywood Reporter*, December 20, 2019, https://www.google.com/search?q=Jane+Fonda+arrested&oq=Jane+Fonda+arrested+&aqs=chrome..69i57j0.2895j1j7&sourceid=chrome&ie=UTF-8.

17. Well worth a listen here is Karina Longworth's podcast series, "You Must Remember This," http://www.youmustrememberthispodcast.com/episodes

/category/Jean+and+Jane. Episodes 106–14 detail the parallel counterculture backstories of Seberg and Fonda.

18. Cara Buckley, "Jane Fonda at 81, Proudly Protesting and Going to Jail," *New York Times*, November 3, 2019, https://www.nytimes.com/2019/11/03/arts/television/04jane-fonda-arrest-protest.html.

19. Patricia Bosworth, *Jane Fonda: The Private Life of a Public Woman* (New York: Houghton-Mifflin, 2011), 367.

20. The segment is available online: https://www.oprah.com/own-master-class/jane-fondas-unforgivable-mistake-video_2.

21. Colby Itkowitz, "How Jane Fonda's 1972 trip to North Vietnam earned her the nickname 'Hanoi Jane,'" *Washington Post*, September 21, 2018, https://www.washingtonpost.com/news/retropolis/wp/2017/09/18/how-jane-fondas-1972-trip-to-north-vietnam-earned-her-the-nickname-hanoi-jane/.

22. The relevant biographical sources here are Bosworth (above) and Fonda's autobiography, *My Life So Far* (London: Ebury Press, 2005).

23. For more details on Henry Fonda's postwar career and politics, see: Scott Eyman, *Hank and Jim: The Fifty-Year Friendship of Henry Fonda and James Stewart* (New York: Simon and Shuster, 2017), 190–92.

24. Roger Vadim, *Memoirs of the Devil* (New York: Harcourt Brace Jovanovich, 1977), 167.

25. Fonda as quoted by Bosworth, 218.

26. Bosely Crowther, "Screen: *Hurry Sundown*," *New York Times*, March 24, 1967, 22.

27. Wilfried Sheed, "Films," *Esquire*, September 1, 1967, https://classic.esquire.com/article/1967/9/1/films-september-1967.

28. Bosworth, *Jane Fonda*, 250.

29. Bosworth, 280–87.

30. Martin Kasindorf, "A Restless Yawning Between Extremes," *New York Times*, February 3, 1974, https://www.nytimes.com/1974/02/03/archives/fonda-a-person-of-many-parts-a-restless-yawing-between-extremes.html.

31. E. Ann Kaplan's 1978 feminist collection, *Women in Film Noir* (London: BFI, 1978) featured two essays on *Klute*, both by Christine Gledhill ("Klute 1: A Contemporary Film Noir and Feminist Criticism," and "Klute 2: Feminism and Klute.")

32. Jonathan Rosenbaum, "*Letter to Jane*" (1975 review), https://www.jonathanrosenbaum.net/2019/09/letter-to-jane-1975-review/.

33. Bosworth, *Jane Fonda*, 395.

34. Bosworth, 399.

35. The speech is posted on YouTube: https://www.youtube.com/watch?v=1rZyCvQFBt4.

36. A lot of the story here is taken from Hart's conversation with David Adams in "An interview with Dolores Hart," *Elvis Australia*, March 5, 2017, https://www.elvis.com.au/presley/an-interview-with-mother-dolores-hart.shtm

37. Cal York, "You Read it First: Gossip Section," *Photoplay*, January 1963, 4.

38. Hedda Hopper, "Under Hedda's Hat," *Photoplay*, February 1963, 34.

39. Hedda Hopper, "Under Hedda's Hat," *Photoplay*, May 1963, 24.

40. Hedda Hopper, "Under Hedda's Hat," *Photoplay*, July 1963, 22.

41. Michael Joya, "I Want to Be a Nun," *Photoplay*, September 1963, 56–58, 84.

42. "Readers Inc.," *Photoplay*, November 1963, 8.

43. Jessica Pickens, "An interview with the actress who left Hollywood to become a nun," *Comet over Hollywood*, September 14, 2013, https://cometoverhollywood.com/2013/09/14/leaving-hollywood-for-a-new-habit-an-interview-with-dolores-hart/; and Dolores Hart, *The Ear of the Heart: An Actress' Journey from Hollywood to Holy Vows* (San Francisco: Ignatius Press, 2013).

44. Perry remains the sole credited director; the DGA insisted upon it. But no one disputes the fact that Pollack finished the film for him.

45. There are available stills of Loden on the set, but no remaining viewable footage, so we'll never get the chance to judge the performance for ourselves.

46. See Maya Montanez Smukler, *Liberating Hollywood: Women Directors and the Feminist Reform of 1970s American Cinema* (New Brunswick, NJ: Rutgers University Press, 2019), 96–102.

47. "Barbara Loden's Own Film Project: On Set Hubby Raps Television Mutilators of Celluloid," *Variety*, September 3, 1969, 17.

48. Vincent Canby, "*Wanda*'s a Wow; So is *THX*," *New York Times*, March 21, 1971, D1.

49. Elia Kazan, *Elia Kazan: A Life* (New York: Da Capo, 1997), 571–73.

50. Kazan, 668–69.

51. Kazan, 692.

52. Molly Haskell, "The Mad Housewives of the Neo-Woman's Film: The Age of Ambivalence Revisited," in *When the Movies Mattered: The New Hollywood Revisited*, edited by Jonathan Kirshner and Jon Lewis (Ithaca, NY: Cornell University Press, 2019), 18–20.

53. Haskell, 25–27.

54. McLandish Phillips, "Barbara Loden Speaks of the World of *Wanda*," *New York Times*, April 25, 1971, D32.

55. Kevin Thomas, "Miss Loden's Wanda—It's Very Much Me," *Los Angeles Times*, April 8, 1971, G1.

56. Rex Reed, "Watch Out for Barbara's '*Wanda*,'" *Los Angeles Times*, February 21, 1971, 52.

57. Pauline Kael, "The Current Cinema," *New Yorker*, March 20, 1971, 138-40.

58. Smukler, *Liberating Hollywood*, 101.

59. A. H. Weiler, "News of the Screen," *New York Times*, April 28, 1974, 59.

60. Madison Women's Collective, "Barbara Loden Revisited," *Women and Film*, nos. 5-6 (1974): 68, 69.

61. Madison Women's Collective, 68.

62. Don DeLillo, "Woman in the Distance," *Black Clock* 4 (2005), 56-59.

63. Nathalie Leger, *Suite for Barbara Loden*, translated by Natasha Lehrer and Cecile Menon (St. Louis: Dorothy Project, 2016). See also: Berenice Reynaud, "For Wanda," in *Last Great American Picture Show*, edited by Thomas Elsaesser, Alexander Horwath, and Noel King (Amsterdam: Amsterdam University Press, 2004), 223-47; Chuck Kleinhans, "Wanda and Marilyn Times Five: Seeing through Cinema Verite," *Jump Cut* (1974), 1-6; and E. Bahr-de Stefano, "Whatever Happened to *Wanda*? Barbara Loden's Unique Vision of Women's Cinema," Academia.edu, http//www.academia.edu/20418447/Whatever_Happened_to_Wanda_Barbara_Lodens_Unique_Vision_of_Womens_Cinema.

Chapter 4. Charles Manson's Hollywood

1. See Robert Giroux, *A Deed of Death* (New York: Knopf, 1990); and Sidney D. Kirkpatrick, *A Cast of Killers* (New York: Dutton, 1986).

2. See Bruce Long's exhaustive website, Taylorology: http://www.taylorology.com/.

3. Simon Louvish, "Silent Victim," *The Guardian*, October 23, 2003, https://www.theguardian.com/film/2003/oct/24/3.

4. See Jon Lewis, *Hard-Boiled Hollywood: Crime and Punishment in Postwar Los Angeles* (Oakland: University of California Press, 2018).

5. Michael Rosenwald, "Charles Manson's Surreal Summer with the Beach Boys, Group Sex, Dumpster Diving and Rock and Roll," *Washington Post*, November 20, 2017, https://www.washingtonpost.com/news/retropolis/wp/2017/11/20/charles-mansons-surreal-summer-with-the-beach-boys-group-sex-dumpster-diving-and-rock-n-roll/?utm_term=.ac5535c3f158.

6. Hadley Freeman, "The Second Summer of Charles Manson: Why the Cult Murders Still Grip Us," *The Guardian*, August 16, 2016, https://www.theguardian

.com/us-news/2016/aug/16/second-summer-charles-manson-why-cult-murders-still-grip-us.

7. Karina Longworth, "You Must Remember This," http://www.youmustrememberthispodcast.com/episodes/?category=CharlesManson%27sHollywood. I listened to Longworth's multi-episode podcast several years ago—they first aired back in 2015—and unlike a book I would have underlined and could then cite verbatim, a podcast is a trickier medium to attribute. The podcast has stayed with me and it no doubt informs a lot of what I've got to say about Manson. Going back over my written source work, I see that Longworth remarked to Hadley Freeman in *The Guardian* in 2016, that the "era-defining tragedy [that was the Manson murders] happened at least in part because [Manson] got so close to becoming famous, but just couldn't get there." That is a big part of the argument I put forward here.

8. The entire transcript of *The People v. Charles Watson* can be found on CieloDrive.com, http://www.cielodrive.com/terry-melcher-trial-testimony.php.

9. Dan Sinykin, "Charles Manson and the Apocalypse to Come," *Los Angeles Review of Books*, November 24, 2017, https://blog.lareviewofbooks.org/essays/charles-manson-apocalypse-come/.

10. Ed Sanders, *The Family* (New York: Avon, 1971), 151.

11. See Tracy Daugherty's terrific biography of Joan Didion, *The Last Love Song* (New York: St. Martins, 2015), 307.

12. Vincent Bugliosi, *Helter Skelter* (New York: Norton, 1974), 388.

13. I've written about Manson before, albeit in a very different context, in: Jon Lewis, *The Road to Romance and Ruin: Teen Films and Youth Culture* (New York: Routledge, 1992), 35–39. The biographical information here covers some of the same ground and it is drawn from a variety of sources, most of them written right around the time of Manson's arrest and murder trial, including Steven Roberts, "Charlie Manson: One Man's Family," *New York Times Magazine*, January 4, 1970, 24–29 and Ed Sanders, *The Family*. Just as I was putting the finishing touches on this chapter, I watched the nearly six-hour, six-episode MGM/Epix docuseries, *Helter Skelter: An American Myth* (Leslie Chilcott, 2020), which included a lot of biographical information, most of it based on Jeff Guin's, *Manson: The Life and Times of Charles Manson* (New York: Simon and Shuster, 2014). No doubt the docuseries also informs the bio sketch here.

14. Most of the early press, including the always well-fact-checked *New York Times*, got the birthdate wrong. The birth certificate for Charles Miles Maddox sets the birthdate as the 12th.

15. Roberts, "Charlie Manson: One Man's Family."

16. Roberts.

17. Joan Didion, *The White Album* (New York: Farrar, Giroux, Strauss, 1979), 42.

18. Didion, 16–18.

19. Peter Biskind, *Easy Riders, Raging Bulls* (New York: Bloomsbury, 1998), 77–80.

20. Roberts, "Charlie Manson: One Man's Family."

21. Bugliosi, *Helter Skelter*, 415.

22. Adam Gopnik, "Measuring Man," *New Yorker*, June 22, 2020, 77–78.

23. See Lewis, *The Road to Romance and Ruin*, 35–39.

24. Bugliosi, *Helter Skelter*, 461–62.

25. Bugliosi, 489.

26. Travis Hirschi, *The Causes of Delinquency* (Berkeley: University of California Press, 1970), 26.

27. Kenneth Keniston, *The Uncommitted: Alienated Youth in America* (New York: Harcourt, Brace, and World, 1965), 84–103.

28. Bruno Bettelheim, "The Problem of Generations," in *The Challenge of Youth*, edited by Erik Erikson (New York: Doubleday, 1965), 89–92.

29. Erik Erikson, "Youth, Fidelity and Diversity," in *The Challenge of Youth*, 24.

30. Schowalter as cited by David Gelman, "A Much Riskier Passage," *Newsweek* (*The New Teens: What Makes Them Different*, special edition) Summer/Fall 1990, 15.

31. *Helter Skelter: An American Myth* featured interviews with the former "Manson girls" Dianne Lake and Catherine Share, Melcher sidekick Gregg Jakobson, and assorted journalists who covered the story back in 1969. At this writing, the series is the latest attempt to tell the real story of Charles Manson. But I'm willing to bet, it won't be the last.

32. Jeffrey Melnick, "Keeping Faith with the Manson Women," *New Yorker*, August 1, 2018, https://www.newyorker.com/culture/cultural-comment/keeping-faith-with-the-manson-women. See also: Melnick, *Creepy Crawling: Charles Manson and the Many Lives of America's Most Infamous Family* (New York: Simon and Shuster, 2018).

33. Much of van Houten's story is drawn from Faith's 2001 book, *The Long Prison Journey of Leslie van Houten: Life Beyond the Cult* (Boston: Northeastern University Press, 2001).

34. For sticklers: The timecodes here and elsewhere are inexact; they match the running time posted on my VLC player as I closely watched a DVD of the film.

That said, my point about leaving things late ("the 129-minute mark") nonetheless holds. It takes Tarantino over two hours to cut to the chase. The duration of screen time that passes once everyone converges on Cielo Drive is just under fifteen minutes—give or take a second or two or three. Tarantino makes us wait for the night of August 8, 1969, and then wait again for Watson, Atkins, Krenwinkel, and Kasabian get on with things (albeit at the wrong house on Cielo Drive).

35. Johnny Brayson, "These Are the Hollywood Legends Who Inspired Leonardo DiCaprio's Latest Character," *Bustle*, July 22, 2019, https://www.bustle.com/p/is-rick-dalton-based-on-a-real-actor-once-upon-a-time-in-hollywood-had-some-famous-influences-18176044.

36. "You're Too Hip Baby" is a quite brilliant short story by the quite brilliant sixties writer Terry Southern, published in *Esquire Magazine* in April 1963. See: https://classic.esquire.com/article/1963/4/1/youre-too-hip-baby.

37. Brayson, "These Are the Hollywood Legends."

38. This came up in a graduate class I taught on the counterculture in the spring of 2020—in a Canvas discussion post by Andrea Schuster. I liked the notion (of Hollywood as a cult) so much I've included it here.

39. Yes, this is a thing. See: Adrienne Tyler, "What's Up with Quentin Tarantino and Feet?" *Screen Rant*, September 8, 2019, https://screenrant.com/quentin-tarantino-feet-explained/.

40. Dianne Lake was a runaway and just fourteen when she fell in with Manson and the Family. Her memoir, *Member of the Family* (New York: Harper Collins, 2017) is well worth a look. She turned state's evidence, though she was at the time quite conflicted. She really liked a lot of the "girls" she met at the Spahn Movie Ranch. And she does still—evident in a 2019 interview with Tarply Hitt at *The Daily Beast*, August 15, 2019 (https://www.thedailybeast.com/ex-manson-family-member-dianne-lake-reviews-quentin-tarantinos-once-upon-a-time-in-hollywood), in which Lake objected to Tarantino's harsh treatment of Fromme, "who wasn't like that."

41. "Clem" Grogan was in the car on August 10 that dropped off Watson, Krenwinkel, and van Houten at the La Bianca house. He was later implicated in and convicted for the murder of the ranch hand, Donald "Shorty" Shea. Grogan got the death penalty, but it was later commuted to life when Judge James Kolts concluded that Grogan was "too stupid and hopped up on drugs to decide anything on his own." Tarantino and Hébert get the "stupid and hopped up" part right.

42. See, for example: Richard Brody, "Quentin Tarantino's Obscenely Regressive Vision of the Sixties in *Once Upon a Time in Hollywood*," *New Yorker*,

July 27, 2019, https://www.newyorker.com/culture/the-front-row/review-quentin-tarantinos-obscenely-regressive-vision-of-the-sixties-in-once-upon-a-time-in-hollywood. Filmgoers wanting political correctness would do well to pass on Tarantino's entire oeuvre; but Brody goes where his magazine sends him. Brody criticizes Tarantino for freighting the word *hippie* with negative connotations, imposing standards that might apply to comments made by a writer today in the *New Yorker*. Fact is: in 1969 the term *was* freighted with negative connotations. Manson was dubbed a "hippie guru" in the press, and not because he was enlightened. In another scene, Rick refers to Mexicans as "Beaners." Rick says the word in character, reading lines written for a sixties TV show—he is a bad actor playing a TV bad guy delivering a racist monologue (in character) for a bad TV show. En route to the Ranch, Cliff brusquely dismisses Pussycat's offer of a blowjob because she's under age. Men in Hollywood have historically exploited women, Brody notes—even and especially much younger women. What Brody asserts here is of course true, but it is also irrelevant. Cliff is a fictional character. Moreover, he is not a producer or director. He has nothing much to offer Pussycat career-wise in exchange for the sexual favor (not that she's asking). And he's not the kind of guy to court trouble with "jail bait."

Epilogue

1. A reference to Oates's 1966 short story, "Where Are You Going, Where Have You Been?" https://www.cusd200.org/cms/lib/IL01001538/Centricity/Domain/361/oates_going.pdf.

2. "12 Plus 1," *Variety*, December 31, 1969, https://variety.com/1969/film/reviews/12-plus-1-1200422298/.

3. Joan Didion, *The White Album* (New York: Farrar, Giroux, Strauss, 1979), 21–25.

Index

Abernathy, Carrie, 153
Academy of Motion Picture Arts and Sciences (AMPAS), 17
Actors Studio, New York: Barbara Loden, 206, 207, 208, 209; Christopher Jones, 99, 107; communists and progressives at, 180; Jane Fonda, 180, 183, 188, 223; Sally LeRoy, 123
Adler, Renata, 50, 116
The Adventures of Robin Hood (1938), 108, 198
After the Fall, 207–8, 211–12
AIP. *See* American International Pictures (AIP)
Airport (1970), 53, 172, 173
Albee, Edward, 7
Alice Doesn't Live Here Anymore (1974), 214
Alice's Restaurant (1969), 49
All the President's Men (1976), 189
Alpert, Richard, 78–79
Altamont, California, 279–80
Altman, Robert, 55
Altobelli, Rudy, 148–52, 239
American Film Institute (AFI), 196–97
The American Friend (1977), 89
American Graffiti (1973), 47, 55

American International Pictures (AIP), 113*fig*; Christopher Jones and, 30, 101, 110–11; cross-marketing with music, 122; drive-in movie venues, 111; eye for talent, 114–15; focus on teens and teen culture, 111–12; low-budget genre picture model used by, 111–12; *Ryan's Daughter* (1970), 100, 142–48, 147*fig*; *3 in the Attic* (1968), 111, 131–39, 135*fig*; *The Wild Angels* (1966), 111–16; *Wild in the Streets* (1968), 111, 115–32, 117*fig*. *See also* Arkoff, Samuel Z.
American Psycho (2000), 265
American Zoetrope, 46–47
Anderson, Adrienne, 156
Anderson, Eric, 187
Anderson, Julie, 204
Andrews, Benedict, 166
antiwar movement. *See* Vietnam War
Antonioni, Michelangelo, 38*fig*; arrest of, 71–72; *Blow-Up* (1966), 27, 29, 33–36; *Blow-Up* (1966), MPAA production code and, 39–41; Communist politics of, 66–68; Daria Halprin and Mark Frechette, casting of, 72–75; on keeping actors

[311]

Antonioni, Michelangelo (*continued*) off-guard, 96; on the loneliness of youth, 84–85; MGM, three-picture deal with, 29, 38, 56–58, 94–97; new wave of foreign art films in U.S., 37–39; *The Passenger* (1975), 95–97; *Zabriskie Point* (1970), 41–42, 56–58, 75; *Zabriskie Point* (1970), analysis of final scenes, 90–94; *Zabriskie Point* (1970), Ebert interview on, 75, 84–85; *Zabriskie Point* (1970), production challenges, 58–68
Apocalypse Now (1979), 47, 89, 284
Arbuckle, Fatty, 99
Archerd, Army, 129
Arkoff, Samuel Z., 113*fig*; as cofounder of AIP studios, 110–11; music and film cross-marketing, 122; *Riot on the Sunset Strip* (1967), 128–29; role in emergence of the New Hollywood, 114–15; *3 in the Attic* (1968), 132, 134; use of actual news footage in films, 128–29; *The Wild Angels* (1966), 112–14; willingness to court controversy, 119. *See also* American International Pictures (AIP)
Atkins, Susan, 236, 249, 251, 255, 261, 266–68
Aubrey, James, 68–72
Avalon, Frankie, 112
Avatar, 80, 84
Avildsen, John, 49

Bacon, Sosie, 266
Bailey, Ella Jo, 233
Bakare, Lanre, 23–24
Ballard, Carroll, 46
Bancroft, Anne, 6, 7–9
Barbarella (1967), 186, 187*fig*
Bardot, Bridget, 182

Barefoot in the Park (1967), 7, 185–86
Barrett, Rona, 50
Barrymore, John Jr., 156–58, 302n46
Basil, Toni, 45
Bazin, Andre, 99
BBS production company, 20–21, 25–26, 46, 50; *Drive He Said* (1971), 20, 53, 54–55; *Five Easy Pieces* (1970), 20, 51–53; *The Last Picture Show* (1971), 21, 48, 54, 55, 114; *A Safe Place*, 54
Beach Party films, AIP, 112
Beardsley, Ed, 72–73
Beatles, 121, 126–27, 244
Beatty, Warren, 4*fig*, 5, 17, 172, 207
Beaty, Madisen, 270
Beausoleil, Robert "Bobby," 249
Beauvoir, Simone de, 186
Beck, Jeff, 35
Belafonte, Harry, 183
Benedek, Laszlo, 111
Benedict Canyon, 11, 148, 187–88, 226. *See also* Manson murders
Benton, Jessie, 79, 84
Benton, Robert, 3
Bergen, Candice, 241*fig*
Bernhard, Sheldon T., 90
Bernson, Harry, 206
Berry, Dennis, 173
Berry, John, 173
Bettelheim, Bruno, 263, 300n20
Betz, Carl, 109
Beverly Hills Seven, 23–24
Bhagavan Das, 79
The Bible (1966), 114
Billodeau, D. C., 45
Birkin, Jane, 35
Birth of a Nation (1915), 129
Bishop, Larry, 124, 162–63
Biskind, Peter, 23, 253
Black, Karen, 30, 45, 51–53, 101

Black Americans: Blaxploitation genre, 15; demographics in 1969, 11; L.A. Rebellion, 15–16; Melvin van Peebles's road to nowhere, 10–16; UCLA Black Studies program, 15–16. *See also* Black Panther Party; race and racism, film portrayals of; race and racism, in film industry; specific individual names
The Blackboard Jungle (1955), 111
Black Dahlia (Elizabeth Short), 232
Black Guerrilla Family, 24
blacklist era: Abel Meeropol, 18; Arthur "Artie" Ross, 23; Artie Shaw, 19; Dalton Trumbo, 195; Elia Kazan, 211; Frank Sinatra, 18–19; Henry Fonda and, 180; John Berry, 173; Maltz, Albert, 18; studio use of blacklisting to control celebrities, 99; Waldo Salt, 27
Black Panther Party, 15–16; Hollywood celebrities, fundraising from, 166–69; Huey Newton, 21–24, 22*fig*; Jean Seberg and, 165–76, 171*fig*, 175*fig*; Kathleen Cleaver work in *Zabriskie Point* (1970), 59
The Black Stallion (1979), 46
Blauner, Steve, 20, 21, 22–24, 46, 51–53
Blaxploitation, 15
Bloody Mama (1970), 123
Blow-Up (1966), 27, 29, 33–36
Blue Velvet (1984), 89
B-movies, 33–34; *vs.* A-movies, 132; Blaxploitation films, 14–15; Cannon Films and, 49; drive-in venues, 111. *See also* American International Pictures (AIP); *Easy Rider* (1969)
Bob and Carol and Ted and Alice (1969), 138
Bogdanovich, Peter, 21, 48, 54, 114, 115
Bonjour Tristesse (1958), 171, 172

Bonnie and Clyde (1967), 3–6, 4*fig*, 114, 221–22
Bono, Sonny, 129
Boston, MA. *See* Fort Hill Community
Boston Globe: interview with Mark Frechette, 75
Bosworth, Patricia, 186, 188, 196
Bottoms, Sam, 55
Bottoms, Timothy, 55
Boyd, Stephen, 202
Boyle, Kay, 79
Brando, Marlon, 10, 100, 139–40, 167, 167*fig*, 183–84
Bray, Charles, 179
The Breakfast Club (1985), 48
Breathless (1960, Jean-Luc Godard), 171*fig*, 172, 174, 220
Breathless (1983, Jim McBride), 46
Bridge Films, 34, 40–41
Bridges, Jeff, 55
A Brief Season (1969), 142
British-based classical training, studio preference for, 139–40
Brooks, Richard, 111
Brown, James, 112
Brunner, Mary, 249, 257
Bugliosi, Vincent, 237–42, 247
Buñuel, Luis, 220
Burkhead, William, 179
Burnett, Charles, 15
Burstyn, Ellen, 30, 101, 115
Burton, Richard, 7, 139
Bush Mama (1979), 15
Butler, Austin, 275
Bye Bye Birdie (1960), 131
Byrnes, Edd, 272

Cabot, Susan, 154–55
Caine, Michael, 139, 140
Cammisa, Rebecca, 204
Campus, Michael, 15

Canby, Vincent: on *3 in the Attic* (1968), 138–39; on *Hearts and Minds* (1975), 25; on *The Last Picture Show* (1971), 54; on *Ryan's Daughter* (1970), 145–46; on *Sweet Sweetback's Baadasssss Song* (1971), 14; on *Wanda* (1970), 210; on *Zabriskie Point* (1970), 71
Cannes awards: *Blow-Up* (1966), 35; *Easy Rider* (1969), 45; *Elvira Madigan* (1967), 142; *L'Avventura* (1960), 37; *Once Upon a Time in Hollywood* (2019), 265–66, 277; *The Passenger* (1975), 95; *Wanda* (1970), 215
Cannon Films, 49
Carlo Ponti British-Italian Productions, 40–41
Carroll, Diahann, 184
Carter, Alprentice "Bunchy," 16
Casablanca (1942), 198
Castellano, Renato, 142
Catholic Legion of Decency, 41
The Causes of Delinquency (Hirschi), 263
Cavett, Dick, 75–76
celebrity: dark side of, 101–2; failure and the celebrity bargain, 235; *A Hard Day's Night* (1964), 121; Phil Ochs and, 118–19; public fascination with movie stars, 98–99; risky diversions of celebrities, 229–35, 245, 251, 253; Roger Ebert on politics and pop idols, 120–21; varying responses to, 99
Chaikin, Joseph, 61
Champlin, Charles, 71
Charlie Says (2019), 265–68
Chateau Marmont, 108, 149
Cheever, John, 208

Chinatown (1974), 114
Christ, Judith, 218
Christopher Lee, 110
Chubasco (1967), 110
Cimino, Michael, 26–27, 27*fig*, 47, 294n63
Circle of Love (1965), 183
Cisco Pike (1972), 49
Clarke, Gary, 202
Cleave, Maureen, 126–27
Cleaver, Eldridge, 59, 167, 169
Cleaver, Kathleen, 59, 292n31
Cleopatra Jones (1973), 15
Clifford, Clark, 26
Coffy (1973), 15
Cohen, Larry, 115
Cohen, Melinda, 82
Cohen, Richard, 71
Colgems, 51
Columbia Pictures: *Bob and Carol and Ted and Alice* (1969), 138; *Cisco Pike* (1972), 49; Colgems, 51; *Five Easy Pieces* (1970), 20, 51–53; *Getting Straight* (1970), 49, 51; *Hearts and Minds*, termination of contract with BBS, 21, 25; *The Looking Glass War* (1970), 139–42, 142*fig*. *See also Easy Rider* (1969)
Coming Home (1978), 26–27
Committee for the First Amendment (CFA), 18, 180
Communist Party: Actors Studio in New York, 180–81. *See also* blacklist era; House Un-American Activities Committee (HUAC)
Compulsion (1959), 123
Conan the Barbarian (1982), 46
Congress of Racial Equality (CORE), 184
Contini, Alfio, 59–60

The Conversation (1974), 46, 47, 48–49
Cooper, Gary, 123
Coppola, Francis Ford, 39, 48, 89, 115, 213
Corman, Roger, 14, 30, 111, 123, 154
Corsaro, Frank, 106, 107
Cortazar, Julio, 34
Cosby, Bill, 13
counterculture: Black American cinema, industry response to, 15–16; Hollywood's first encounters with, 2–10; major studio shifts after success of *Easy Rider*, 45–55, 132; Oscar nights 1968 and 1975 as counterculture frame, 16–20
Covell, Mitchell, 202
Cronenberg, David, 115
Crosby, Bing, 20
Crowley, Aleister, 230
Crowther, Bosley, 5, 36, 185
Curtiz, Michael, 198, 201

Dacy, Mike, 239
Daisy Miller, 48
Dakota, Bill, 154
Daley, Richard, 129
Dallesandro, Joe, 219
Dalton, David, 78–79, 83*fig*
Damiano, Gerard, 193
Darling, Candy, 187
Da Silva, Howard, 18
Dass, Ram, 79
David, Johnny, 45
Davis, Bette, 107
Davis, Peter, 16–17, 25–26
Davison, Bruce, 86
Day, Doris, 35, 235
Dean, James, 30, 102–3, 103*fig*, 105, 106–7

Death Valley National Park Rangers, 62–66
Death Valley Superstars: Occasionally Fatal Adventures in Filmland (Haney), 153–54
Dee, Sandra, 200
Deeley, Michael, 27*fig*
Deep Throat (1971), 193
The Deer Hunter (1978), 26–27, 47
The Defenders (television show), 254–55
Degermark, Pia, 141–42
DeLillo, Don, 221
DeLong, Owen, 79
Demme, Jonathan, 115
Democratic National Convention (1968), 16, 23–24, 118, 129
Deneuve, Catherine, 182
De Niro, Robert, 115
Dennison, Sally, 72, 73
De Palma, Brian, 115
Dern, Bruce, 30, 101, 114, 115, 116, 162, 276
Dern, John, 26–27
Des Barres, Pamela, 148–49, 154–55, 160
Diary of a Mad Housewife (1970), 213
DiCaprio, Leonardo, 268, 273
Dick Cavett Show, 75–76
Didion, Joan, 1, 49, 251–53, 279, 283–84, 286
Directors Company, 48–49
Doctor Zhivago (1965), 147
documentary-style filming, effect of, 59–60
Dodd, Sherry, 152–53
Dolan, Tony, 85
Dolemite (1975), 15
Dolenz, Mickey, 50
Donovan, 124

Don't Look Back (1967), 120
Doran, Ann, 109
Dowd, Nancy, 27
Dracula Has Risen from the Grave (1968), 110
Dr. Doolittle, 9
Dreifuss, Arthur, 111, 128–29
Dreyfuss, Richard, 55, 115
Drive He Said (1971), 20, 53, 54–55
drive-in movie venues, 111
Duke, Patty, 282*fig*
Dulles, John Foster, 26
Dunaway, Faye, 4*fig*, 181
Dunham, Lena, 275
Dunne, Irene, 205
Dunne, John Gregory, 49, 252
Dunne, Philip, 123
Duras, Marguerite, 222
Dylan, Bob, 45, 78, 119, 120, 124
Dymytrk, Eddie, 173

Eastman, Carole, 51–53
East of Eden (1955), 103*fig*, 105
Eastwood, Clint, 172, 273
Easy Rider (1969), 20, 27, 33–34, 41–46, 43*fig*, 114; box office gross, 46; production backstory, 44–45; Zabriskie Point (1970), comparisons to, 56–57
Easy Riders, Raging Bulls (Biskind), 253
Ebert, Roger: on The Last Picture Show (1971), 54; on Privilege (1967), 120–21; Samuel Arkoff interview, 115–16; on Wild in the Streets (1968), 120–21, 122; on Zabriskie Point (1970), 56, 57, 71, 84–85
Edwards, Vince, 203, 272
Ellsberg, Daniel, 21, 26
Elvira Madigan (1967), 142
"The End" (Jim Morrison), 284–86
Erikson, Erik, 263

Ernie Kovacs (television show), 207
Esalen Institute, 86
Esquire Magazine: on Hurry Sundown (1967), 185
European New Wave, 33–34; Dennis Hopper's techniques in Easy Rider, 57; foreign art films in U.S., 37–39; MGM studios and, 35–36. See also Blow-Up (1966)
Everett, Ronald (Maulana Karenga), 15–16
Exner, Judith, 20

A Face in the Crowd (1957), 210
Fahrenheit 451, 3
Faith, Karlene, 266
The Family (1971, Sanders), 244
Fanning, Dakota, 275–76
FBI (Federal Bureau of Investigation): COINTELPRO investigations, 169; Jean Seberg and the Black Panthers, 31, 166–70, 176; Zabriskie Point (1970), complaints about film production, 65
Fear and Loathing in Las Vegas, 81, 296n86
Feitshans, Fred, 116
Fell, Norman, 9
Fellini, Federico, 37
Felton, David, 78–79, 81–82, 83*fig*
feminism: Dolores Hart, 206; Jane Fonda in Klute (1970), 188–94, 192*fig*; Wanda (1970) and, 219–23, 224
Ferguson, Paul, 252–53
Ferguson, Thomas, 252–53
film industry. See Hollywood; studios
Finney, Albert, 139
Five Easy Pieces (1970), 20, 51–53
Flatley, Guy, 64, 66
Fleischer, Richard, 9, 123

Floyd, Randy, 26
Flynn, John, 86
Folger, Abigail, 237, 262
Fonda, Henry, 180–81
Fonda, Jane, 30, 31, 223–24, 281; *Barbarella* (1967), 186, 187*fig*; *Barefoot in the Park* (1967), 185–86; Black Panthers, financial support for, 167, 186; dual life in US and Paris, 186–88; early acting career, 181–82; early life of, 180–81; *Hurry Sundown* (1967), 184–85; *Klute* (1970), 188–94, 192*fig*; *Letter to Jane* (1972), 194–95; Life Achievement Award (AFI), 196–97; Oscars 1979 appearance, 27–28; political awakening of, 183–84; protesting Trump administration, 177; Roger Vadim and, 182–83; Sharon Tate and, 187, 188; Tom Hayden and, 195–96; Vietnam War protests by, 177–80, 178*fig*
Fonda, Peter, 42–46, 43*fig*, 114, 115
Fontaine, Gwen, 24
Ford, Harrison, 72
foreign art films, rise of in U.S. market, 37–39
Forman, Milos, 49
Forte, Fabian, 272
Fort Hill Community, 76; backstory of, 77–79; establishment of and early days, 79–82; Mark Frechette and, 84–85, 90–92; *Rolling Stone* cover story, 78–79, 81–82, 83*fig*
The 400 Blows, 220
Foxy Brown, 15
Francis, Freddie, 110
Francis of Assisi (1961), 201–2
Franckenstein, Faith, 79
Frank, Barney, 80
Frankenheimer, John, 35

Frechette, Mark, 91*fig*, 280; arrest and death in prison, 90–92; casting decisions, 72–75; Fort Hill Community and, 84–85; post-film life of, 29, 75–85; post-film press tour comments, 75–76, 85; in *Zabriskie Point* (1970), 57–58, 58*fig*
freeze frame, as trope, 55
The French Connection (1972), 48
Friedkin, William, 48
Fromme, Lynette "Squeaky," 256–59
From the Journals of Jean Seberg (1995), 173–74
Frykowski, Wojciech, 237
Funicello, Annette, 112

Garcia, Jerry, 78
Gardner, Fred, 59
Garfield, John, 18
Garris, Mick, 151
Gary, Romain, 169, 173, 176
Gazzara, Ben, 207
generation gap, 131–32. *See also Wild in the Streets* (1968)
Gerima, Haile, 15
Getting Straight (1970), 49, 51
Giancana, Sam, 20
Gibson, Margaret, 230–31
Gidget (1959), 200
Gilliate, Penelope, 42
Gimme Shelter (1970), 279
Glass, Philip, 188
The Glass Bottom Boat (1966), 35
Godard, Jean-Luc, 3–5, 171–74, 171*fig*, 194–95, 220
The Godfather (1972), 29, 48, 68, 139
God Is the Bigger Elvis (2012), 204
Golden Globe awards: *Lilith* (1964), 172
Good, Sandra, 257
Goodman, Paul, 131–32

Gopnik, Adam, 260
Gorin, Jean-Pierre, 194-95
Gorson, Arthur, 118
The Graduate (1968), 6-9, 8*fig*, 116-17, 137
Grand Prix (1966), 35
The Great Escape (1963), 140
Green, Guy, 10
Greenspun, Roger, 14
Gregory, Dick, 184
Grier, Pam, 15
Griffith, D. W., 129
Growing Up Absurd (Goodman), 131-32
Gude, David, 79
Guerra, Tonino, 59
Guess Who's Coming to Dinner (1968), 9-10, 11
Gun Crazy, 3
Gustaitas, Rasa, 74-75, 77
Guthrie, Arlo, 49, 119

Haber, Joyce, 69-70, 170
Haigh, Nancy, 277
Halprin, Daria, 29, 280; Dennis Hopper and, 85-90, 89*fig*; *The Jerusalem File* (1972), 86; life as therapist, 86-87; Mark Frechette and, 72-76; *Zabriskie Point* (1970), 57-58, 58*fig*
Halston, 188
Hamilton, George, 200
Hammer Films, 110
Hampton, Fred, 168-69
Haney, Duke, 152, 153-54, 158-59, 160
A Hard Day's Night (1964), 121
Hardin, Ty, 203, 272
Harris, Richard, 139
Harrison, Rex, 139
Harron, Mary, 265-68
Hart, Dolores, 30, 197-206, 198*fig*, 201*fig*, 224, 281

Hart Benton, Thomas, 79, 84
Hartman, Elizabeth, 10
Haskell, Molly, 213
Haver, June, 205
Hawaii (1966), 114
Hawke, Maya, 270
Hayden, Tom, 195-96
Hayes, Helen, 53
Hayward, Brooke, 87
Hayworth, Rita, 184
Head (1968), 20, 50, 51
Hearst, William Randolph, 19
Hearts and Minds (1975), 16-17, 21, 25-26
Heaven's Gate (1980), 71, 294n63
Hébert, James Landry, 277
Hellman, Monte, 114
Helter Skelter, Manson's vision of, 242-45, 265
Hemmings, David, 34, 36*fig*
Henreid, Paul, 19
Henry, Buck, 253
Hepburn, Katharine, 9, 19
Herriman, Damon, 272, 272*fig*
Hershey, Barbara, 115
Hewitt, Raymond, 170
HHH Rainbow Productions, 219
HICCASP (Hollywood Independent Citizens Committee of the Arts, Sciences, and the Professions), 19
Higgins, Michael, 215
Hill, George Roy, 114
Hill, Jack, 15
Hinman, Gary, 248-49
hippies: in *Alice's Restaurant* (1969), 49; in Boston, MA, 73, 80; in *Drive He Said* (1971), 53; in *Easy Rider* (1969), 43, 44; Fort Hill Community, 76, 80; Haight Ashbury, 248; Manson Family, 188, 227, 232, 233, 238-40, 242, 243, 248, 249, 255, 258,

259; Mark Frechette, death of, 91–92; in *Once Upon a Time in Hollywood* (2019), 269, 275, 277, 310n42; in *Revolution* (1968), 72; use of term, 240, 310n42; *Wild in the Streets* (1968), 128–32
Hirschi, Travis, 263
Hochman, Joel, 261
Hoffman, Abbie, 21
Hoffman, Dustin, 7–9, 8*fig*, 116–17, 140, 181
Holbrook, Hal, 125–26
Holiday, Billie, 18
Hollywood: Black Hollywood, 10–16; Conservative Hollywood, Frank Sinatra as representative of, 17–20; first encounters with counterculture, 2–10; Oscar night 1975, Hollywood discovers Vietnam, 16–24. *See* movie stars; studios
The Hollywood Reporter: on Jane Fonda protesting Trump administration, 177
Hooks, Robert, 184
Hoover, J. Edgar: Jean Seberg and, 31, 166, 169–70, 174–75, 223
Hope, Bob, 17
Hopkins, Anthony, 139
Hopper, Dennis, 27, 29–30, 33–34, 280; acting roles after *Easy Rider*, 87, 88–90; Charles Manson and, 254–55; Daria Halprin and, 85–90, 89*fig*; *Easy Rider* (1969), 41–46, 43*fig*; *The Legend of Jessie James* (television show), 108–9, 298n4; life in Taos, 87–88, 89*fig*; Michelle Phillips and, 87–88
Hopper, Hedda, 202
Hopper, Marin, 87, 88
Horne, Lena, 19

The House I Live In (1945), 18
House Un-American Activities Committee (HUAC), 18–19, 23, 173, 180. *See also* blacklist era
Howard, Ron, 55
Howard, Trevor, 143
HUAC. *See* House Un-American Activities Committee (HUAC)
Huggins, John, 15–16
Hughes, John, 48
Humphrey, Hubert, 20
Hunter, Tab, 272
Huppert, Isabelle, 222
Hurry Sundown (1967), 184
Hussey, Olivia, 101, 145, 150–52
Huston, John, 114
Hutton, Lauren, 16
Hutton, Robert "Lil' Bobby," 167, 167*fig*
Huyck, Willard, 46

Inside Daisy Clover (1965), 189
In the Heat of the Night (1968), 9–10, 11, 11*fig*, 185
Ishihara, May, 124
I Shot Andy Warhol (1996), 265
Izzo, Lorenza, 268

Jackobson, Gregg, 238, 239, 240, 241, 242
Jaglom, Henry, 25, 219
Jakobson, Gregg, 238, 240
Jamal, Hakim, 166–68, 170
James, Jessie, 108–9, 298n4
Jaws (1975), 47
The Jerusalem File (1972), 86
Jewison, Norman, 9
Jim Kweskin Jug Band, 77–79, 81
Joe, 49
Johnson, Ben, 54
Johnson, Don, 115

INDEX [319]

Jones, Christopher, 30, 104*fig*, 280; AIP (American International Pictures) and, 110–16; career overview, 99–102; Carrie Abernathy, relationship with, 153; children of, 154–55; *Chubasco* (1967), 110; death of Jim Morrison and, 149–50; death of Sharon Tate and, 145, 148, 149, 159–60; decision to drop out, 160–63; downfall of, 148–63; *The Looking Glass War* (1970), 139–42, 142*fig*; nervous breakdown, 149–50; Olivia Hussey, relationship with, 150–52; origin story, 102–10; Pamela Des Barre, interview with, 148–50; Paule McKenna, relationship with, 153; Quentin Tarentino and, 158–59; Rudy Altobelli and, 148–52; *Ryan's Daughter* (1970), 142–48, 147*fig*; Sherry Dodd, relationship with, 152–53; on "Skip E. Lowe Looks at Hollywood," 156–58; Susan Cabot, relationship with, 154–55; *3 in the Attic* (1968), 131–39, 135*fig*; *Wild in the Streets* (1968), 116–17, 117*fig*, 122

Jones, Davy, 50
Jones, Paul, 121
Jones, Robert C., 27
Jones, William Franklin. *See* Jones, Christopher
Joseph Chaikin's Open Theater, 61–66, 62*fig*
Joya, Michael, 203–4
Judd for the Defense, 109

Kael, Pauline, 42, 54, 70, 146–47, 148, 218–19
Kafka, Franz, 13
Kanfer, Stefan, 54

Kantner, Hal, 198, 198*fig*
Karenga, Maulana (Ronald Everett), 15–16
Kasabian, Linda, 236, 256
Katz, Gloria, 46
Kaufman, Stanley, 37
Kaye, Danny, 19
Kazan, Elia, 105, 181, 206, 207, 209–12
Kazan, Molly, 212
Keith, Maxwell, 239–42
Kellerman, Sally, 108, 115
Kelly, Grace, 203
Keniston, Kenneth, 263
Kennedy, John F., 19–20
Kennedy, Robert, 20, 79
Kerkorian, Kirk, 68, 71
Kerouac, Jack, 29, 43
Kershner, Irvin, 213–14
Kidder, Margot, 115
Kilgallen, Dorothy, 183
Killer of Sheep (1978), 15
King, Henry, 108
King Creole (1958), 198
The King of Marvin Gardens, 21, 51
Kinsey Reports, 132
Klaus, Olivia, 261
Klein, Stanley, 80
Klute (1970), 188–94, 192*fig*
Koster, Henry, 35
Kovacs, Laszlo, 51–53
Kramer, Stanley, 9
Krenwinkel, Patricia, 233, 236, 255, 258, 261–63, 266–68

Ladd, Diane, 114
La Dolce Vita (1960), 37
Laemmle, Carl, 98
Lancaster, Burt, 184, 208, 209*fig*
La Notte (1961), 37
La Permission, 12

L.A. Rebellion, 15–16
Larner, Jeremy, 53
The Last Movie, 30, 34, 51, 88
The Last Picture Show (1971), 21, 48, 54, 55, 114
Laurie, Piper, 5
L'Avventura (1960), 37, 38*fig*, 96
Lawford, Patricia, 19
Lawford, Peter, 20
Lawson, Johns Howard, 19
Leachman, Cloris, 54, 55
Lean, David, 100, 142–44, 147
Leary, Timothy, 79
Le Carre, John, 139
L'Eclisse (1962), 37
The Legend of Jesse James (television show), 108–9, 298n4
Leger, Nathalie, 222
Lennon, John, 126–27, 216–18
Lester, Richard, 121
Let It Be (1970), 53
Letter to Jane (1972), 194–95
Levin, Henry, 111, 199, 201*fig*
Lewis, Damien, 274
Lewis, Jerry, 35
Lewis, Joseph, 3
Life Achievement Award, AFI, 196–97
Life after Manson (2014), 261–62
Lilith (1964), 172, 173
Ling, Barbara, 277
Liston, Sonny, 50
Lockwood, Gary, 108
Loden, Barbara, 30, 209*fig*, 216*fig*, 224–25; Broadway career, 206–8; Elia Kazan, relationship with, 209–12; *The Swimmer* (1968), 208–9, 209*fig*; *Wanda* (1970), 209, 210, 213–23, 216*fig*
Logan, Joshua, 172, 182

Longworth, Karina, 236
The Looking Glass War (1970), 139–42, 142*fig*
Los Angeles Times: interview with Christopher Jones, 161–62; on Jean Seberg's pregnancy, 170; on *Wanda* (1970), 216; on *Zabriskie Point* (1970), 69–70, 71, 77
Los Olvidados, 220
Louvish, Simon, 231
Love Means Always Having to Say You're Sorry, 219
Loving You (1957), 198, 198*fig*
Lowe, Skip E., 156–58
LSD use: Fort Hill Community, 78–79; in *Once Upon a Time in Hollywood* (2019), 269, 271; in *Wild in the Streets* (1968), 123, 129, 130
Lucas, George, 46, 47, 55
Lyman, Mel, 73, 76; Fort Hill Community, creation and early days of, 79–82; in Jim Kweskin Jug Band, 77–79; *Rolling Stone* cover story, 78–79, 83*fig*
Lynch, David, 89

The Mack (1973), 15
MacLaine, Shirley, 17
MacMurray, Fred, 205
Mad Dog Time (1996), 162–63
Maddox, Kathleen, 246–47
mad housewife films, 213–14, 219
Madison, Mikey, 270
Magnum Force (1973), 23
Maharis, George, 272
The Making of Ryan's Daughter (2005), 143
Malle, Louis, 114
Maltz, Albert, 18
Manfred Mann, 121

INDEX [321]

The Man from U.N.C.L.E., 109
Mann, Barry, 122
Mann Act (1910), 65, 69
Manson, Charles, 29, 32, 226–28; arrest for Tate murders, 250; Dennis Wilson and, 232–35; followers of, 255–58, 258*fig*; Gary Hinman, murder of, 248–49; Helter Skelter vision, 242–45; importance of music to, 234, 242; life before moving to California, 246–48; making meaning of Manson, 258–64; planning for his biopic, 254–55; Spahn Movie Ranch, residence at, 249–50, 249*fig*; Terry Melcher, court testimony of, 237–42; Terry Melcher and, 233–45, 236*fig*
Manson, William, 246
Manson murders, 1–2; as American folklore, 264–65; arrests for, 250; Charles Manson, overview of, 226–28; Gary Hinman, murder of, 248–49; Hollywood's response to, 253–54; Joan Didion on, 1, 251–53, 279, 283–84, 286; making meaning of the Manson Family, 258–64; Manson followers, overview of, 255–58, 258*fig*; *Once Upon a Time in Hollywood* (2019), 158–59, 265–78, 272*fig*, 278*fig*; Sharon Tate, murder of, 31–32, 145, 149, 150, 159–60, 187, 188; Terry Melcher, court testimony of, 237–42; Terry Melcher as target of, 236–37
Mapplethorpe, Robert, 188
Marathon Man (1976), 140
Maron, Marc, 116, 162
Martin, Dino, 151
Martin, D'Urville, 15
Marvin, Lee, 167, 172

Marx, Groucho, 19
Mature, Victor, 50
May, Elaine, 6
Mazursky, Paul, 138, 214
McBride, Jim, 46
McCarthy, Eugene, 26
McGee, Garry, 166
McGuinn, Roger, 45
McNeil Island Penitentiary, 247–48
McQueen, Steve, 140, 273
Medium Cool (1969), 49
Meeropol, Abel, 18
Melcher, Terry, 32, 150, 228, 234–45, 241*fig*
Melnick, Jeffrey, 265
Melvin and Howard (1980), 48
Merv Griffin Show, 85
Method acting: Ben Gazzara, 207; bias against in Hollywood, 139–40; Christopher Jones, 109, 139, 152; Jane Fonda, 188; Konstantin Stanislavski, 182; Olivia Hussey, 152
MGM Studios: Antonioni, three picture deal with, 29, 38, 56–58, 94–97; *Blow-Up* (1966), 35–36; *Blow-Up* (1966), MPAA production code and, 39–41; James Aubrey, leadership of, 68–72; Kirk Kerkorian take-over, 68–69; *Zabriskie Point* (1970), 34, 56–68
Midnight Cowboy (1969), 70, 294n55
Mike Douglas Show, 216–18
Miles, Sarah, 143
Milius, John, 46, 115
Millbrook community, 79
Miller, Arthur, 207–8, 211–12
Mills, Bart, 170–71, 172, 173, 175–76
Mills, John, 143, 145
Mimieux, Yvette, 134, 135*fig*, 200, 201*fig*
Mineo, Sal, 108

[322] INDEX

Miner, Allen H., 110
Minnelli, Liza, 188
Minter, Mary Miles, 230
miscegenation, 168–70
mise-en-scène, 57
Mister Roberts (1955), 181
Mitchum, Robert, 143–44
The Monkees (TV show, 1966-1968), 20, 50–51
Montand, Yves, 183, 194
Montparnasse Cemetery, 176
Moore, Rudy Ray, 15
Morgenstern, Joseph, 5
Morricone, Ennio, 275
Morris, Jan E., 150
Morrison, Jim, 30, 122, 126, 149–50, 284–86, 285*fig*
Morrison, Van, 80
Mother McCree's Uptown Jug Champions, 78
Motion Picture Association of America (MPAA): *Blow-Up* (1966), production seal for, 40–41; Jack Valenti on concern over foreign-made films, 38–39; *Midnight Cowboy* (1969), 294n55; production code, history of, 290n10; *Zabriskie Point* (1970), production seal for, 68, 292n37
MPAA. *See* Motion Picture Association of America (MPAA)
Mulligan, Robert, 189
Mulvey, Laura, 174
Murch, Walter, 46
Murray, Hannah, 266
music: AIP movies use of, 112; Altamont, California, 279–80; *Don't Look Back* (1967), Bob Dylan and, 120; *A Hard Day's Night* (1964), 121; Jim Morrison, 122, 284–86, 285*fig*; John Lennon's comments on rock and roll and Christianity, 126–27; Phil Ochs as voice of counterculture, 117–20; in *Wild in the Streets* (1968), 119–20, 122; Woodstock, 279–80

National Catholic Office for Motion Pictures (NCOMP), 41
The National Enquirer: on Dolores Hart, 204–5
NCOMP (National Catholic Office for Motion Pictures), 41
Neal, Patricia, 205
Needham, Hal, 272
Neem Karoli Baba, 79
Nesmith, Michael, 50
New Hollywood: BBS and, 21; *Blow-Up* (1966), 34–39; Christopher Jones and, 100–101, 108; *Easy Riders, Raging Bulls* (Biskind), 253; Jane Fonda and, 182, 184; Oscar night 1975, 16–17, 20; Samuel Arkoff and, 115–16; *Time* magazine cover story, 5. *See also* American International Pictures (AIP); *Easy Rider* (1969); *Zabriskie Point* (1970)
Newman, David, 3
Newman, Eve, 116
Newman, Paul, 10, 120, 167, 183, 184
New Republic: on *L'Avventura* (1960), 37; on *Zabriskie Point* (1970), 42
Newsweek: on *Bonnie and Clyde* (1967), 5; on *The Last Picture Show* (1971), 54
Newton, Huey, 21–24, 22*fig*, 167, 169
New York Daily News: on *Hearts and Minds* (1975), 25
New Yorker: on 50th anniversary of Manson murders, 265; on *Easy Rider* (1969), 42; on *Ryan's Daughter* (1970), 146–47; on *Wanda* (1970), 218–19

New York Film Critics: on *Five Easy Pieces* (1970), 52
New York Times: on *Blow-Up* (1966), 36; on *Bonnie and Clyde* (1967), 5; on *Chubasco* (1967), 110; on *Dracula Has Risen from the Grave* (1968), 110; on *Head* (1968), 50; on *Hearts and Minds* (1975), 25; on *Hurry Sundown* (1967), 185; on Jane Fonda's 2019 arrest, 177; Jean Seberg interview, 170-71; on *The Jerusalem File* (1972), 86; on *The Looking Glass War* (1970), 140; on *Sweet Sweetback's Baadasssss Song* (1971), 14; on *3 in the Attic* (1968), 138-39; on *Wanda* (1970), 210, 216; on *Wild in the Streets* (1968), 116; on *Zabriskie Point* (1970), 71
Nichols, Mike, 6-9, 8*fig*, 117
Nicholson, Jack, 30, 44-45, 50, 101, 115; *Drive He Said* (1971), 53; *Five Easy Pieces* (1970), 51-53; *The Passenger* (1975), 95-97
Nielson, Blackie, 247
Night of the Iguana (1961), 107
Niven, David, 171
Nixon, Richard, 20, 49, 179
Nolte, Nick, 115
Normand, Mabel, 230
Norris, Chuck, 115
Norton, B. L., 49
Novarro, Ramon, 31, 252-53

Oates, Joyce Carol, 279-80
Ochs, Phil, 117-20, 299n14
O'Connell, Jack, 72
The Odd Couple, 7
Olivier, Laurence, 139, 140
Once Upon a Time in Hollywood (2019), 158-59, 265-78, 272*fig*, 278*fig*
O'Neill, Tatum, 48

Ono, Yoko, 216-18
On the Road, 29, 43
O.P.E.R.A, 12
Orbach, Jerry, 107-8
Orbach, Marta, 107-8
Orbison, Roy, 65
Oscars: *Blow-Up* (1966), 34; *Bonnie and Clyde* (1967), 5; *Coming Home* (1978), 26-27; counterculture films in 1970, lack of awards for, 53; *The Deer Hunter* (1978), 26-27; *Easy Rider* (1969), 45; *Five Easy Pieces* (1970), 52-53; *The French Connection* (1972), 48; *The Graduate* (1968), 6; *Guess Who's Coming to Dinner* (1968), 9; *Hearts and Minds* (1975), 16-17, 21; *In the Heat of the Night* (1968), 9, 10; Hollywood discovers Vietnam, Oscar night 1975, 16-24; *The House I Live In* (1945), 18; *Klute* (1970), 188; *The Last Picture Show* (1971), 48, 54; *Once Upon a Time in Hollywood* (2019), 277; *Paper Moon* (1973), 48; preference for classical training *vs.* Method acting, 139-40; *Ryan's Daughter* (1970), 145; *They Shoot Horses Don't They* (1969), 188; *Wild in the Streets* (1968), 116
O'Toole, Peter, 139, 140

Pace, Judy, 134
Pacino, Al, 49, 181, 273
Packard, Vance, 132-34
Paint Your Wagon (1969), 172, 173
Pakula, Alan, 188, 189, 193
Panic in Needle Park (1970), 49
Paper Moon (1973), 48, 114
The Parallax View (1974), 189
Paramount Pictures Studio: Dolores Hart and, 197-98; Frank Yablans,

leadership of, 48; *Medium Cool* (1969), 49
Parent, Steven, 237
Parkins, Barbara, 282*fig*
Parks, Gordon, 15
Parks, Gordon Jr., 15
A Passage to India, 147
The Passenger (1975), 95–97
The Passover Plot (Schonfield), 126–27
A Patch of Blue (1965), 10
Pather Panchali, 220
Patton (1970), 53
Patton, George III, 26
Pauling, Linus, 19
Peavy, Henry, 230, 231
Penitentiary (1979), 15
Penn, Arthur, 4*fig*, 49, 183
Pennebaker, D. A., 120
The People of the State of California vs. Charles Denton (Tex) Watson, 237–42
Peploe, Clare, 59
Perkins, Anthony, 151
Perry, Frank, 208, 213
Peyton Place (1957), 123
Phillips, John, 250
Phillips, McLandish, 216
Phillips, Michelle, 87–88
Photoplay: on Dolores Hart, 202, 203–6
Pierson, Frank, 139, 140
Pitt, Brad, 268, 277
Platt, Polly, 114
Play It As It Lays (1972), 213
The Pleasure of His Company (1959), 199
Poitier, Sidney: *Guess Who's Coming to Dinner* (1968), 9–10, 11; *In the Heat of the Night* (1968), 9–10, 11, 11*fig*; *A Patch of Blue*, 10
Polanski, Roman, 32, 114, 150, 250–51
politics: Antonioni on politics, 66, 67, 93–94; Antonioni on sexual revolution as form of protest, 62; Democratic National Convention (1968), 16, 23–24, 118, 129; *Easy Rider* (1969), appeal across political spectrum, 43; of Frank Sinatra, 17–20; of Henry Fonda, 181; of Jane Fonda, 177–80, 181, 183–84, 186, 187, 188, 189, 195–96, 281; *Klute* (1970), gender politics in, 193–94; L.A. Rebellion, 15; Mark Frechette, on robbery as political protest, 90; of Marlon Brando, 10, 167, 167*fig*, 184; Oscar night 1975, 16–20; Phil Ochs and, 118; radical chic, 30–31, 165–66, 175–76, 177, 195–96; Roger Ebert on politics and pop idols, 120–21; *Wild in the Streets* (1968), 125–26, 127–32. *See also* blacklist era; Black Panther Party; Vietnam War
Pollack, Sydney, 188, 208
Pollard, Michael J., 114
Ponti, Carol, 34
Post, Ted, 23
Power, Tyrone, 108
Premier Films, 40–41
Preminger, Otto, 168, 171, 173, 184
Presley, Elvis, 198–99, 198*fig*, 203
Pretty Baby (1978), 114
prison films: *Penitentiary* (1979), 15
Privilege (1967), 120–21
Proferes, Nick, 221
Pryor, Richard, 115, 124
Psycho IV: The Beginning (1990), 151–52

Q (1982), 115
Qualley, Margaret, 274

race and racism, film portrayals of: Blaxploitation films, 15; *Guess Who's Coming to Dinner* (1968), 9–10; *In the Heat of the Night* (1968), 9–10;

race and racism, film portrayals of (*continued*)
  Hurry Sundown (1967), 184–85; L.A. Rebellion, 15–16; *A Patch of Blue*, 10; *Sweet Sweetback's Baadasssss Song* (1971), 13–14; *3 in the Attic* (1968), 134–38; *The Watermelon Man* (1970), 12–13
race and racism, in film industry: Black Panther fundraising in Hollywood, 166–69; celebrity support for racial equality, 184; FBI investigations of Jean Seberg and Black Panthers, 168–70; Frank Sinatra and, 18; *Hurry Sundown* (1967), 184–85; Melvin van Peebles's road to nowhere, 10–16
race war, Manson's vision of Helter Skelter, 242–45
radical chic, 30–31, 165–66, 175–76, 177, 195–96
Rafelson, Bob, 20, 21, 45, 46, 50; *Five Easy Pieces* (1970), 51–53
Rainbow Releasing, 25–26
The Rain People (1969), 213
Rappaport, Mark, 173–74
ratings system: *Midnight Cowboy*, 70, 294n55; *Sweet Sweetback's Baadasssss Song* (1971), 14, 288n11; Voluntary Movie Rating System, 41, 146; *Zabriskie Point* (1970), 61, 68, 292n37
Rauschenberg, Robert, 5
Ray, Nick, 108, 111
Ray, Satyajit, 220
Raybert Productions, 45, 46, 50
RCA: Colgems, Columbia co-venture, 51
Reade, Walter, 183
Reagan, Ronald, 19

Rebel without a Cause (1955), 109, 111
Red Desert (1964), 37
Redford, Robert, 185, 207
Redgrave, Vanessa, 35
Reed, Rex, 25, 76, 216
Regina Laudis monastery, 199, 204
Reid, Wallace, 99
Reitman, Ivan, 115
Rendon, Marianne, 266
Revolution (1968), 72
Reynolds, Burt, 272
Reynolds, Debbie, 35
Richardson, Ralph, 139
Riley, Clayton, 14
Riot on the Sunset Strip (1967), 111, 128–29
road trip: as setting for countercultural adventure, 56–57
Robbie, Margot, 268, 277–78, 278*fig*
Roberts, Steven, 247, 250–51, 255, 257
Robinson, Don, 202, 203
Robinson, Tyrone, 24
Robson, Mark, 123, 282*fig*, 283
rock and roll: AIP movies use of, 112, 119–20; *Bye Bye Birdie* (1960), 131; *Don't Look Back* (1967), Bob Dylan and, 120; *A Hard Day's Night* (1964), 121; Jim Morrison, 122, 283–96, 285*fig*; John Lennon's comments on rock and roll and Christianity, 126–27; The Monkees, 50–51; *Wild in the Streets* (1968), music in, 119–20, 124; *Wild in the Streets* (1968), rock and roll fascism, 122; in *Zabriskie Point* (1970), 70
Rocky (1976), 49
Rolling Stone: Daria Halprin interview, 86; on *Head* (1968), 50; Mel Lyman cover story, 78–79, 81–82, 83*fig*
Romeo and Juliet (Zeffirelli, 1968), 101

[326] INDEX

Roos, Fred, 72
Rosenbaum, Jonathan, 194
Ross, Arthur "Artie," 23
Ross, Elaine, 8*fig*
Rossen, Robert, 172, 173
Rostow, Walt, 25, 26
Rule, Janice, 208
Rush, Richard, 49
Russell, Kurt, 268
Ryan's Daughter (1970), 100, 142–48, 147*fig*

A Safe Place, 54
Saint Joan (1957), 168, 171, 173
Saks, Gene, 185
Sanders, Ed, 244
Sands, Edward, 230
Sarandon, Susan, 115
Sarris, Andrew, 36, 37, 54
Sartre, Jean-Paul, 185–86
Schatzberg, Jerry, 49
Schickel, Richard, 54
Schlesinger, John, 70, 140
Schneider, Bert, 16–17, 20–21, 25, 45, 46, 51–53, 219
Schonfield, Hugh J., 126–27
Schowalter, John, 263
Schumacher, Michael, 117–18
Scofield, Paul, 139
Scorsese, Martin, 39, 115, 214
Scott, George C., 53
Scott, Lizabeth, 198*fig*
SDS (Students for a Democratic Society), 195–96
Seale, Bobby, 21, 167
Seaton, George, 172
Seberg (2020), 166
Seberg, Jean, 30, 31, 171*fig*, 175*fig*, 223, 281; Bart Mills interview with, 170–71, 172, 173, 175–76; death of, 176; Dennis Berry and, 173; FBI investigations of, 168–70, 176; Hakim Jamal, relationship with, 166–70; Jean Luc Godard and, 171–74; Mark Rappaport's 1995 documentary on, 173–74; Otto Preminger and, 171–74; pregnancy of, 169–70, 176; Romain Gary, relationship with, 169–70, 173–74, 176

Sebring, Jay, 237
Seeger, Pete, 119
Sellers, Peter, 139
Sennett, Mack, 231
Setlowe, Rick, 12
Seven Arts: *Chubasco* (1967), 110
sexual revolution: *3 in the Attic* (1968), 131–39, 135*fig*; *Bob and Carol and Ted and Alice* (1969), 138; *The Graduate* (1968), 7–9, 8*fig*; Karina Longworth on free love and the cost to women, 236; *Klute* (1970), gender politics in, 193–94; sex acts on film, legal issues, 65–66, 293n45; *The Sexual Wilderness* (Packard), 132–34; *Where the Boys Are* (1960), 199–201, 201*fig*; *Zabriskie Point* (1970), Death Valley love scene, 60–66, 62*fig*, 293n45
The Sexual Wilderness (Packard), 132
Shaft (1971), 15
Shampoo, 51
Shaw, Artie, 19
Shear, Barry, 111
Sheed, Wilfrid, 185
Shelby, Charlotte, 230
Shepard, Sam, 58–59
Shephard, Cybil, 48, 55
Short, Elizabeth (Black Dahlia), 31, 232
Shrimpton, Jean, 121

Shuster, Harry, 215
Sidney, George, 131
Siggins, Bob, 77
Sight and Sound: Top Ten Best Films list, 37
Sigma Productions, 184
Signoret, Simone, 183, 185
Simmons, Jack, 153
Simon, David, 78
Simon, Neil, 7, 185–86
Simonelli, James, 65–66
Sinatra, Frank, 17–20, 53
Sinatra, Nancy, 114
The Singing Nun (1966), 35
Sinykin, Dan, 243
Sixteen Candles (1984), 48
"Skip E. Lowe Looks at Hollywood," 156–58
Smith, David, 261
Smith, Gerald L. K., 19
Smith, Kathleen, 22
Smith, Matt, 267
Smith, Patti, 188
SNCC (Student Nonviolent Coordinating Committee), 184
Southern, Terry, 45
Spahn Movie Ranch, 227, 249*fig*; Terry Melcher, court testimony of, 237–39
Spiegel, Sam, 208
Spielberg, Steven, 47
Spikings, Barry, 27*fig*
spiritual quests: Antonioni on suspicion of cult leaders and gurus, 84; of Daria Halprin, 86, 87; of Dennis Hopper, 87; Dolores Hart, 197–206; LSD and, 78–79; Mel Lyman and Fort Hill Community, 78–79, 81, 84–85; Richard Alpert/ Ram Dass, 78–79
Splendor in the Grass (1961), 181, 207
Stanislavski, Konstantin, 182

stardom. *See* celebrity
Stark, Ray, 219
Starr, Harrison, 67, 73
Starr, Ringo, 127
Starrett, Jack, 15
Star Wars (1977), 47
Steele, Walter S., 19
Steiger, Rod, 10, 11*fig*
Stevenson, Michael, 143
Stewart, Kristin, 166
Stock, Dennis, 105
Stockton, Joe, 102–3
The Story of a Three-Day Pass (1967), 12
"Strange Fruit" (Meeropol), 18
Strasberg, Lee, 181–82
Strasberg, Susan, 107–8, 151, 181
Streisand, Barbra, 214
Student Nonviolent Coordinating Committee (SNCC), 184
Students for a Democratic Society (SDS), 195–96
studios: approaches to teenage story lines, 111–12; on audience preferences for film heroes, 52; blacklisting and, 18–19, 23, 99; Blaxploitation films, 15; first encounters with counterculture, 2–10; generation gap, trivialization of, 131–32; major studios and B-movie studios, different business models for, 111, 132; plastic surgery, use of, 182; preferences for classical training *vs.* Method acting, 139–40; scandals, managing of, 99; Vietnam War films, 25–28, 128, 130; view of counterculture as a passing fad, 49–50. *See also* specific studio names
Sturges, John, 140
Sunset Strip, 108
Super Fly (1972), 15

Supremes, 112
Sutherland, Donald, 186, 189
Sutherland, Shirley, 186
Sweeney, Sydney, 274
Sweet Sweetback's Baadasssss Song (1971), 13–14, 288n11
The Swimmer (1968), 208–9, 209*fig*

Taking Off (1971), 49
Tamalpa Institute, 86–87
Tanen, Ned, 47–48
Tarantino, Quentin, 158–59, 265
Tashlin, Frank, 35
Tate, Debra, 262
Tate, Sharon: career of, 281–83, 282*fig*; Christopher Jones and, 145, 149, 150, 159–60; Jane Fonda and, 187, 188; murder of, 31–32, 237; press coverage of murder, 250–51
Tavoularis, Dean, 63
Taylor, Elizabeth, 7
Taylor, Samuel, 199
Taylor, William Desmond, 31, 99, 229–32
teenagers: generation gap, trivialization of, 131; major studies and B-movie studios, storyline differences, 111–12
Tenney, Jack, 19
Ten North Frederick (1958), 123
Tet Offensive, Vietnam, 16
They Shoot Horses Don't They (1969), 188
Thien, Chris, 90
Thomas, Danny, 16
Thomas, Kevin, 161, 216
Thompson, Howard, 110, 140
Thompson, Hunter S., 81, 296n86
3 in the Attic (1968), 111, 131–39, 135*fig*
Three the Hard Way (1974), 15
Thrett, Maggie, 134

THX-1138, 47
Time: on *Barefoot in the Park* (1967), 185; on *Bonnie and Clyde* (1967), 5; on *The Last Picture Show* (1971), 54
To Kill a Mockingbird (1962), 189
Tork, Peter, 50
Totaro, Donato, 60
Tout va bien (1972), 194
Towne, Robert, 53
Tracy, Spencer, 9
The Trip (1967), 111
Truffaut, François, 3, 171–72, 220
Trumbo, Dalton, 19
Tuttle, Frank, 173
Twentieth Century Fox: *The Legend of Jesse James* (television show), 108–9; *Panic in Needle Park* (1970), 49
Two-Lane Blacktop (1971), 114

UCLA (University of California Los Angeles): Black Studies program, 15–16
The Uncommitted: Alienated Youth in America (Keniston), 263
Universal Studios: Carl Laemmle on role of movie stars, 98; *The Last Movie* release, 88; Ned Tanen, leadership of, 47–48, 49
An Unmarried Woman (1978), 214
Up the Down Staircase (1967), 189
Up the Sandbox (1972), 214

Vadim, Roger, 182–83, 186–87, 187*fig*, 196
Valenti, Jack, 38, 40–41
Valley of the Dolls (1967), 282*fig*, 283
van Houten, Leslie, 250, 257, 266–68
van Peebles, Melvin, 11–16
Variety: on Barbara Loden, 210; on *Barefoot in the Park* (1967), 185; Jack Valenti on *Blow-Up*'s defiance of

Variety (continued)
  production codes, 40–41; Jack
  Valenti on foreign-made pictures,
  38; on Martin van Peebles, 12; on
  Wild in the Streets (1968), 115–16
Varsi, Diane, 123
Venice Film Festival: *Wanda* (1970),
  215; *The Wild Angels* (1966), 114, 116
Veruschka, 35
Vidal, Gore, 195–96
Vietnam War: *Bush Mama* (1979), 15;
  Coming Home (1978), 26–27; *The
  Deer Hunter* (1978), 26–27; *Hearts
  and Minds* (1975), 25–26; Hollywood's hearts and minds, 25–28;
  Jane Fonda's activism, 177–80,
  178*fig*, 183, 194–96; Oscar night
  1975, Hollywood discovers
  Vietnam, 16–24; Phil Ochs as voice
  of counterculture, 118–20; Tet
  Offensive, 16; *Wild in the Streets*
  (1968), 119–20, 125, 130
Village Voice: on *The Last Picture Show*
  (1971), 54
"Visual Pleasure and Narrative
  Cinema" (Mulvey), 174
Viva, 187
Voight, John, 27
Voluntary Movie Rating System, 41

Wadleigh, Michael, 53
Walken, Christopher, 26–27
Walker, Beverly, 64
Wallis, Hal, 197, 203, 205–6
Walsh, Ryan, 74
Walters, Barbara, 195
Wanda (1970), 209, 210, 213–23, 216*fig*
Warhol, Andy, 187, 216
Warner, Jack, 5, 182
Warner Bros. Studios: *Chubasco*
  (1967), 110; Francis Ford Coppola

and, 46–47; *Hearts and Minds*
  (1975), 26
Washington Post: Jane Fonda,
  interview with, 179–80
The Wasp Woman (1959), 154
Watergate tapes, 49
The Watermelon Man (1970), 12–13
Watkins, Peter, 120–21
Watson, Tex, 32, 227, 236; Terry
  Melcher, court testimony of, 237–42
Weill, Claudia, 122
Welles, Orson, 19, 134
Wendkos, Paul, 200
Westmoreland, William, 26
Wever, Merritt, 266
Wexler, Haskell, 49
Where the Boys Are (1960), 111,
  199–201, 201*fig*
White, Kevin, 80
white supremacy, Charles Manson
  and, 242–45
Who's Afraid of Virginia Woolf, 7
Widerberg, Bo, 142
Wier, Bob, 78
The Wild Angels (1966), 111–14
Wild in the Streets (1968), 111, 115–32,
  117*fig*; music in, 119–20, 122; Phil
  Ochs as potential lead actor,
  117–19; *Privilege* (1967), comparisons to, 120–22, 124–26; storyline of,
  127–31
The Wild One (1953), 111
Wild River (1960), 207
William Conrad Productions, 110
Williams, Paul, 79
Williams, Tennessee, 107, 188
Williamson, Nichol, 86
Willis, Rosalie, 247
Wilson, Dennis, 228, 233–35, 233*fig*;
  Terry Melcher, court testimony of,
  237–42

Wilson, Earl, 183
Wilson, Richard, 111, 134
Winfrey, Oprah, 179
Winn, Kitty, 49
Winters, Shelley, 107, 131, 153
Wolfe, Tom, 30–31, 165–66, 195
women in Hollywood: job opportunities for, 164–65; Karina Longworth on free love and the cost to women, 236; mad housewife films, 213–14, 219. *See also* individual names
Women's Wear Daily, 71
Wonder, Stevie, 112
Wood, Natalie, 108, 181
Woodstock, 279–80
Woodstock (1970), 53
Woodward, Joanne, 167
Wright, Elinor, 3–4
Wright, Norton, 3–4

Yablans, Frank, 48
York, Cal, 202
Young, Freddie, 145
Young, Loretta, 205
The Young and the Damned, 220

Youth International Party (yippies), 118

Zabriskie Point (1970), 29, 34, 41–42, 56–58, 91*fig*, 292n37; Antonioni's comments on American life, 66–68; box office gross, 71; Daria Halprin and Mark Frechette, casting of, 72–75; Death Valley love scene, controversy over, 60–66, 62*fig*, 293n45; final scenes in film, Antonioni's vision of, 90–94; Grand Jury investigations, 65–66; James Aubrey, PR efforts, 69–72; MGM's three picture deal, fulfillment of contract, 29, 38, 56–58, 94–97; MPAA rating system, 292n37; post-film press tour, 75–77, 85; production budget, 68; production challenges, 58–68; release of film, 70–72; Teamster delays, 63–64; use of multiple screenwriters, 59
Zeffirelli, Franco, 101
Zimmerman, Paul, 54
Zucker, Howard, 25

Founded in 1893,
UNIVERSITY OF CALIFORNIA PRESS
publishes bold, progressive books and journals
on topics in the arts, humanities, social sciences,
and natural sciences—with a focus on social
justice issues—that inspire thought and action
among readers worldwide.

The UC PRESS FOUNDATION
raises funds to uphold the press's vital role
as an independent, nonprofit publisher, and
receives philanthropic support from a wide
range of individuals and institutions—and from
committed readers like you. To learn more, visit
ucpress.edu/supportus.